The Devil of Great Island

Witchcraft and Conflict
in Early New England

Emerson W. Baker

First published in 2007 by
PALGRAVE MACMILLAN™
175 Fifth Avenue, New York, N.Y. 10010 and
Houndmills, Basingstoke, Hampshire, England RG21 6XS.
Companies and representatives throughout the world.

PALGRAVE MACMILLAN is the global academic imprint of the Palgrave Macmillan division of St. Martin's Press, LLC and of Palgrave Macmillan Ltd. Macmillan® is a registered trademark in the United States, United Kingdom and other countries. Palgrave is a registered trademark in the European Union and other countries.

ISBN-13: 978–1–4039–7207–1
ISBN-10: 1–4039–7207–9

Library of Congress Cataloging-in-Publication Data
Baker, Emerson W.
    The devil of Great Island : witchcraft and conflict in early New England / Emerson W. Baker.
        p.   cm.
      ISBN-13: 978–1–4039–7207–1
      ISBN-10: 1–4039–7207–9
      1. Witchcraft—New Hampshire—New Castle—History—17th century.   I. Title.

BF1576.B25   2007
133.4'3097426—dc22
        2007005084

A catalogue record of the book is available from the British Library.

Design by Letra Libre, Inc.

First edition: October 2007

10 9 8 7 6 5 4 3 2 1

Printed in the United States of America.

Dedicated

to

Peggy, Megan, and Sarah.

Contents

List of Figures

Principal Characters in
The Devil of Great Island

Mary Agawam and her son William (sometimes known as William Indian): Native American servants to George and Alice Walton.

John "the Greek" Amazeen: A Mediterranean sailor who finds a home in Portsmouth, he marries Mary Walford after the death of her husband, Jeremiah.

Joseph Andrews: A Harford resident and son-in-law of Elizabeth Strickland Desborough, he is involved in a dispute with Nicholas Desborough.

Captain Walter Barefoot: A neighbor of the Waltons on Great Island, Barefoot was a physician and deputy collector of customs who supported the Mason family.

Richard Chamberlain: London-trained lawyer and secretary of the colony of New Hampshire, he boards at the Walton tavern and is a representative of the Mason family.

Nicholas Desborough and his second wife, Elizabeth Strickland Desborough: Residents of Hartford, Connecticut, their household suffers a lithobolia attack in 1682.

John Emerson (uncle and nephew): The uncle is the minister in Gloucester, Massachusetts, and the nephew is the minister in Berwick, Maine, when the Fortados undergo a lithobolia attack.

Mary Start Fortado and her husband, Antonio Fortado: She is the daughter of a York, Maine fisherman, and he is a native of

Fayal, in the Azores. They reside in Berwick, not far from the Shorts.

Sir Ferdinando Gorges: He is the proprietor of the Province of Maine and a close associate of Captain John Mason.

Hannah Walford Jones and her husband, Alexander Jones: Hannah was the daughter of Thomas and Jane Walford. Alexander is a fisherman, and Hannah is a midwife. Her parents give them land on Great Island that is in dispute with George Walton.

Captain John Mason and his wife, Ann: John is the promoter and would-be proprietor of New Hampshire; his death in 1635 leaves the colony in turmoil.

Joseph Mason: Kinsman of Captain John Mason, during the 1650s and 1660s he lives in Portsmouth, representing the family interests.

Robert Tufton Mason: Grandson of Captain John Mason, he attempts to reinstate the family claim to New Hampshire in the 1670s and 1680s.

Thomas Maule: A prominent Quaker from Salem, Massachusetts, he witnesses the lithobolia attack on the Walton tavern.

Reverend Joshua Moody: Puritan minister in Portsmouth, he provides Reverend Increase Mather with information about lithobolia for his book *Remarkable Providences*.

Elizabeth Morse and her husband, William: Residents of Newbury, Massachusetts, who suffer a lithobolia attack that results in Elizabeth being accused of witchcraft.

Obediah Morse and Joseph Morse: Residents of Portsmouth Obediah is the son of Elizabeth and William Morse, and Joseph is their nephew.

Edward Randolph: A Royalist and supporter of the Mason family, Randolph was the collector of customs for New England. He occasionally boards at the Walton tavern.

Henry Robie: Hampton merchant and business associate of George Walton.

Mary Walton Robie and her husband, Samuel Robie: The daughter and son-in-law of George and Alice Walton. Samuel, a Great Island cooper, is the younger brother of Henry Robie.

Major Nicholas Shapleigh: A wealthy Quaker merchant, ship owner, and a leading supporter of the Royalist cause and of the Mason family.

Mercy Short: The daughter of Clement and Faith Short, neighbors of the Fortados in Berwick.

Joseph Strickland: The son of Elizabeth Strickland Desborough and stepson of Nicholas Desborough, he lives at the Desborough home in Hartford and observes the lithobolia attack there.

Abishag Walton Taprill and Robert Taprill: The daughter and son-in-law of George and Alice Walton; Robert is a mariner, and Abishag runs a shop on Great Island.

Dorcas Walton Treworgy and Samuel Treworgy: The daughter and son-in-law of George and Alice Walton; he is a Portsmouth mariner and nephew of Major Nicholas Shapleigh.

Major Richard Waldron: A leading merchant and magistrate of Dover, he is particularly known for his harsh dealings with both Native Americans and Quakers.

Jeremiah Walford and his wife, Mary: Live on Great Island on land abutting the Waltons' property. Jeremiah is the only son of Thomas and Jane Walford. His son, Jeremiah Jr., inherits the family lands.

Thomas Walford and his wife, Jane: Anglicans and early settlers of Portsmouth; Thomas was a blacksmith, and Jane was repeatedly accused of witchcraft. They have six children who survive to adulthood: Jeremiah, Jane, Hannah, Elizabeth, Mary, and Martha (see family tree in chapter five).

George Walton and Alice Walton: Quakers and tavern keepers on Great Island (present-day New Castle), New Hampshire. They have six children who survive to adulthood: Abishag, Martha, Dorcas, Mary, George, and Shadrach (see family tree in chapter four).

George Walton Jr. and his wife, Mary: George was a shipmaster, captaining vessels for Nicholas Shapleigh.

Shadrach Walton: Probably the youngest child of George and Alice Walton; in 1682 he and his family resided on his father's property on Great Bay in the Piscataqua.

Martha Walton West and Edward West: The daughter and son-in-law of George and Alice Walton, they take over the family's tavern from the Waltons.

Introduction

For the entire summer of 1682, George and Alice Walton's tavern in Great Island, New Hampshire, was the target of what one eyewitness called "lithobolia, or the stone-throwing devil." Hundreds of flying stones plagued the tavern and its proprietors and guests for months on end, causing considerable damage. Amazingly, no one ever saw anyone throwing the rocks. At the same time other mysterious if not magical events of all sorts took place that summer. People heard strange demonic noises and observed objects moving inexplicably about the tavern.

The Waltons accused their neighbor Hannah Jones of using witchcraft to carry out the attacks. The elderly widow quickly responded by declaring that George Walton was a wizard—a male witch. Finally, in the fall of 1682, the lithobolia attacks subsided and the courts dismissed all charges of witchcraft. But this was not before they had spawned copycat incidents in Maine and Connecticut.

Although the strange events on Great Island and their repercussions in the social life of the town are now relegated to the historical footnotes, the drama caused a great sensation when it originally took place. The prominent Boston minister Increase Mather first authored a description of the incident in his book *Illustrious Providences* (1684), and eyewitness Richard Chamberlain published a detailed 7,000-word pamphlet on it in 1698. Yet over time this gripping and unexplained episode was forgotten by all except a few local historians, overshadowed by the Salem witchcraft outbreak that overwhelmed Massachusetts ten years later.

Today it is hard to believe that the peaceful seaside community on Great Island could have been the scene of such mayhem. Indeed, most current residents of the island would not even recognize it by its seventeenth-century name. In 1693 Great Island achieved its independence from Portsmouth, becoming the town of New Castle, New Hampshire, and with the change, the name "Great Island" soon passed out of usage. Lying at the mouth of the Piscataqua River, New Castle today consists of a little over 1,000 residents living on 512 acres of land. The smallest town in New Hampshire, it is a classic picturesque New England village, complete with a white church steeple, old cemeteries, a lighthouse, and ancient cottages built by the fishermen who founded the community. Next to the village, on the grounds of a Coast Guard station, lie the ruins of Fort Constitution; in earlier times it guarded the mouth of the Piscataqua, along with the ships and wharves that once made the region prosperous. Fishing and commercial activity are now gone from New Castle, and there is not even a gas station or a general store. Most residents leave New Castle to go to work, driving over bridges that make life far easier than it was for the colonial residents. The only major business on the island today is Wentworth by the Sea, a grand ocean resort hotel that hosted the 1905 negotiations that ended the Russo-Japanese War. Nearby, the town beach and park offer spectacular views of the waves crashing on the rocky coastline. On a hot summer evening it is the perfect place to go to enjoy a picnic supper, a gentle breeze, and a refreshing walk on the beach.

However much I enjoy visits to New Castle, they are probably more restful for my family than for me. For, when I visit Great Island, I can't help but envision stone-throwing devils and the whole host of other oddities that populate this story. Of course, such images should seem commonplace to a historian such as myself who teaches at Salem State College, in the country's one and only "Witch City." Salem, Massachusetts, is rich in historic houses, museums, and heritage; it was the first settlement of Massachusetts Bay, an early center of the China trade, and home to author Nathaniel Hawthorne, master architect Samuel McIntyre, and the practical navigator Nathaniel Bowditch. Despite this amazing past, however, people consistently focus on the brief, unfortunate months in 1692 when Salem was the site of a series of witch trials and executions. Today, the heritage of the trials is both a blessing and a curse for the City of Salem. With the decline of traditional industry, tourism has become a strong economic force in the city, and the majority of it is focused on witchcraft. The annual highwater mark is Halloween and the accompanying weeks of "Haunted Happenings." (Never mind that there is no historical connection between the 1692 outbreak and Halloween.) Salem even added another dimension in 2006, hosting the international *Harry Potter* festival for the first time.

Since the mid-1970s historians have devoted much attention to colonial witchcraft, producing a pile of books, mostly on Salem, that explore the outbreak through a variety of approaches. So when people asked me about this book, I said I am doing something no one in Salem has done before: writing a book about witchcraft . . . but not about Salem! This invariably gets their full attention, which gives me a chance to explain that, despite its focus on earlier events, in some ways the book actually is about the outbreak of 1692. For when it comes to witchcraft in early New England, all roads eventually lead to Salem.

There still are important lessons to be learned about witchcraft in early New England. *The Devil of Great Island* aims to break down common stereotypes of witchcraft and of early New England society. When the American public thinks of witchcraft, they tend to think of stern New England Puritans recoiling in horror as satanic specters afflict young girls. But the phenomenon cannot be typecast so easily. For several decades, historians have been demonstrating that accusations of witchcraft occurred in Europe and the Americas throughout the early modern era amid peoples of a wide variety of faiths. Furthermore, evil specters were just one form of witchcraft associated at the time with Satan. In fact, scholars agree that the very size and scope of the Salem witch trials suggest that what happened there was atypical of New England witchcraft and therefore not the most instructive case to examine. To really understand the broader phenomenon, you need to look elsewhere.[1]

In some ways, the events of 1682 are similar to those in Salem ten years later. This classic case of witchcraft panic contained most of the expected elements: neighborly and communal conflict, political uncertainty, ethnic division, and religious antagonism. In other important ways, however, lithobolia highlights the differences between Puritan Salem and other outbreaks of witchcraft. Despite what was believed to be the presence of Satan, no evil specters afflicted or possessed anyone on Great Island. With flying rocks appearing and other objects disappearing, lithobolia actually seems closer to what we might call a haunting or a poltergeist. Many other accounts of witchcraft in Britain and New England include stone throwing and similar supernatural events. For example, the famous "Demon Drummer" disturbed a house in Tedworth, England, for months in 1661. In 1679 the Morse family of Newbury, Massachusetts, suffered a supernatural assault of stones and mischief quite similar to lithobolia. A few stones were even thrown in Salem in 1692—a fact that historians have overlooked.

Just as numerous cobblestones came together to form the paved streets of early America, so the stones cast at the Walton tavern were part of a larger pattern of witchcraft and supernatural events in Europe and America over a very long time. *The Devil of Great Island* will start at the Walton tavern and follow these patterns outward to their logical conclusion. Beyond the identity and motive of the tavern's assailants, mysteries will still remain. The origins of lithobolia will need to be explored, as will two amazing copycat incidents later in 1682—one located over 150 miles away. Finally, there are some fascinating links between the events of 1682 and witchcraft in Salem ten year later.

The Devil of Great Island demonstrates the truly diverse nature of early New England society. It is a narrative peopled with Native Americans, Portuguese, Greeks, Scots, and others. This diverse society was a recipe for conflict: Native American versus European, Puritan versus Royalist, and Puritan orthodoxy versus its many challengers. The book is also a story about this clash, as well as the differences between Puritan Massachusetts and northern New England. At Salem, the outbreak began in the parsonage of the Puritan minister. Lithobolia took place in a Quaker tavern. Our story also includes Puritans, Royalists, Baptists, Catholics, Antinomians, and "godless" fishermen.

Recently, historians have worked hard to shed light on the Native Americans, Africans, Antinomians, Quakers, and others who brought diversity to early New England. Some scholars have even pointed to the influence of such "outsiders" in Salem in 1692. However, these groups have usually received this recognition within the framework of Puritan southern New England. When people speak of seventeenth-century New England, most really mean Massachusetts. The founding myths of Plymouth Colony and Massachusetts stand as part of our national epic, embedded deep in every schoolchild's memory. Indeed, as the first settlement established by the Massachusetts Bay Colony, Salem had secured a place in American history long before the witch trials took place. While Salem and Massachusetts have been given a central place in the narrative of American history, New Hampshire and Great Island have been pushed to the margins. It is time to refocus our vision of early America, for as the events in this book show, northern New England has a rich and overlooked history that can teach us a great deal about the foundations of America, and in the process perhaps reveal something about our present situation as well.

One

⟨ornament⟩

The First Stone Is Cast

It was ten o'clock at night on June 11, 1682—the end of a Sunday evening on the peaceful island at the mouth of New Hampshire's Piscataqua River. The light of the full moon shimmered on the ocean as aged George Walton and several companions were strolling toward his home and tavern. The serenity was shattered unexpectedly however, when invisible assailants furiously assaulted them with a barrage of flying stones. As they ran into the tavern, the stones slammed repeatedly into the building. The noise woke Walton's sleeping family and guests, and soon a terrified household had gathered at the entry of the enclosed porch. Boarder and attorney Richard Chamberlain was one of those who observed the stones, some as big as his fist, flying into the porch. The onslaught soon forced everyone to retreat to a more protected part of the tavern. Still they could not escape the fury. Flying rocks appeared inside the tavern and struck two boys in the legs, and Chamberlain was nearly hit in the head. Outside, the rocks continued to batter the Walton tavern, breaking windows and causing other considerable damage. Chamberlain noted that some of the missiles were hot, as if the unseen thrower had snatched them from the fire. The meticulous lawyer even gathered nine of the stones on a table and labeled them. Yet, some of them were soon flying about the room again.[1]

The attack of these "lapidary salutations" continued for over four hours without abatement or explanation. As they peered out the windows into the moonlit night, Chamberlain and his companions were not able to see the culprits. Admittedly, it would have been difficult even in broad daylight to see clearly through typical seventeenth-century windows, which were composed of small imperfect panes of greenish glass held together by lead strips. Still, the invisibility of the attackers seemed to imply something ominous and possibly supernatural, an impression made even stronger by the full moon overhead. In part, the assault seemed to originate inside the house itself. Stones came down the chimney, a large hammer flew across the room, and rocks drove a candlestick off the table top. Several rocks seemed to fall out of the ceiling and others forced the lead strips and frames of the windows outward, suggesting that they had been thrown from inside. In the absence of any logical explanation for what they observed, the household believed it was a supernatural attack perpetrated by the devil himself.

At two in the morning, an exhausted Chamberlain bid goodnight and retired to his chamber hoping to get some sleep. No sooner had he dozed off than he was awakened by a noise so great that it made him think his room was in danger of collapse. Getting out of bed, he realized that the largest stone yet, weighing eight and a half pounds, had broken through his chamber door. He again went back to bed, only to be jarred awake by another missile: a whole brick that clattered down his chimney. Fortunately, the clay intruder was the last of the night. As dawn approached, Chamberlain was finally able to drift off to a brief slumber.

The next morning the stones continued to fly, and more objects moved around the house. The spit disappeared from the fireplace, only to come clanging down the chimney later in the day, while a vanished clothes iron miraculously reappeared in the yard. Still George Walton did not let the mayhem keep him from his tasks. He may have been over sixty, but he was also stubborn and industrious. He and several of his workers headed out to the fields to tend his crops, but the flying stones followed them, as did a mysterious black cat. More rocks inexplicably hit the tavern at ten o'clock on both Monday and Tuesday nights. The long siege that

Chamberlain would dub "lithobolia, or the stone-throwing devil" had begun.

Throughout the summer of 1682, the stones continued to fly, occasionally even seeming to follow George Walton when he left his home on Great Island. Walton would often sail eight miles up the Piscataqua River and into Great Bay to the farmstead he owned at Herrod's Cove, in present-day Newington, New Hampshire. Walton's son Shadrach and his young family occupied the property, which also served as the family's woodlot. One time George and several workmen were cutting trees when they were caught in a hail of stones. Walton painstakingly gathered up a hatful of the rocks and then carried a load of firewood to his boat. Upon his return the hat and stones had disappeared, and rocks soon took to the air again. Meanwhile, back at Shadrach's house, a brick bat flew into a cradle just a moment after one of the Walton grandchildren had been removed from it. On another trip upriver, Walton's boat nearly sank when the bilge plug mysteriously disappeared.

Even the Walton's farm produce suffered an attack. Unknown agents removed and broke up a cheese press, cut down corn crops, and destroyed haystacks, leaving the hay scattered all about—even in the trees. On another occasion, as the Waltons were reaping hay, flying rocks broke three sickles in the hands of workers, as if demanding the harvest be halted. Near the fields people repeatedly heard an eerie snorting and whistling. Others working in the field and orchard heard a humming that sounded like a bullet fired from a gun, yet they heard no gunfire. Despite these supernatural events, and despite being hit over forty times with stones, old George Walton obstinately continued to work in his fields.[2]

Richard Chamberlain attributed the events to supernatural forces, pointing to such evidence as the black cat, the strange noises, and the fact that no one had been seen throwing even one of the thousands of rocks. George Walton and his wife, Alice, shared the belief that witchcraft was at work. After suffering nearly two months of lithobolia, they finally attempted a traditional form of countermagic in hopes of stopping the attacks. They cooked a pot of bent pins in a pot of urine, a concoction often bottled and placed under the hearth of a house to ward off

Figure 1.1 The village on Great Island and the recently constructed Fort William and Mary are seen in this detail of a 1699 drawing by Colonel Wolfgang Romer. Courtesy of the Maine State Archives (Baxter Rare Map 47).

witches. Unfortunately, though, the forces of evil would not stand such a remedy being applied this time: As the liquor grew hot, a stone fell down the chimney, broke the mouth off the pot, and spilled the contents. When the Waltons refilled the pot, a second stone flew in, breaking the handle and again spattering the contents on the floor. They mounted a third and final try, only to have a stone hit the pot once again, this time shattering it to pieces.

The Waltons must have been truly desperate to resort to countermagic. Although such well-intentioned folk remedies had been around for hundreds of years, ministers and magistrates still classified them as illegal and dangerous satanic magic. The Waltons risked public reprimand or even punishment for their failed efforts. The old couple had recently suffered a series of family tragedies and the last thing they needed was more trouble.[3]

By this time, the family had already decided who was responsible, and George Walton publicly accused neighbor Hannah Jones of witchcraft. The family of this poor and elderly—but far from de-

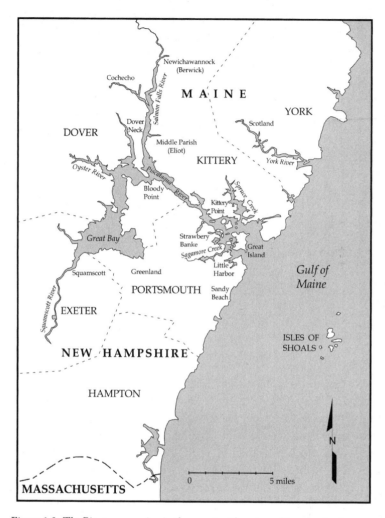

Figure 1.2. The Piscataqua region in the seventeenth century. Drawing by the author.

fenseless—widow had been involved in a bitter thirty-year-old property dispute with the Waltons over the ownership of a mere two acres of marshy field. The fishwife retaliated by calling George Walton a wizard, and her family accused him of trespassing.[4]

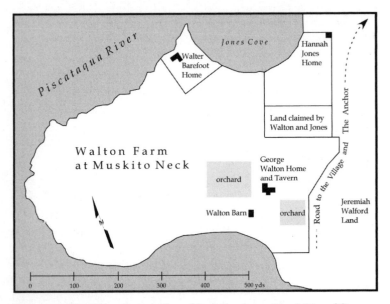

Figure 1.3. The Walton farm on Great Island. Based upon Sketch Map of Great Island, 1699, by Colonel Wolfgang Romer, National Archives of the United Kingdom (CO 700/New Hampshire 4). Drawing by the author.

Despite the charge and countercharges, the stone throwing continued intermittently through August and came to an end only in September after one final assault on George Walton. Early in the month, Walton took his canoe from Great Island to the mainland of Portsmouth to attend the Governor's Council, which was finally scheduled to discuss the case. En route, Walton was battered by three fist-sized cobbles. One blow fractured his skull. He would be in pain from this and the other attacks for the rest of his life. After this incident, the devil made just one more appearance, briefly reemerging to carry off some axes that the Waltons had securely locked up. This was the last recorded incident at the Walton tavern, though people in the region continued to complain of strange events for months to come, including the "monstrous birth" of a baby delivered stillborn with severe physical defects. Seventeenth-century New Englanders considered such births punishment for past sins, as well as portents of terrible events to come.[5]

On the surface, lithobolia appears to be an easy phenomenon for the modern-day observer to explain: Hannah Jones or her family engineered the attacks as a part of her ancient land feud with the Waltons. Whether or not George Walton really believed he was under attack from a "stone-throwing devil" or knew that his tormentor was just an angry neighbor, the accusation of witchcraft was an effective tactic. As one modern observer has suggested, Walton used witchcraft as his ultimate legal weapon against Jones in their endless property dispute.[6]

When looked at closely, however, the pieces just do not fit. Lithobolia was far more than a simple dispute among neighbors. First, Richard Chamberlain's and Increase Mather's published accounts of the episode suggest that Hannah Jones was probably innocent—indeed, she may have been framed for the crime. Even if she was involved, the elderly woman would have needed a legion of accomplices to carry out such vigorous and prolonged attacks in a variety of settings, including the distant home of Shadrach Walton. For the culprits behind such public assaults to remain "invisible" on a small, populous island, numerous witnesses would have had to maintain silence and perhaps even join the attack. Many people would have had to despise the Waltons to allow the attack to continue. Moreover, the family's enemies would have had to include an insider—an employee or boarder who threw things about the inside of the tavern and made axes under lock and key disappear. Clearly, a multitude of residents of Great Island, including possibly even Walton family members, had to actively participate in or silently support the conspiracy.

The identities and motives of the attackers are part of a story that provides a seldom seen view of New England. The tale bubbles with political and legal intrigue, religious controversy, and criminal activity—ranging from fornication to ax murder—carried out by a multicultural cast. The principle setting is the Walton tavern, a place filled with mystery. Why was Richard Chamberlain, the agent for the Mason family (the would-be royalist proprietors of New Hampshire), boarding at the tavern? Why did some of the leading Quakers in America also gather at the tavern that summer? Why was the tavern an issue in Great Island's efforts to separate from Portsmouth? Before investigating these questions, we first need to look back to long before 1682. To modern observers, lithobolia appears bizarre and unusual. The eyewitnesses on Great Island would have had a very different reaction for, in their minds, demons and witches had been throwing stones and other objects for centuries, if not millennia. Such supernatural occurrences were all too real to people in 1682.

Two

Evil Things

Men and spirits have thrown stones in anger since before the dawn of recorded history. Stoning was often a ritualized form of violence, a collective means to punish wrongdoers and to purge community tensions. In this ancient practice we can find the inspiration for the attack on the Walton tavern. Chamberlain drew the name of his pamphlet from the festival of Lithobolia, annually held in Trozen in ancient Greece to commemorate the mythical sacrifice of sixteen maidens who were stoned to death in order to resolve community conflict. Greek writer and traveler Pausanias described Lithobolia in the second century A.D. Supernatural stone throwers may have been at work centuries earlier for the Roman historian Livy recorded the numerous showers of stones that terrified the Romans during the Second Punic Wars (218 B.C. to 201 B.C.). Modern observers have suggested that these were fragmented meteorites, but the Romans saw them as evil omens.[1]

Saint Daniel the Stylite encountered stone-throwing devils in fifth-century Syria. After learning that a coastal church was inhabited by demons who threw stones, sinking ships and injuring passersby, he went to the chapel to do battle with them. When night fell, the imps threw stones at him and caused an uproar. On subsequent nights, the demons became even more menacing, appearing as screaming phantoms and brandishing swords at Daniel. Eventually, however, he drove the demons out of the church.[2]

The first recorded incident of supernatural stone-throwing in Western Europe occurred in A.D. 858, when a demon threw stones, hammered at walls, and sent terror through the community of Bingen on the Rhine River. In the late twelfth century Gerald of Wales reported attacks on houses in Pembrokeshire in his *Itinerary through Wales*. In the early thirteenth century, Gervase of Tilbury recorded similar incidents in his *Otia Imperialia*, a lengthy work on history, theology, and popular piety written for his patron, Holy Roman Emperor Otto IV. Gervase called the stone-throwing demons *foletti*. They were invisible and threw sticks, stones, and household implements at those who dared enter any home they haunted. By the fourteenth century, Englishmen were recording the use of St. John's wort and other remedies to keep "evyll thynges" out of their houses.[3]

Authorities might not have agreed on a name for such phenomena, yet from an early time there seems to have been consensus that the evils existed. Satan could unleash a range of supernatural agents on mankind: fairies, pixies, kobolds, gnomes, boggarts, staines, bilwiz, and goblins are just a few of the names given to these harmful spirits. Elves, foletti, ghosts, or stone-throwing devils wreaked havoc in homes and churches. Probably the most common term for them today is the German word *poltergeist*, which was first used in England and America in the nineteenth century. Today, many of these demons are known through J. K. Rowling's novels, where they are usually tamed by Harry Potter's magic. In earlier times, they seemed much more menacing and real.

The first detailed European descriptions of poltergeist-like activity date to the late 1500s. A local priest, for example, recorded the 1581 affliction of a family in Tuttelstadt, Germany. Unseen hands began to throw lumps of dirt, clay, and rocks at the family and their home. Over time the violence escalated, as plates, spoons, dishes, a range of household goods, and even a two-pound iron ball flew about. Demons spooked the family's cattle and horses and freed them from their stalls. They knotted the horses' tails and hailed the mother with stones when she tried t cows. One night something tried to strangle her oldes next day the family vacated the house amid a shower of objects, including axes, hatchets, excrement, and many of the household furnishings. The assaults only ended after the Catholic bishop came to the house, set up an altar, and celebrated Mass.[4]

A similar attack took place eleven years later in North Ashton, Oxfordshire—the first English case of lithobolia for which there is a substantial contemporary account. For several months, mysterious stone throwing took place in the farmhouse of a prominent local family. Inexplicably, stones ranging from two to more than twenty pounds crashed through the roof of the house. The assaults, witnessed by numerous people, temporarily drove the family from their homestead. When a son came back to stay in the house to see if the danger had passed, his blankets were pulled off his and other beds in the middle of the night. Failing to heed this warning, the family returned and soon the disturbances were worse than ever. In addition to the stone throwing, bloodstains appeared on the hall table, the house was lit up as if by fire, and strange apparitions were observed. Even the high sheriff of Oxford came to investigate. The attacks seemed to be aimed at the homeowner himself, for the stones followed him around and flew most violently when he was in the house. When he died, the violence came to an immediate halt. Perhaps this man's enemies were harassing him just as George Walton's enemies would pester him a century later.[5]

It is difficult to determine what influence the somewhat obscure Tuttelstadt and North Ashton cases had on subsequent events in England and America. The similarities in these and later cases, however, suggest that such incidents may have been common throughout Europe, with stories of them circulating widely though local folklore and the popular press. Comparable incidents continued throughout the seventeenth century in England, and some of these were known to Increase Mather, Richard Chamberlain, and the residents of Great Island.

Odd occurrences like lithobolia attacks, comets, and great tempests, along with mermaids, witches, and other supernatural beasts, were all a part of the seventeenth-century imagination. God could unleash powerful and unexplained forces to vent his anger, or he could give providential signs to warn of troubles ahead. Some people attributed the harm not to God but to the evil spirit itself. Other observers believed that such attacks, while carried out by inhuman forces, had their origins in human witchcraft. A witch called upon Satan to inflict damage on homes and to harm the people who lived in them, generally as a way to seek revenge for a perceived wrong committed against the sorcerer.

The modern American public's view of witchcraft has been so strongly affected by the image of young girls possessed or afflicted by invisible specters that it is hard to imagine any other kind of witchcraft; yet in the seventeenth century, people held witches accountable for a much wider range of miseries. This tremendous power to harm in many different ways accounted for the high terror instilled by a witch. A few souls, however, resisted the scare stories and sought rational explanations for such phenomena. While they were still a small minority in the early 1600s, by the end of the century, a growing number of educated Englishmen were rejecting supernatural explanations for natural phenomena.

Regardless of their personal beliefs, authors and printers loved to publish such accounts, for they were surefire bestsellers among the growing literate masses. Stories of witches, hauntings, and tales of wonder filled the publications of the century. Whether they were Puritan, Anglican, or some other Protestant faith, most New Englanders were religious people familiar with the rich lore of wonder stories in the Bible. Other sensational tales attracted a wide readership, thanks to the printing houses of London. With much of the world still unexplored and unexplained, most people accepted without question the existence of unusual phenomena ranging from witches and goblins to mermaids and monsters. Today people consider comets and eclipses to be harmless natural occurrences; in the seventeenth century, these were acts of providence, divine omens of things to come.[6]

Puritan reformers tried to curb such popular beliefs, superstitions, and celebrations, which they linked to the excesses of the Catholic Church. They preferred conduct that manifested self-control, orderliness, and piety. Massachusetts Puritans viewed the northern New England frontier as a particularly wicked place in need of moral reformation. The lack of ministers and the surplus of ungodly citizens and "heathen" Native Americans led to fears that the region would revert to paganism or Catholicism. In 1641, Puritan Reverend Thomas Jenner complained that when he arrived in Saco, Maine, he found his new parishioners addicted to papist practices.[7]

From 1638 to 1639, and again from 1663 to 1671, John Josselyn resided with his brother Henry in Scarborough, Maine. Upon returning to England he wrote two accounts of the region's flora, fauna, and history. Mixed in with descriptions of birds and fishes, Josselyn discusses such beasts as a triton (a male mermaid) and a giant sea serpent or snake seen coiled up on a rock at Cape Ann. When a triton grabbed onto a canoe in Casco Bay, the surprised canoeist chopped off one of the beast's hands with a hatchet. The dying triton's purple blood quickly stained the sea. Some travelers to unknown parts of the New World brought home tales retold by Josselyn and others. Such was the case in 1671 when the *Falcon of Amsterdam* arrived in Dover, New Hampshire, after sailing for two years in the South Atlantic. The ship's master told of discovering islands occupied by hairy men who stood eleven feet tall. The ocean was a particularly mysterious place, whether at the mouth of the Piscataqua or in the middle of the South Atlantic. Sailors have always been notorious for their tall tales of distant lands. As members of the maritime community on Great Island, the Waltons surely heard their share of these.[8]

John Josselyn and other New Englanders were not only intrigued by stories of strange beasts; they were also fascinated by such natural phenomena as eclipses, comets, thunderstorms, floods, and earthquakes. Despite a growing body of scientific explanations for these events, people often still regarded them as evidence of the power of God and signs of his pleasure or displeasure. Josselyn, for example, suggested that a great sickness that overtook the region might have something to do with the death of the prominent Puritan minister John Cotton. In 1663, a year of several earthquakes in New England, was also the year when three leading ministers died. The next year, when a great comet blazed across the sky, Josselyn pointed out that mildew and blight destroyed much of the region's crops.[9]

While today one might label such linking of events superstitious, in colonial times even educated members of the community accepted these connections as signs of God's providence. For example, in 1684 the Trustees of Harvard College moved the date of graduation when they learned a solar eclipse would take place on July 2, the originally chosen day. Seven months before the graduation, Harvard's president and two college officers expressed concern when they realized the coincidence. Although not superstitious by the standards of the day, these men understood the power of providential signs such as eclipses. The overseers soon moved the commencement date to July 1. The ceremony went without incident, but when the college president died the next day, just as the sun started to emerge from the eclipse, many took this as a sign that concern over the solar phenomenon had been entirely justified.[10]

Increase Mather, the prominent Boston minister and the deceased Harvard president's successor, must have been particularly interested in the eclipse, for he had just completed *An Essay for the Recording of Illustrious Providences*. In 1681 Mather revived the project, first put forward in the late 1650s by the English Presbyterian Matthew Poole, of creating a register of providences. The project was formally initiated in May 1681 at a gathering of all the ministers of Massachusetts. Clerics throughout New England would report to Mather any "Divine judgments, tempests, floods, earthquakes, thunders as are unusual, strange apparitions, or whatever else shall happen that is prodigious, witchcrafts, diabolical possessions, remarkable judgments upon noted sinners, eminent deliverances, and answers of prayer, are to be reckoned among illustrious providences."[11]

Mather undertook his project in reaction to efforts made by Anglican leaders in Restoration England to de-emphasize providential acts and instead accent reason and rationality in religion. In addition to being a Puritan theologian, Increase Mather was a talented amateur scientist who believed that there was still a place for wonders. He saw his book as an opportunity to scientifically observe and catalog acts of providence in order to better understand their place in God's plan. Mather was not alone in a renewed interest in providence. Between 1672 and 1698 four English ministers turned their attention to the topic, publishing books on acts of providence in the Bible.[12]

It was no coincidence that Mather took on this effort in the early 1680s, when people in Massachusetts were still reeling from the disaster of King Philip's War. Many viewed the war as a terrible sign of God's displeasure with New England, and rumors of renewed Indian attacks panicked the land well into the decade. Threat of attack came from England as well, for the Royalist assault on Massachusetts had grown particularly intense. In 1680, New Hampshire had been taken away from Massachusetts Bay, and the colony's charter was under increased threat of revocation. The religious situation in England did not look much better. Puritans were particularly concerned that the aging Charles II would be succeeded by his younger brother James, a man who threatened to bring Catholicism back to England. Meanwhile on the Continent, the growing power of Louis XIV meant a resurgence of Catholicism and a threat to the French Huguenots and other Protestant groups. In January 1682 Reverend Timothy Woodbridge preached in support of the French Huguenots at a prayer vigil held at Boston's South Church. In a mournful sermon full of dark imagery, he lamented that "We know not how soon our own turn may come." By that summer Woodbridge had moved to the Piscataqua where he witnessed the lithobolia attack on the Walton tavern. He must have thought his turn had indeed come.[13]

Under these spiritual conditions, it makes sense that the early 1680s were ripe with omens and prodigies for New England Puritans. Comets, terrible storms, even a rare tornado were all precursors to 1682, a year that was particularly remarkable for tempests and portents. February's blood-colored eclipse of the moon was followed in the summer by the arrival of a great comet. English astronomer Edmund Halley saw the comet and predicted that it would return in seventy-six years—hence Halley's Comet. In 1682, however, New Englanders took it as another sign of trouble. It is no surprise that many saw the devil's hand in lithobolia that summer.[14]

By the 1680s, there were numerous cases of lithobolia and other hauntings well known to both Englishmen and New Englanders. The tumultuous years of the English Civil Wars, the creation of the Commonwealth, and the restoration of the monarchy seem to have been a time particularly fraught with the supernatural. The worst outbreak of witchcraft in English history took place in East Anglia during the civil wars of the mid-1640s, resulting in more than 100 executions. More would follow in the years to come, as would publications popularizing the events.[15]

Joseph Glanvill's 1668 *A Blow at Modern Sadducism, or Philosophical Considerations touching the being of Witches and Witchcraft* was a widely read source for supernatural tales in this era. This Anglican scholar was a skeptic and a defender of the new natural philosophy of Robert Boyle and others. Glanvill believed that the existence of witchcraft had to be determined on empirical, not metaphysical, grounds. Only by examining the factual evidence could one determine whether or not witches, ghosts, goblins, and related phenomena actually existed. Glanvill and others believed that a science of witchcraft was possible, and that the presence of witches could be a valid scientific explanation of paranormal phenomena. These views demonstrate that the emergence of the scientific revolution in England in the later seventeenth century did not guarantee the dismissal of belief in the supernatural. Glanvill and his colleagues believed that it was possible for witches to exist in a scientific world. Even the great scientist Robert Boyle wrote that "one circumstantial narrative fully verified" could prove the existence of witches.[16]

Glanvill's work remained an influential best-seller long after his death in 1680. Henry More edited and republished it as *Saducismus Triumphatus: Or, Full and Plain Evidence Concerning Witches and Apparitions* just a year before lithobolia hit the Walton tavern. The most popular story in *Saducismus Triumphatus* was the Demon Drummer of Tedworth, a spectacular haunting on the scale of the Walton's lithobolia. In March 1661, John Mompesson was visiting the village of Ludgersall, Wiltshire, when he ran across William

Drury, a former soldier who was fraudulently trying to raise alms for the poor—drawing attention to his cause by constantly rattling out songs on his drum. Mompesson exposed the man, seized his drum, and had him arrested. He then took the drum to his home in the neighboring village of Tedworth, only to be assailed repeatedly by supernatural drumming and knocking on the walls. The problem in the house continued off and on for months. At times it included sulfurous smells (the brimstone associated with the devil) and glimmering lights. Chairs walked about the house, shoes flew, and a bedstaff hit the town's minister when he came to address the problem. The Mompesson children seemed to be particularly susceptible to attack. The drummer would beat their bedsteads and throw off their bedclothes. The children became so terrified they had to seek refuge at a neighbor's house. At other times, the beds would levitate in the air as servants tried to sleep in them. On Christmas Day, a Bible was buried in the hearth ashes. The sounds of people walking in hallways were heard, and doors were seen to open and shut, but the observers saw no one.[17]

Similar to the spirit that haunted North Ashton, the demon drummer emptied chamber pots into beds and then smeared fireplace ashes across the mess. As with other cases, animals were present—possibly "witch's familiars." A dog's panting and scratching were heard under the children's bed. Another time the bed itself seemed to purr like a cat. A linen bag moved as if a rat or mouse was in it, but the bag proved to be empty. The afflictions continued for months.

Drummer William Drury was suspected of carrying out these acts, especially after he confided to a fellow jail inmate that Mompesson would continue to suffer for taking away his drum. Being jailed for another crime during the attacks was not an effective alibi in the seventeenth century. Officials merely assumed that he had used diabolical means to afflict the Mompesson house. A grand jury indicted Drury for witchcraft, though he was ultimately acquitted of the crime.[18]

The Drummer of Tedworth was one of the most infamous cases of witchcraft in English history. Word quickly spread of the disturbance, and people came from far and wide to see and hear the mischief. Even the king and queen sent their representatives to observe the strange happenings. A broadside ballad was immediately published about the drumming, and Glanvill's account soon followed. The drummer incident occurred at a time in England when there was increasing skepticism over witchcraft, hauntings, and related wonder stories. Glanvill was a true believer, but others pointed to several suspicious aspects of the tale that suggested Mompesson had faked the incident. When officials came to investigate the case, they found no unusual phenomena.

The controversial story of the Drummer of Tedworth was well known to Americans as well as Englishmen. Increase Mather published a brief account of it in his *Illustrious Providences*, including it in the same chapter with his report on the lithobolia attacks on Great Island. Even in the increasingly skeptical eighteenth century, people still remembered the demon drummer. Two letters published in the *Pennsylvania Gazette* in 1730 described a copycat incident in Pennsylvania. While these may have been a literary hoax designed to ridicule superstition—possibly written up by none other than Benjamin Franklin—the author clearly depended upon his audience's familiarity with the Tedworth tale.[19]

Mather compared the case of the demon drummer to the demonic possession of the Morse family home in Newbury, Massachusetts in 1679 and 1680. The strange events that occurred in the house of William and Elizabeth Morse would be one of the longest lasting and best known cases of witchcraft in early New England. They would also have direct ties to the Waltons' lithobolia attack several years later just a few miles up the coast in Portsmouth.

In December 1679, a series of lithobolia-like attacks commenced at the Morse house. Spirits tossed sticks and stones at the walls, windows, and roof of the humble home. Chairs flew about, a chest moved, and a bedstead lifted off the floor as a terrified Elizabeth tried to make the bed. Unseen agents hurled a cat at Elizabeth. Late one night a great noise awoke the Morses, who soon found a hog crashing about the house. The entire household—William, Elizabeth, and their young grandson, John Stiles, suffered constant attack. Stones, a box, a board, and even a bag of hops hit them while they tried to sleep. Ashes flew out of the fireplace to ruin meals. In fact, much of the disturbance took place around the hearth and chimney. Bricks flew about, an apron was thrown into the fire, and, most amazingly, a long staff danced in the chimney. One night, William left a shoe downstairs only to have an invisible agent fill it with charcoal and ashes and throw it upstairs after him.[20]

While the modern observer would see the shoe as just more mischief, Mather and his contemporaries would have recognized this as an effort at counter magic. People left shoes near fireplaces and hearths, believing that an empty shoe could capture evil spirits. Since chimneys were an easy entry point into a house for malevolent beings, the shoe was intended to catch the evil as it entered the house. This folk belief persisted well into the eighteenth century. In 1999 in York, Maine, workers found a cache of eighteenth-century shoes in a hollow adjacent to the chimney and hearth while carrying out repairs to the 1719 Old Gaol museum. Many other cases of witchcraft and counter magic in early New England focused on chimneys.[21]

Soon the afflictions in the Morse house centered on young John Stiles. When he was put to bed, a great noise was heard in his chamber, and he claimed that his bed was jumping up and down. He began to suffer odd twitches and seizures, so the Morses twice took their grandson to a doctor for treatment. On both occasions he improved, but the fits came back when they returned to the Morse residence. Upon homecoming the second time, Stiles cried out in pain, and when his grandparents looked to see what was wrong, they "found a three-tin'd fork sticking strangely there." The Morses recognized the fork as coming from the doctor's house, though the physician's servant claimed to have seen it in its proper place after Stiles's departure. If so, the implication was that the fork had not been stolen by Stiles; rather, it had been supernaturally transported from the doctor's house to the Morse home and lodged in Stiles's back. Soon, other objects were found sticking in the poor boy's back, including an iron spindle, a spoon bowl, and several knives. One knife even seemed to come out of his mouth. The fits continued, sometimes causing Stiles to bark like a dog or cluck like a hen.[22]

Such cases of possession had taken place before in both old and New England. The erratic behavior of the boy was reminiscent of the 1671 performances in Groton, Massachusetts, of Elizabeth Knapp, who many believed to be bewitched. People who were allegedly afflicted often appeared to be pricked by pins, knives, nails, and other sharp objects. Sometimes the objects even appeared in their mouths. The most notorious case was that of Anne Gunther, an English girl who had the attention of much of England in 1606. Indeed, her case was studied personally by King James I, himself an amateur demonologist. Eventually authorities determined that, under her father's guidance, Anne was faking her possession, and that the pins were being produced through sleight of hand. John Stiles was clearly doing the same thing.[23]

The first thing to allegedly pinch Stiles was the doctor's three-tined fork, a unique luxury item. Though today we take table forks for granted, they were still novelties in early New England. By the mid-seventeenth century, most Englishmen had begun to eat with forks, which were invented in Renaissance Italy. This new utensil took much longer to be adopted in New England. Still rare throughout most of the seventeenth century, forks were usually owned only by the upper classes. In the 1680s, a doctor—that is, a prominent and wealthy member of the community—might have been one of the few residents of Newbury to own a fork. A three-tined fork would have been particularly rare. Most early forks were two-tined iron forks with bone or wooden handles. The only known surviving three-tined fork from this time period in New England was uncovered from the 1690 shipwreck of the *Elizabeth and Mary*, a ship transporting members of the Dorchester, Massachusetts, militia home from Sir William Phips's unsuccessful expedition against Quebec. The three-tined fork from the *Elizabeth and Mary* is a fancy specimen, made out of silver. Such a rare and valuable curiosity must have proved an irresistible temptation for the troubled young John Stiles. When he got home, the lad must have realized his theft would soon be revealed—after all, not just anyone owned a three-tined fork. To avoid detection and punishment, he feigned the supernatural attack by stabbing himself in the back. The doctor's servant may have been his accomplice in the theft or perhaps was just taking pity on the poor boy by supporting his story.[24]

Soon, an acquaintance of the Morses' named Caleb Powell, a transient seaman temporarily residing in what is now Newburyport, seemed to offer them hope. He volunteered to help the boy, who initially seemed to respond to the efforts. Powell sent Stiles away from the Morse home, and the afflictions and the lithobolia attacks immediately ended, returning only when Stiles came back to the house. It seemed that Powell had come up with the cause of the disturbances: John Stiles. Ironically, the Morses began to hold Powell responsible for their problems. After all, if he was able to control Stiles, perhaps Powell was also to blame for the boy's outbursts. Furthermore, Powell had hinted that he had access to counter magic, or perhaps sorcery itself. One observer testified that Powell had been trained in the dark arts by Francis Norwood, Sr. Norwood lived in nearby Gloucester, where he was widely believed to be a wizard—probably because he was a prominent Quaker. On Wednesday, December 3, 1679, William Morse went to the local magistrate to make a formal complaint of witchcraft against Caleb Powell.[25]

By spring, Powell had been acquitted, and instead Elizabeth Morse stood charged with witchcraft for afflicting her own grandson and attacking her own home. In the extensive testimony that followed, people expressed their long-held suspicions of Elizabeth. One witness said that even William Morse called his wife a witch and claimed she was capable of both healing and harming people with magic. At least Morse had the good sense to suggest that his wife could help people with her magic. Still, bewitching your home and family was quite unusual. Hannah Jones may have been thinking of Elizabeth Morse as well as the Quaker Francis Norwood when she accused Quaker George Walton of being a wizard willing to attack his own home.

Despite the fact that her own house and family had been damaged, Elizabeth Morse was found guilty of witchcraft in May 1680 and sentenced to death by hanging by the Court of Assistants. Some of the assistants must have expressed doubts over the conviction, for a few days later the court issued a stay of execution until their next meeting. A second stay was granted in October, and in the spring of 1681, Elizabeth was allowed to go home under house arrest, ordered not to go beyond sixteen rods (264 feet) from her house and land, except to go to church. Though the death sentence still officially lay over her head, it would never be carried out.

Even aside from the supernatural events that took place in the Morse house, it was, as John Demos has indicated, a deviant and unhappy household. Grandson John Stiles was apparently a bastard, and another Morse daughter had a child out of wedlock as well. A third daughter was absent from the household, showing up only in her father's will. Rather than dutifully staying near their parents, the Morses' two sons, Jonathan and Obediah, both fled Newbury at an early age.

Obediah Morse provides one of several direct links between the events at his parents' house and the lithobolia attack on Great Island, for in 1670 he abandoned Newbury and bought land in Portsmouth. At the time Morse was about twenty-five years old. He probably migrated to Portsmouth with his cousin, Joseph Morse, a fellow blacksmith who first showed up in the town at about the same time. (Mechanical skills must have been a strength of the Morse family: Joseph's great-great-grandnephew was the inventor and painter Samuel F. B. Morse.) While Obediah lived on the mainland, Joseph Morse bought a house and land on Great Island from none other than George Walton. The house was located on present-day Walbach Street, close to the fort. It was also next to "The Anchor"—the old Walton tavern that at the time was owned and operated by the Walton's daughter Martha West and her husband Edward. When Joseph Morse died from smallpox in January 1679, Obediah bought the home from Joseph's widow. Obediah apparently remained in his home in the Strawbery Banke neighborhood and did not reside in his cousin's house. Still, while the supernatural events at his parents' house and on Great Island were taking place, Obediah Morse was the owner of a former Walton home, located literally a stone's throw from one of their taverns. When the Walton tavern was attacked by a stone-throwing devil, Obediah's mother, Elizabeth Morse, was under house arrest for witchcraft, including a lithobolia assault.[26]

The Morse family had their differences with George Walton. In the spring of 1678, Joseph Morse was a plaintiff in an unspecified court case against the Quaker. When the court met on June 25, Morse withdrew the charges, though Walton must have been at fault, for he agreed to pay the four shillings in court costs. The two families certainly held opposing political views. Obediah Morse signed the 1677 petition asking the king to keep New Hampshire under Massachusetts's jurisdiction. Several years later Obediah sued royal customs agent Edward Randoph for breaking open the door to his house in search of smuggled goods. Morse clearly supported Massachusetts and opposed the Royalist cause. He was also a leading member of the Puritan church. In 1671 he contributed ten shillings to the voluntary subscription to pay the salary of Reverend Moody. Perhaps an average donation, it was still a significant amount for a young tradesman who had only recently moved to town. Wealthy George Walton was notably absent from the list, as were all members of his family except son-in-law Edward West, who offered to "pay what he can."[27]

By the late 1670s, Obediah Morse had become a well respected member of Moody's congregation. In 1678 the town entrusted him to serve as one of the tithingmen to enforce the Sabbath. His task was to make sure his neighbors attended worship services, snooping inside their houses if necessary to root out shirkers. Perhaps these differences over religion and royal allegiance led Obediah to initiate or encourage the assaults on the Walton tavern. Even if he was not responsible for the attacks, Obediah Morse would have known the specifics of the attack on his parent's home. His stories about the incident may have inspired others to attack the Waltons.[28]

When Increase Mather described the Morse case in *Illustrious Providences*, his source for the story was none other than Portsmouth's Puritan minister, Reverend Joshua Moody. Moody regularly corresponded with Mather, providing him specifics of similar events in the Piscataqua for Mather's book. Furthermore, Joshua was raised in Newbury, and both his father William and brother Caleb played a role in the Morse case. Caleb deposed against Elizabeth Morse, suggesting she had used black magic to kill his pig some sixteen years earlier. William Moody twice took down a horseshoe over the doorway at the Chandler house. The shoe had been placed there specifically as counter magic to keep Elizabeth Morse out, for it was feared that she was bewitching Mrs. Chandler. The first time he simply removed the shoe, calling it "a piece of witchery." When William next visited the house and saw the shoe restored, he pocketed it to prevent more of the counter magic that he considered witchcraft. Joshua Moody was close enough to the Morse case to acquire a description of the incident written by William Morse himself.[29]

The Woodbridge family provided another link between Newbury and Portsmouth. Retired minister and Newbury magistrate John Woodbridge witnessed many of the depositions made in the Morse case. His son, Reverend Timothy Woodbridge, was living on Great Island or across the river in Kittery, Maine, in 1682. Most likely Timothy resided with his sister Dorothy and her husband, Nathaniel Fryer, a Great Island merchant. So, not only were there members of the Morse family living in Portsmouth in 1682; two local ministers also had family involved in the case. Plenty of people in the Piscataqua knew the details of the Morse case, which could have inspired them to carry out the lithobolia attack on the Waltons.

While early New England was filled with wonders, not every odd occurrence required a supernatural explanation. Sometimes mobs or gangs of youths openly threw stones at the targets of their anger. A dramatic example of such collective violence took place at the same time as the attack on the Morses, less than twenty miles away from their Newbury home. On Christmas Night 1679, four young men entered the house of John and Mary Rowden in Salem Village (present-day Danvers, Massachusetts). In the tradition of Christmas wassailing, the men sang several songs and demanded a cup of perry from Rowden. "Perry" or "peary" was the pear equivalent of apple cider—both of these fermented beverages were quite popular in early New England. Proper Puritan New Englanders did not celebrate Christmas, so John Rowden denied the men's request and told them to be gone. The lads became indignant and offered to pay Rowden for perry if he would not give it to them. This time Mrs. Rowden answered the men, telling them that she and her husband did not run a tavern and demanding that they leave. The crew departed, only to return with another offer to pay for their perry; the coins they produced this time, however, turned out to be slugs of lead. The Rowdens and their adopted son finally managed to convince the visitors to leave the house. However, the rowdies did not go far, retreating about forty feet from the house and shouting at the Rowdens, daring the son to come out and fight. When it became clear that he could not be baited, the men assaulted the house.[30]

For an hour and a half, they bombarded the Rowden residence nonstop with stones, bones, and other objects. They also tore down a stone wall, broke the door off the root cellar, and stole five or six pecks of apples. The damage sounds very similar to that caused by the lithobolia attack on the Waltons. The only difference was that this time the assailants made their identity all too clear. They proved to be four young men between the ages of seventeen and twenty-one, from some of the poorer families of Salem Village. One wonders, however, if the young men had stealthily assaulted the house with stones from the cover of the woods, whether this too might have been considered a case of witchcraft. Instead, Salem Village would wait thirteen years for the first of such accusations, when the community became the focus of the Essex County witchcraft outbreak of 1692.[31]

At any rate, a long tradition of stone-throwing, by agents natural or supernatural, had long been in place at the time of the Walton incident. New Englanders had fresh knowledge of lithobolia and similar mischief and would have recognized it as witchcraft.

Three

The Waltons

Historians have provided several glimpses of the controversial George Walton and the lithobolia attack on his tavern, but the case has never been explored in any detail. Like most of his contemporaries in early New England, Walton left behind a very modest paper trail. No letters, business papers, or other family documents survive, leaving sizable gaps in his story to be filled with historical guesswork. Still, a fascinating picture of a seventeenth-century New England settler and his family emerges from the fragments.[1]

George Walton was born about 1615, somewhere in England; no other facts about his origins are known. In later documents, his occupation is listed as tailor. Presumably, he completed his apprenticeship in this profession when he was in his early twenties and then joined the Great Migration of Puritans and other Englishmen who would populate the new Massachusetts Bay Colony. George first appeared in the records in Boston, Massachusetts, on December 4, 1638, when Suffolk County magistrates convicted him for swearing. This unbecoming behavior suggests why he soon left Boston, and perhaps even hints at Walton's involvement in the so-called Antinomian Controversy that gripped Boston at this time.[2]

The Antinomian Controversy demonstrates the range of beliefs held by nonconforming (or dissenting) Protestants in England in the first half of the seventeenth century. Thousands of Englishmen agreed that the Church of England needed reform, but they hotly debated the exact nature of the changes to be made. These people held a broad spectrum of beliefs all labeled "Puritan"; they did not subscribe to some monolithic "Puritan Church." Some reformers, including those who migrated to Plymouth in 1620, believed the Church of England had become so corrupt that they had to completely break with it. Others, including the settlers of Massachusetts Bay, thought that they could best reform the church from within. They formally maintained membership in the Church of England, even though they were separated from it by the Atlantic Ocean as well as by theological differences.

Once in Massachusetts, the Puritan settlers adopted numerous different interpretations of the Bible, and during the 1630s the government fought several battles to create and maintain a religious orthodoxy and a political hierarchy. Roger Williams, the brilliant and mercurial young minister of Salem, fell victim to this quest when he challenged government and church officials on several points. In 1635, after authorities ordered him to quit the colony, he moved south to Narragansett Bay, founding what would become the new colony of Rhode Island. The next major controversy arose in Boston, Massachusetts, over the individual's role in achieving salvation. One of the two ministers of the Boston Church, Reverend John Cotton, disagreed with the majority view that people must actively seek faith before they could receive God's grace. Rather, Cotton argued that God gave salvation to sinners without conditions. These ideas were expanded upon and actively promoted by Cotton's followers, including Anne Hutchinson and her brother-in-law, Reverend John Wheelwright. Historians would later dub these people "Antinomians."[3]

The Antinomian interpretation of Scripture disturbed many Massachusetts Puritans. They believed that the saved had to lead morally pure lives, maintain a godly society, and serve as examples for the unregenerate. Even though Cotton and his followers agreed that everyone should lead godly lives, the idea that this was not an absolutely necessary condition for salvation seemed to some to encourage amoral behavior and, ultimately, to threaten a breakdown of civil society. Faced with a growing social, religious, and political challenge from the Antinomians and those who supported them in the name of religious freedom, the magistrates decided to take action. In 1637, Massachusetts Bay banished Hutchinson and Wheelwright and disarmed and disenfranchised many of their followers. John Cotton managed to avoid prosecution.[4]

The two banished leaders soon split company. Anne Hutchinson, her family, and some of her followers went south to Aquidneck, in what would eventually become the colony of Rhode Island. Meanwhile, Reverend John Wheelwright and about twenty families moved north to found Exeter, New Hampshire. Wheelwright was a popular and charismatic leader and Puritan intellectual. He was also an imposing presence. He was known for his wrestling at Cambridge University, where he was a classmate of Oliver Cromwell, the future leader of Parliament's cause in the English Civil Wars. Cromwell is supposed to have said that he was never afraid of meeting any enemy army in combat as much as he feared meeting the daunting figure of John Wheelwright on the football (or soccer) field.[5]

New Hampshire had actually been established as a colony before Massachusetts Bay, but when Wheelwright arrived in early 1638 it was still a loosely settled frontier. The colony had been without effective government since the death of John Mason three years earlier. Mason held title to lands in the Piscataqua region and invested much time and money in establishing settlements. He died while he was preparing to leave England to come lead the fledgling colony. His untimely death left New Hampshire in a fragile and uncertain state.

At the time New Hampshire consisted of small settlements at Strawbery Banke (later renamed Portsmouth) and Dover. In July 1639, Wheelwright and the thirty-four other adult male church members signed the Exeter Compact. Like the more famous Mayflower Compact, the Exeter document was a social contract written by people who wanted to establish order in a new land, far from English authority. The residents agreed to grant themselves liberties similar to those of Massachusetts Bay and to live peacefully under Christian law in a godly manner. George Walton was one of the signers of the Exeter Compact.[6]

Walton had been in Boston as late as December 1638, which means that he did not leave with Wheelwright and the other initial settlers of Exeter. One can only speculate why Walton eventually did follow this northern migration, though several possibilities come to mind. He may have arrived in Boston during the controversy, or perhaps even after the departure of Wheelwright for New Hampshire. Possibly his conviction for swearing precipitated his departure. Most likely he had close ties to Wheelwright or members of his group. Exeter's founding group was dominated by Wheelwright's family and friends, many of whom shared his Lincolnshire origins. George Walton could have been of these, for a man with his name was born in 1617 in Threekingham, a village just fifteen miles from Boston, Lincolnshire, and a hotbed of Puritanism where John Cotton had preached before immigrating. Regardless of the specific reasons, it does seem quite likely that Walton moved to Exeter because he preferred Wheelwright's brand of Puritanism to that of Massachusetts Bay. In 1639, a recent immigrant could select from a number of different settlements in Massachusetts. It is unlikely that someone would choose to go to the small and remote frontier town of Exeter, known for its controversial minister, for reasons other than religious.[7]

An analysis of the Wheelwright followers and the Exeter Compact itself sheds some interesting light on this group. First, its members were considerably less radical in their religious beliefs than Anne Hutchinson and those who moved to Rhode Island with her. None of Hutchinson's vocal supporters belonged to the Wheelwright group, and five Exeter settlers had even received a formal "dismission" from the Boston Church. Rather than being forced out of the church, the dismission certified these Exeter settlers as Puritan church members in good standing who could form their own congregation in their new community. Authorities did not force the Exeter settlers to leave Boston; rather, they chose of their own accord to follow the charismatic Wheelwright. The Exeter group also demonstrated surprising loyalty to Charles I. English Puritans had been the leading opponents of the king throughout the 1630s, and many had migrated to New England because of his efforts to persecute Puritans. The Exeter Compact makes elaborate statements of loyalty to the Crown, and soon after settlement authorities even arrested one resident for making comments disloyal to the king. In April 1640, the town went even further, prescribing the death penalty for anyone who attempted treason or rebellion against the Crown. Royalist tendencies of this sort were unheard of elsewhere in early New England. Presumably, the residents of Exeter hoped the king might check the expansionist ambitions of Massachusetts, for the Bay Colony clearly desired to expand its northern border to include the settlements of New Hampshire. George Walton would support the king and oppose Massachusetts for the rest of his life.[8]

Walton's name appeared in the Exeter town records only when he signed the Exeter Compact. He received no acreage in the first division of land in the fall of 1639, and there is no evidence that he ever owned property in the community. By 1643, he had moved to the adjoining town of Dover, where he established a home and tavern. In 1646 the Dover court fined Walton five shillings for selling beer at three pence a quart, when the colony had set the maximum price at two pence. It must have been a reasonably large tavern, for court was held there several times. In 1648, Dover assessed Walton's real estate and personal property at £84. The fifty-six taxpayers on the rate list owned property ranging from £156 10s down to £4. Only thirteen men were assessed at a higher rate than Walton, which means that he was among the more prosperous men in Dover. He took advantage of the opportunities presented to him to prosper in his new homeland.[9]

The Dover Neck neighborhood where Walton lived and worked was at the crossroads of local commerce. This narrow neck of land separated Great Bay from the Piscataqua River, and the road that ran along the point served as the principle land route for those traveling along the river valley. It was a fine location for a young man to establish a tavern and to seek his fortune. Standing outside his business, George Walton could observe ships sailing along the river, hear the bustle of the shipyard, view his

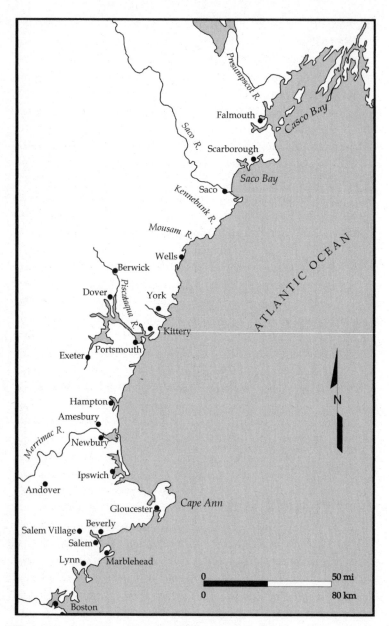

Figure 3.1. Coastal New England from Boston to Casco Bay. Drawing by the author.

neighbor's tanning yard, and smell the drying codfish harvested by local fishermen.[10]

Walton may even have been able to see the nearby Dover meetinghouse. In its first decade, four ministers came and went from the community. Most were religious radicals who departed because of theological disagreements with the community or transgressions of its moral codes. No surviving documents specifically indicate George Walton's personal religious views or his opinions of these clerics. However, when his early years in New England are viewed collectively, an interesting pattern emerges. In a few short years, Walton had moved to three communities—first Boston, then Exeter, then Dover. All three were caught up in religious turmoil, and at each step, Walton was moving to a more radical community. This trend toward extremism became even more pronounced in his later years when Walton joined the Quakers. It is tempting, then, to conclude that his religious views influenced his movement. Alternatively, a woman may have been responsible for his relocation, as is often the case with a young man's behavior.

George Walton probably met and married his wife, Alice, during his years in Exeter and Dover. He would have been in his mid-twenties when he moved to Exeter in 1639, typical marrying age for men in early New England. Unfortunately, all too little is known about his wife, the woman one Quaker writer called "one of the most Godly women thereabouts." Genealogists have speculated that she was the daughter of William Hilton of Dover Point, one of New Hampshire's first settlers. An eighteen-year-old Alice Hilton did indeed migrate to the Americas in 1635, on board the ship *Ann and Elizabeth*, but her parents migrated to New England a dozen years before. Also, the *Ann and Elizabeth* was destined for the Barbados—certainly an indirect route to New Hampshire. Still, circumstantial evidence does suggest that it was Alice Hilton who married George Walton. A year or two younger than George, she would have been the right age. Furthermore, Walton's Dover Point home stood a short walk from the Hilton homestead. From the high ground where he lived, George could look across the cove and down to the end of Dover Point and see the Hilton home. Walton had business dealings with the family as early as

1642. Later connections between the Waltons and Hiltons also suggest ties between the families, so even if she were not William Hilton's daughter, Alice may have been a member of the Hilton clan. If she was, then George Walton married wisely. Brothers William and Edward Hilton owned extensive property and held numerous political and military offices. Their sawmills and merchant activity quickly made them one of the wealthiest families in New England.[11]

The names of six of George and Alice Walton's children survive, and a seventh unnamed child died at an early age. Daughter Mary was born about 1646, making her one of the oldest children. George Jr., the oldest son, was born in 1649. Son Shadrach, born in 1658, was the youngest; in between there were three more daughters: Abishag, Dorcas, and Martha. Quite large by today's standards, the Walton family was fairly typical for early New England.

On November 25, 1648, Walton sold his tavern and another house on seven acres of land on Dover Neck and prepared to move his family. He also sold six acres of marsh in the Cocheco area of Dover and twenty acres of land on Oyster River (present-day Durham). The purchase price of the property was two pipes of wine. A pipe was a very large barrel, usually holding 126 gallons of wine. So, Walton exchanged his lands for 256 gallons of wine, which would have had a wholesale price of approximately £100. This was a substantial sum, roughly equaling the total wealth (house, land, and possessions) of a typical resident of the area at the time. Sold at retail at Walton's tavern, the wine would have been worth far more. By the terms of the deed, Walton was given until April 1649 to turn over the premises. A month before this deadline he purchased a house and one hundred acres of land at "Muskito Neck" on Great Island, in Portsmouth. It was in this home that Walton and his family would suffer the lithobolia attack some twenty-three years later.[12]

At the time Walton acquired the property, the house probably consisted of only one room. Known as the kitchen, this room would have measured twenty feet by twenty feet at the most, and it could have been considerably smaller. The kitchen would have been dominated by a massive hearth and fireplace critical for preparing meals and for keeping the family warm when the cold winter winds whipped across Great Island. A lot of living took place in this one room. A modest loft above would have provided sleeping space, but most daily chores and activities would have been crowded into the kitchen. Here they might gossip with neighbors, share a joke or a prayer, or read with great anticipation a rare letter from family or friends back in England.[13]

Thanks to extensive deforestation, English carpenters had to be frugal in their use of lumber, but settlers to New England were thrilled to find an overabundance of wood. Therefore, New England houses were framed in massive timber beams which often measured twelve inches by twelve inches. Provided the homeowner could afford the hand-forged nails, the ready supply of timber also meant that these homes usually had clapboard exteriors and shingled roofs—features rarely found in England. The clapboards protected thick walls made of wattles (interwoven sticks and branches) covered with daub (a plaster of sorts usually made of mud, clay, animal dung, and straw). The interior walls probably would have

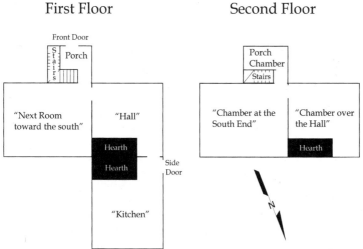

First Floor   Second Floor

Figure 3.2. Conjectural plan of the Walton home and tavern during lithobolia in 1682. Drawing by the author.

been left with the daub exposed and painted white, to brighten up an otherwise dark room.

Glass windows had to be imported from England, so they were expensive. Typically, there might be two or three small windows in a kitchen. The little panes of greenish glass, held together by a latticework of lead, provided only a modest amount of light. The fireplace and a couple of candles or a simple oil lamp did not improve the situation very much. The house probably had an unpleasant odor, too. People rarely bathed, and most kitchen garbage was merely thrown out the door of the house. The only thing that kept down the stink was the overwhelming smell of smoke, coming from the fire that was always burning on the kitchen hearth.

By modern standards, the Waltons and their neighbors lived in small, dark, crowded, and smelly homes. Yet the picture is far more distasteful to us than it would have been to them. Present day historical reenactors and living-history museum interpreters have found that they soon grow accustomed to the smells of early America. People had no expectations of privacy, and they had few furnishings or goods, so houses were not cluttered with possessions. In the seventeenth century, most living took place outside the close confines of the house. Farming went on from sunrise to sunset out in fields or barns. In good weather, many chores and activities would have occurred outside as well.

Still, most settlers did their best to expand their homes as soon as time and money permitted. Sometime before 1682 an entire new wing with front porch and entry was added to the Walton home. This two-story addition provided two additional downstairs rooms. One was a hall meant to serve several purposes. It combined the function of a modern-day formal living room and a master bedroom. It usually contained a family's finest possessions, which would be used to serve and impress guests. It also typically contained the best bedstead in the house. However, in the crowded homes of the day, there was little privacy, and children often slept in the hall along with their parents. Next to the Walton hall was another substantial room, whose function is unclear. Presumably it served as the tavern, at least in the 1680s, when this house was both the family home and place of business. Unfortunately, the only formal mention of the room comes in a probate inventory written long afterward, where it is recorded simply as the "next room toward the south."

Upstairs there were three chambers or bedrooms. Two were sizable rooms, above the hall and the "next room toward the south." The third was a much smaller chamber over the porch. The chamber above the parlor might have been the only one to have a fireplace, so the other rooms may have been particularly cold in the winter. The expanded Walton home, complete with

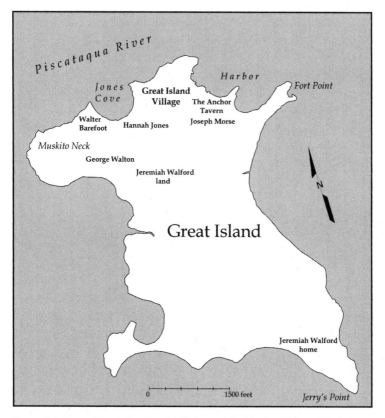

Figure 3.3. Great Island, showing the Waltons and selected neighbors. Based on Romer's 1699 Plan of Great Island. Drawing by the author.

three rooms and three chambers, was a bit larger than most neighbor's homes. Still, as many as nine members of the family lived there, along with several servants. It must have been a very crowded and busy place.

The town of Portsmouth would grant George Walton a piece of land on the waterfront at Great Island, less than a mile northeast of his home. On this site he would soon build a new tavern, named The Anchor. In 1650 he was licensed to keep an ordinary (or tavern) and to sell wine. The next year, the court renewed his license and also gave him permission to keep a ferry. The family would own and operate The Anchor for many years.[14]

On May 5, 1657, a devastating personal tragedy struck the Walton family. Alice Walton prepared dinner for her husband George and went to deliver it to him in the fields where he was working, leaving the children under the care of her eldest daughter, a teenager. When Mrs. Walton returned, one of the younger children was missing. She asked her eldest daughter where the child was, only to receive an answer dreaded by every parent: the child was there a minute ago but now was nowhere to be seen. Mother, daughter, and several neighbors made a hasty search, only to find the child drowned in an unfenced well. Two days later, the family had to undergo the additional trauma of having the body examined by a coroner's jury, who determined that the toddler, whose name is lost to history, had drowned accidentally. This death was the first of numerous family tragedies that George and Alice Walton would have to suffer. The loss probably also damaged the Waltons' reputation in the community. Dangerous unfenced waterholes did not create favorable impressions with neighbors, especially when children were left unattended. Remarkably, the well was still unfenced nine years later, despite the fact that both the Walton's child and a farm animal had drowned in it.[15]

Death was not uncommon for children in early New England. Infant and childhood mortality rates were far higher than they are today. About a quarter of all children born in seventeenth-century New England died before reaching adulthood. But the high incidence of childhood mortality probably did not make the event any less devastating for parents. Considering the circumstances,

George and Alice's mourning must have been tinged by guilt and perhaps even angry accusations at each other or their children. The death may have caused them to look at their spiritual life and to ponder why God would have allowed them to suffer such loss. Self-reflection of this kind leads some people to redouble their faith. In the case of the Waltons, it may have provoked them to alter their religious convictions, for soon after the death, George and Alice Walton would become Quakers—a move that would change their lives.[16]

Four

The Neighbors from Hell

At first glance, George Walton appears an unlikely target for an attack. By today's standards, he would seem to be a model citizen. He worked hard to build a prosperous life and a successful career in a new land. He went to great lengths to find religious freedom. He eventually became a Quaker, a faith renowned today for its commitment to pacifism and egalitarianism. Walton welcomed people of diverse racial and cultural backgrounds as workers and guests at his tavern. Unfortunately for George, though, early New England was vastly different from modern America. Many of Walton's contemporaries would have taken issue with his beliefs, practices, and even his occupation. Furthermore, Walton and his family had a dark, tragic side that further damaged their reputation. His was not the idyllic and peaceful Walton family seen on television in the 1970s. Amazingly, George Walton and his clan were the neighbors from hell.

There were signs of trouble even before the drowning of their child in 1657. Running a tavern often meant inviting problems, for it could be the scene of ungodly behavior. Furthermore, Walton often took a stubborn, pugnacious attitude toward people, as his legal disputes attest. Still, neighbors largely overlooked these concerns until the Waltons underwent their spiritual conversion. Historian Richard

Archer has pointed out that the turning point in George and Alice Walton's lives was their 1664 conviction in court for being Quakers.[1]

Quakers were one of the more radical of the Protestant sects to emerge during the English Civil War. Along with such dangerous religious extremists as the Ranters, the Seekers, and the Fifth Monarchists, the Quakers had their own interpretation of the word of God. Like many of these groups, the early Quakers also preached a social egalitarianism that many Englishmen feared. To the modern-day observer, it is hard to believe that the peaceful group who would come to be known as the Society of Friends was considered a serious social, political, and religious threat to the Puritans of New England. Massachusetts considered Quakers to be such a threat that they put three to death simply for trying to practice and spread their faith.[2]

On February 2, 1664, the court convicted George and Alice Walton of being Quakers, less than a year after their daughter Abishag Taprill, also a Quaker, had been presented at court for not attending worship for several months. Her claim that she was ignorant of the law did not protect her from being fined and admonished to attend in the future. Although official persecutions of this sort soon came to an end, a significant stigma remained attached to the Quakers, in part because they were associated with social radicalism, law-breaking, and even witchcraft. George Walton was no exception. In 1660, he was called as a witness in a case of adultery against a Kittery couple who used his tavern as the scene of their illicit encounters. The court also charged Walton with theft on two different occasions. In 1651 a fisherman testified that Walton had stolen a jar of olive oil, though he later admitted to having fabricated the charge. In August 1676 Walton was called before the court on suspicion of stealing a cloak, though he escaped conviction once again. Thus, while Walton was never convicted of theft, people had their suspicions, and these were magnified by his Quakerism. His new faith seemed to make him the target of legal attacks. As Richard Archer has pointed out, Walton was sued repeatedly after his conversion. After 1666 he did not win one of the ten remaining law suits he would participate in, though six were settled out of court.[3]

Owning a tavern (or ordinary) also singled out the Waltons for trouble. At a Portsmouth town meeting held September 25, 1662, the selectmen raised multiple concerns about the disorderly tavern. Not only had George Walton failed to renew his license at the last county court, he had also done a poor job of running the ordinary. Walton promised to do a better job running the tavern, but this did not satisfy the selectmen, who asked Walton and his wife to live on the premises to maintain proper decorum. Without promising to occupy the ordinary, Walton answered that he would closely monitor the people he hired to do so. The freemen of the town were unhappy with this response and voted to give the tavern license to someone else. No doubt there was concern over one of Walton's recent hires. Earlier that year, George had employed a man to work in the tavern who had recently been convicted of drunkenness, cursing, and swearing, among other offenses. This was not the sort of man the community trusted to draw beer, wine, and liquor for thirsty tavern denizens, especially when the tavern keeper was often absent.[4]

After the town vote Walton must have changed his mind about living on the premises, for several weeks later the county court renewed his license to keep the ordinary. The following July, the license was transferred to his son-in-law, Edward West. The selectmen of Portsmouth recommended that West keep the ordinary because he maintained an orderly tavern and provided civil accommodations to all. At the same court, West confessed to serving strong liquors without a license and paid a £5 fine. Apparently West and his wife, Walton's daughter Martha, had been the resident proprietors of the family tavern for some time, allowing George and Alice to move back to their home at Muskito Neck.[5]

Edward West had recurring legal problems of his own, though he continued to run the tavern until his death in 1677. Soon after he received his license, the Portsmouth constable searched the premises for goods stolen from the ship *Blue Dove*. A witness had tipped off authorities that a thief had shown him some stolen pearls in the tavern. No charges were filed against West, but the incident further contributed to the tavern's unsavory reputation. In 1667, West's servant was whipped fifteen stripes and sentenced to serve his master for another year because he had run away and had been suspected of stealing twenty-four pieces of eight. The next year, West became involved in a lawsuit over a debt of £30 that resulted in his temporary arrest. In 1671, the court found that he allowed gaming, swearing, and drunkenness in his tavern and fined him forty shillings. It could have been worse, for he was also accused of being drunk himself, but the charges were dropped when the court determined that the informant was a slanderous liar.[6]

The busy port of Portsmouth, with its many visiting mariners and other travelers, had more taverns than the surrounding farming communities. Ordinaries served as gathering places where locals could come together, relax, talk, and enjoy a drink. Wine, beer, ale, and liquor would have been the staples of the tavern. Hard apple cider and perry were New England favorites as well. Liquor and wine were imported from England or Europe, while the other potables were produced locally. Edward West was a vintner, and an inventory of his tavern, The Anchor, included a brew house. Early New England taverns had a wide range of characteristics and reputations. Though people did not use the term at the time, some could be considered inns—places providing a bed for the night as well as food and drink for the traveler. Other establishments were primarily used for the drinking and socializing that all too often led to carousing, gaming, and other acts of revelry. By the second half of the seventeenth century, this rowdy sort of tavern was becoming a serious issue. George Walton was sometimes a part of that problem. In 1650, for example, he and Robert Mendum were fined five shillings for delivering excessive amounts of wine to the Isles of Shoals, the fishing islands located in the Atlantic Ocean ten miles off the coast of Portsmouth. They sold the wine to the thirsty fishermen who got drunk and started a brawl. The same court also accused Walton of breach of the Sabbath for transporting a load of lumber to the Isles of Shoals on a Sunday.[7]

In the 1660s, New Englanders observed a sharp increase in drinking and such related crimes as fighting, fornication, and vandalism, particularly among servants, young people, and visiting sailors. These problems were more extreme in large coastal towns like Portsmouth and Salem. Ministers led the attack against excessive consumption of alcohol. In 1673 Increase Mather published two sermons on the sins of drunkenness, to be followed by another publication in 1676. Coming in the midst of King Philip's War, this later jeremiad railed against the slide toward drunkenness of New England's once sober Puritan society. Excessive drink and related vices signified spiritual decline and another reason for God's anger at the New England experiment.[8]

Taverns were a necessary part of society. Courts were often held in them, for they were amongst the largest houses and the only place where food and accommodation were available for the magistrates and others who traveled to court. As selectmen had told the magistrates, a busy port town like Portsmouth needed taverns to serve the numerous visitors to the town, and Walton's was the only tavern on Great Island, a part of Portsmouth that was growing in commercial importance. Coastal tavern keepers, including George Walton, often ran ferry services as well, since weary travelers usually waited for the ferry at a tavern. At the same time, taverns were dangerous places that could threaten a community's order, stability, and godliness.[9]

Walton's problems with the tavern were directly tied to a career change. George aspired to become a merchant and money lender, and these activities eventually left him no time to run the ordinary. In the late 1650s, he accepted mortgages on property to secure several loans. While most of the debts were promptly repaid, George held one mortgage for twenty acres of marsh in Kittery so long that the land became known as George Walton's marsh. In the early 1660s, he gradually made the shift from tavern keeper to merchant. Once he turned the tavern over to the Wests, there was no looking back. But it was not always a smooth transition. For example, in 1664 a Portsmouth trader sued Walton for a debt of £119 and a prominent Boston merchant sued Walton for nonpayment of a £40 bond.[10]

New England merchants depended on personal ties to cement their business relations, so marriage alliances were common between their families. Several of the Walton children made marriages that enhanced their father's business endeavors. The most important of these was daughter Dorcas Walton's marriage into the family of Nicholas Shapleigh, the leading merchant of Kittery, Maine, just across the Piscataqua River from Great Island. George Walton and Shapleigh were old acquaintances who had much in common. They knew each other by 1650, when Walton witnessed the laying out of land in Kittery to Shapleigh. Shapleigh frequented Walton's tavern. A court deposition in 1654 noted that someone seeking Shapleigh found him merrily drinking at Walton's establishment. Aside from business interests, both men supported the king and the royalist cause in New England. Also, both were among the earliest Quaker converts in the Piscataqua.[11]

Dorcas Walton married Samuel Treworgy, Nicholas Shapleigh's nephew. Samuel's parents were Katherine Shapleigh Treworgy and her late husband, James. Samuel's grandfather was Alexander Shapleigh, a wealthy and powerful merchant of Kingsweare, Devon, which was an early investor in Maine. The very name of Kittery was derived from Kittery Quay in Kingsweare, the site of the Shapleigh wharf and warehouses. When Alexander sailed to Maine, he came on one of his own ships—a testament to his considerable wealth and power. As early as 1642, the family's Piscataqua holdings were valued at £1,500, a huge sum at a time when a typical settler's real and personal property was worth about £100. The Shapleigh investments ran the gamut of early New England enterprises, including the fisheries, lumbering, ship building, the fur trade, and land speculation. Alexander only occasionally visited Maine, preferring to leave his investments in the care of his family.[12]

James and Katherine Treworgy brought their six children with them to Maine. Through a series of marriages, the Treworgys and Shapleighs came to be at the hub of a number of important alliances. Daughter Elizabeth married John Gilman, whose family owned sawmills in Exeter. Daughter Lucy married Humphrey Chadbourne, a wealthy merchant, mill owner, and magistrate who was the largest property owner in Berwick, Maine, just upriver from Kittery. After James Treworgy's death in 1650, Katherine married Edward Hilton, another prominent landholder and sawmill owner with extensive holdings on Great Bay, between Exeter and Dover. If Alice Walton was indeed a member of the Hilton family, the Waltons had allied themselves to the Hiltons in two different ways. Together, the Shapleighs, Hiltons, Gilmans, and Chadbournes controlled much of the timber industry of the Piscataqua. It is no wonder that George Walton's wharf included a lumber warehouse. Undoubtedly, son George Walton Jr. docked there many times, for he was captain of Nicholas Shapleigh's bark, *Trial.*[13]

George and Alice Walton's daughter, Mary, born about 1646, married into another Piscataqua merchant family. She wed Samuel Robie, whose brother Henry was a business partner of her father's and a fellow signer of the Exeter Compact. In 1649, Henry helped to build the sawmill in Exeter. He soon moved to the adjoining town of Hampton, where he became a civic leader, serving repeatedly as selectman, constable, justice of the peace, and a justice of the court of sessions. Born in 1628, Samuel was eleven years younger than Henry and apparently followed him to New England at a later date. In 1662 he bought five acres of land in Hampton, adjoining to his brother's holdings. The following year he moved to Great Island and practiced his trade as a cooper. About this time, he married Mary Walton, who was roughly eighteen years his junior. Samuel's move to Great Island may have been related to a major business venture initiated that year by his brother and George Walton. His marriage to Mary would have cemented this partnership.[14]

To gain capital for the venture with Henry Robie, George Walton mortgaged his tavern and all his property on Great Island for £254. The substantial property involved in this deal indicates his growing wealth. The tavern property included wharves and other buildings, while the farmstead at Muskito Neck included a barn and outbuildings. Walton's business focused on lumber and fish—the chief exports of the Piscataqua and the driving force behind the growing prosperity of early New England. For example, in 1662 Humphrey Wilson acknowledged himself indebted to George Walton for 13 shillings and 4 pence, and 900 feet of pine boards. Three years later, George sued another man over an investment in a fishing voyage.[15]

Daughter Abishag Walton wed a ship's captain, Robert Taprill, another useful son-in-law for a merchant to have. Presumably

Robert was some relation to the William Taprill who was noted as a servant of the Waltons in 1652. By 1672 the Taprills and their three daughters lived in Boston, occupying the home of Alexander Waldron, who may have been a kinsman of the Walton family. However, it was an unhappy marriage, and not long after 1672, Abishag left her husband and returned to her parent's home on Great Island. Robert died in November 1678 at sea, as captain of the ketch *Providence*. He left no will, so as death approached him, his crew asked him about his estate. Taprill said that while he had a wife and three children, "they never were a penny ye better for him." He gave his entire estate to a friend and nothing to his wife and daughters. Abishag Taprill lived and died in a house provided by her father. She made a living for her family by operating a shop out of the home. It was a modest business at best, for Abishag did not even own any of the goods for sale; rather the items were on consignment from her father, her sister Martha, and others. When asked how her property should be disposed of in the event of her death, she lamented that she had no estate.[16]

The deaths of Abishag and Robert Taprill were two of the many family tragedies suffered by George and Alice Walton in the late 1670s. These would rock the family far more than any criminal accusations, and also damage the Walton's reputation further. Now in their sixties, the Waltons had seen their children marry and start raising families of their own. They were of an age when they could expect to slow down and rely on the younger members of the family to do the bulk of the work. However, within a few short years most of the Walton's grandchildren would be left parentless. Abishag passed away several months after her estranged husband, leaving their three daughters as impoverished orphans. Oldest son George Walton Jr. was alive in June 1678 but dead by the summer of 1679, the year of his widow's remarriage. She and her only surviving child, Samuel, moved to the Rye home of her new husband, Samuel Rand. Daughter Dorcas and son-in-law Samuel Treworgy also must have died in the mid-1670s, when they disappear from the records without a trace. It is quite possible that they were among the unrecorded victims of King Philip's War (1675–1678), the devastating conflict between the English and Native American

The Waltons and their Relations

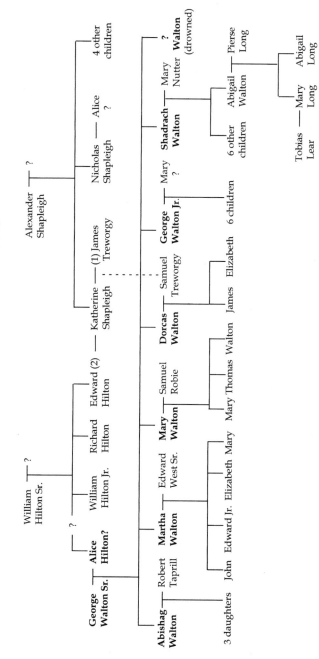

Figure 4.1. The Waltons and their Relations

residents of New England. The Treworgys left two young children. Son-in-law Edward West also died in 1677, to be followed by the Waltons' daughter, Martha, in 1679. The Wests left four young children. Thus, in a few short years, George and Alice lost four of their six children and three sons-in-law. Nine young grandchildren had been orphaned. Life in the seventeenth century was uncertain, and few people who lived into their sixties did not suffer the loss of close family members, including children and grandchildren. However, this string of deaths must have left the entire family reeling. The elderly Waltons now had responsibility for numerous grandchildren, and they also had to resume the challenge of running the family tavern.[17]

The death of almost an entire generation of the Walton family soon led to problems. Take the example of Edward and Martha West's young son, John. On June 27, 1679, soon after he became an orphan, the court accused him of theft. Indeed, John West faced charges of stealing from his late mother's clothes chest. Amazingly, his accomplice was his own aunt—Mary Walton, the recently widowed wife of George Walton Jr. John acknowledged stealing £1 17s from the chest and was assessed triple damages, making his total debt £35 11s, payable to the estate's administrator, his grandfather George Walton Sr. The court also committed Mary Walton to jail until she paid a £5 fine. It is notoriously difficult to translate historical currencies into modern day equivalents. However, £5 was certainly substantial. At the time it would have bought an ox, or a good horse with saddle.[18]

A family member would typically have been appointed guardian of a young child; however the court chose non-relatives to serve in this capacity for both John and Edward Jr. These appointments suggest that either George and Alice had their hands full looking after the rest of their orphaned grandchildren or that the community did not entirely trust the elderly Waltons to care for a toddler. Some of the grandchildren were servants and maids at the tavern, but the grandparents certainly did not need the help of nine children. It may have been too much to look after all of these youngsters. Teenaged granddaughter Alice Taprill seems to have been particularly troublesome. In 1685, officials issued a search warrant for George Walton's house to find the fetus or child that Alice had delivered. Years later, Alice's sister would bear an illegitimate child.[19]

There also may have been some tension between the Wests and the Waltons behind the court's decision to appoint an outsider as guardian. In 1669, George Walton had sued Edward West for debt. It must have been a serious public conflict to have led Walton to sue his own son-in law, who ran the family tavern.[20]

Inevitably controversy swirled around these people, for in addition to their troubled family relations, the Waltons also had difficulties with a series of indentured servants and hired hands. In 1666, servant Walter Weymouth was in court, attempting to gain freedom from his indenture to George Walton. Weymouth had exclaimed to Dorcas Walton that he absolutely would not stay with her father, even if it meant going to the highest court in the land to be free of his indenture. One deposition in the case hints that George had beaten and verbally abused Weymouth. Perhaps Weymouth felt that Walton had taken advantage of him. This was the case of John Davis, another indentured servant of the Waltons, who had deposed against Weymouth in 1666. Six years later, Davis would be in court himself, trying to win his freedom from Walton. The court ordered Davis released, after it determined that he had served eleven years of an indenture that was supposed to last only five. Incredibly, Walton had tricked Davis into believing that the terms of the indenture allowed Walton to extend his service. In 1663, a court of inquest was called to look into the death of another servant of George Walton's; the verdict of the court in this case is unknown.[21]

In addition to his indentured servants, Walton also employed others to work at his tavern and other enterprises. In 1665, for example, he hired Dermon O'Shea, who was still working for him fifteen years later. O'Shea was an older man of forty-five when Walton hired him, and he stood out as one of the few Irishman in the Piscataqua region. As such, he had probably been raised as a Catholic, which would have further distinguished him from his neighbors. O'Shea was convicted of abetting the indentured servants of prominent Portsmouth merchant Richard Cutts in robbing their master.

Dermon hid the stolen goods in his home, presumably with the intention of selling them. Great Island blacksmith Joseph Morse seemed to harbor a particular dislike for O'Shea. In 1677, he was imprisoned in the Dover jail for assaulting the elderly man, leaving Dermon's face and head so bloodied that his son feared his brains had literally been beaten out of him. The animosity between Morse and O'Shea came less than a year after Joseph bought his house from George Walton. The beating of a close Walton associate may be another indicator of tensions between the Walton and Morse families.[22]

Not only did the questionable characters hired by Walton pose a threat to a well-ordered society; on at least one occasion Walton incited other servants to take action against their masters. In 1657, the court fined him £5 for urging an Irish indentured servant to defy his master, John Pickering. Walton must have been reviled for such actions, for Pickering was a wealthy and prominent citizen, and the underclass of servants in early America could be a dangerous element. In 1675, the residents of Portsmouth would learn this all too well when two foreign-born servants murdered their master, a Great Island fisherman. Diarist Samuel Sewall recorded the spectacular crime: "A Scotchman and a Frenchman kill their master, knocking him in the head as he was taking tobacco. They are taken by hew and cry, and condemned: hanged." Two foreigners brutally murdering their master as he was trying to relax with a pipe of tobacco must have shocked and appalled respectable New Englanders, and reminded them of the dangers of unruly servants and outsiders.[23]

Although no Scotsmen or Frenchmen worked for George Walton, he did have two true outsiders—Native Americans—among his servants. Mary Agawam had been employed in the tavern for many years. Her surname suggests she came from the vicinity of Ipswich, Massachusetts, which the natives called Agawam. Mary's bastard son, William, was born in 1659. When magistrates inquired about her fornication with a transient sailor, Mary confessed that William had been conceived in Walton's tavern late on a Sunday afternoon. In 1678, the court bound William to George Walton until he reached the age of twenty-four in 1683.

William served as a constant reminder of how his mother had desecrated the Sabbath at the unruly tavern. Beyond this religious issue, the very presence of Native Americans in the household during and after King Philip's War would have been exceptional. Only one other Native American is known to have been a household servant in the Piscataqua region during these uneasy times on the northern frontier. King Philip's War had only ended in 1678 in Maine and New Hampshire, and the peace that prevailed was a troubled one, punctuated by recurring rumors of new native uprisings. In 1688, these tensions would boil over, resulting in the start of King William's War.[24]

King Philip's War proved to be a bloody turning point in New England's history. The three years of fighting led to a huge loss of life and property that would take years to recover from. Officials estimated that £150,000 of English property was destroyed during the war and that the colonies had spent £100,000 to fight it. Hundreds of Englishman and Indians were killed in a war that spread throughout most of the region but hit the frontier of northern New England particularly hard. Most of the towns of Maine and New Hampshire suffered some sort of attack, and many Maine settlements were completely destroyed. Portsmouth was spared direct attack, though the fort on Great Island did manage to fire its cannon when a Native American raiding party attacked homesteads just across the river at Kittery Point.[25]

Even if Portsmouth avoided destruction, the community's losses were substantial. The Massachusetts General Court raised taxes repeatedly to pay for the war, adding to the burdens of all citizens. The town was flooded with refugees from Maine, who often became dependent on local charity. In addition, local militiamen left the community to go fight in Maine. Even the local fishermen came under threat. In the summer of 1677, Indians began attacking English fishing vessels as they sailed along the coast of Maine. In July alone, Wabanaki warriors seized close to twenty fishing vessels and crews.[26]

The attacks abated enough by September 1677 for George Walton Jr., William Agawam, and several other companions to sail up the Maine coast and into a scandalous war-related incident.

George Jr. led a group of about a half-dozen young men on a plundering expedition to the English farmsteads abandoned by refugees from the war. The party included his younger brother, Shadrach, William Agawam, and three other men, including kinsman William Hilton Jr. The men would later claim that they went to harvest hay, but they did not own any property in the area. They did know that the farms of coastal Maine contained many abandoned acres of planted crops and hay that were ready to harvest. When they sailed into Cape Porpus, they noticed two large, unattended stacks of hay. A couple of local men warned the crew that the hay belonged to Ferdinando Huff, a Cape Porpus selectman who had fled the community along with most of his neighbors. Young George ignored the warning, saying it was better for him to take it than to leave it rotting. So the men filled their boat with the harvest. Presumably they looted other abandoned farms before sailing back to Portsmouth.[27]

George Jr.'s band would have gotten away with their plundering, but Ferdinando Huff had sought refuge from the war in Portsmouth. When he heard of the theft, the angry Huff charged George Jr. with trespassing and stealing his hay. Walton was brought before the court in December 1677. In his defense, he declared that Cape Porpus tavern keeper Richard Palmer had said the stacks were his and given them to Walton. Unfortunately, Palmer was not the best alibi. Only a few years earlier, the tavern keeper had been fined for marrying while under suspicion of already having a wife in England. Huff won the case against Walton, and the court awarded him £3. Young Walton inherited his father's stubborn streak, for he refused to let the embarrassing case end there. The Court of Associates heard his appeal in June 1678. George Jr.'s new defense rested on a legal technicality: since the alleged trespass and theft had taken place in Maine, the New Hampshire courts had no jurisdiction. The court refused to listen, and Walton was forced to pay the £3 plus £2 4s 6p in court costs.[28]

Most of the residents of Portsmouth had suffered during King Philip's War. Some had lost their homes or family members, while others had to pay higher taxes or serve in the militia. The Waltons must have earned a substantial black eye from the Cape Porpus affair. William Agawam's presence on the expedition would have been particularly damning. Many of the homes of Maine had been sacked and destroyed by raiding Wabanaki Indians. Rather than fighting Indians like most able-bodied young men, the Walton clan had gone looting with an Indian. If William and his mother had tried to keep a low profile in Portsmouth during the war, this sorry affair ended all hope of anonymity. There can be no doubt that the presence of Native Americans in the Walton household would have caused considerable consternation among the English population.

Richard Chamberlain may have been referring to Mary Agawam as the "Negro Maid hit on the Head . . . with a Porringer" during the lithobolia attack. A man straight from England in the 1680s would have had little previous exposure to Africans, and had probably never seen a Native American. It is certainly possible that he confused the two, particularly in this era when racial lines had not completely hardened in the minds of Englishmen. Alternatively, the Walton household may have also included a slave from Africa or the Caribbean. Although traditionally associated with the southern colonies, in the seventeenth century slaves were shipped to the north as well. New England merchants imported slaves in small numbers, generally using them as household servants. There were a handful of slaves in the Piscataqua region in the second half of the seventeenth century. When Nicholas Shapleigh died in 1682, his probate inventory included five slaves, valued at £90. Tellingly, they show up in the inventory right after the swine—but just before the two Irish indentured servants. So it is possible that George Walton owned a slave; however, Chamberlain does not mention the Agawams or any Native Americans in his account, so most likely the Negro maid was in fact Mary Agawam.[29]

All together, the Walton household was a wild, barely controlled mix of people—Native Americans, Irishmen, Quakers, criminals, and possibly even an African slave. Such a household was the absolute antithesis of the orderly English Puritan homes sought by the civic leaders of Portsmouth. A contentious and controversial figure, George Walton had poor relations with many of those in his employ. His choice of servants and employees, the charges against him, and the death of an unsupervised child were all signs of the disorder under Walton's roof. His family even stole from each other. Even worse, George Walton was a religious radical who attempted to incite turmoil in other households. The family tavern, The Anchor, operated at the fringes of legitimate society. A place of drunkenness and fornication, its very name advertised its desire to cater to the rowdy mariners who sailed into Portsmouth from all over the Atlantic. In sum, there were more than enough reasons for neighbors to dislike the Waltons, throw rocks at them, and even accuse them of practicing witchcraft inside their unruly tavern.

Five

⟨⟨⟨⟨⟨⟨⟨⟨⟨⟨⟨⟨⟩⟩⟩⟩⟩⟩⟩⟩⟩⟩

Fences and Neighbors

Something there is that doesn't love a wall,
. . . 'Good fences make good neighbors'.

—Robert Frost, "Mending Wall"

New England's great poet Robert Frost understood Yankee ambivalence toward boundaries. People worry about what is being fenced in and what is being fenced out, and argue over who has the right to decide. In "Mending Wall," Frost suggests that there is no real need for the stone wall between his apple trees and his neighbor's pines, yet the two men meet every year to repair their wall. They maintain this physical and social boundary because his neighbor believes in the Yankee truism passed down from father to son: "Good fences make good neighbors." Robert Frost's direct ancestor, Nicholas Frost, was one of the earliest settlers in the Piscataqua, and Frosts still live on Frost Hill in present-day Eliot, Maine. The Frost homestead even shared a boundary with George Walton's in-laws, the Treworgys. Certainly these early families would have understood the poet's interest in fences, for they witnessed many struggles over boundaries.

These arguments struck at the heart of a town, for they put in conflict the importance of neighborliness and community with the rights and prosperity of individual families. It should come at no surprise that combative George Walton was frequently involved in the Portsmouth land disputes. His quarrel with the Walford family was at the very center of the lithobolia attack.

Land troubles frequently clogged the courts and dominated the town meetings of early New England. The relative simplicity of the temporary court systems and the roughness of the methods for parceling out land added to the confusion. Sometimes land was granted to prospective settlers on the condition that they find a location to claim it, as in Portsmouth in 1660 when the selectmen granted several men an acre of land each on Great Island "somewhere not yet given already." The imprecise methods and temporary markers used to lay out land were often invitations to future disputes. Consider the bounds of the twenty acres of land laid out on Great Island to Jeremiah Walford in 1658: "forte pole or rod from the east of a pale of the garden Due north to a forked pine and a hemlock tree growing out of the side of the pine near the stum(p) as it is marked at the stumpe noched in with an axe and then(ce) Due east to the sea sore with the neck of land layinge out to the mouth of the little harbour." Not only were these inexact bounds open to multiple interpretations, but the cutting down of a tree, or the collapse of a rotted fence could quickly lead to a heated argument over a boundary.[1]

The disputes were not limited to individuals, for entire towns often debated their boundaries with one another. Portsmouth, for example, had a recurring conflict with Dover over its border. Both communities claimed an area that came to be known as Bloody Point, after the fierce but actually bloodless confrontation over the land. After years of arguing, a 1643 commission awarded the area to Dover. The town won the case because its boundaries, including Bloody Point, had been guaranteed when Dover submitted to Massachusetts two years earlier. Portsmouth had no such confirmation of any of its bounds, so property concerns lingered and festered there, even contributing to a plot to overthrow the authority of Massachusetts Bay in 1651. The rebellion never took place.

Rather, residents put their various concerns into a petition to Massachusetts Bay, including a request that authorities confirm the town borders.[2]

The General Court responded by formally establishing the line between Portsmouth and Hampton. This settled one uncertain boundary, though problems persisted with Dover over lands fronting on Great Bay. The town requested that George Walton accompany two selectmen to Dover to try to resolve the outstanding boundary differences. Although Walton held no official office, his neighbors must have felt that, as a former resident of Dover, he could help mediate the disagreement. Unfortunately, a resolution eluded Walton and his associates, and the next year residents of Portsmouth again asked the General Court to recognize their ownership of the disputed lands along Great Bay. With no answer coming, the community changed tactics. In 1657, the Portsmouth town meeting simply awarded much of the disputed land—from Herrod's Cove to Welchman's Cove—to George Walton and five other men. The selectmen made the grant under the condition that the men would defend the claim in court if necessary. Walton and his partners further acknowledged that the land was part of Portsmouth, and that they would only pay property taxes to Portsmouth. Eventually the General Court would award much of the disputed territory to Portsmouth, and 112 acres at Herrod's Cove would be laid out to George Walton, who would turn it over to his son Shadrach. The lithobolia attacks would follow George Walton to the property in 1682.[3]

Disputes over property division and land use gripped many towns in the seventeenth century, largely because these transplanted Englishmen came from a country with numerous regional landscapes, each with its own system of agricultural landholding and social structure. For example, farmers in East Anglia, who mostly grew cereal crops, did not have much in common with West Country dairy farmers. When people from far corners of the realm came together to found a new town and divide its land, problems inevitably arose. In some areas of England, the prevailing system was still the open field, in which farmers cooperated with the neighbors to work their own strips of land situated within large fields farmed in common. Elsewhere, men enclosed their individual holdings and worked their farms largely independently of their neighbors. Some Englishmen farmed commercially, exporting to the growing English cities, while others struggled for subsistence. These diverse people would have different ideas of how to treat common land, how to fence their holdings, and how many acres of land they needed to farm. Hence, disagreements were common.[4]

Tensions over land became more acute in the later seventeenth century. Growing populations led to a scarcity of land in coastal New England. Some of this pressure had initially been eased by the establishment of towns in the interior. But in 1675 the outbreak of King Philip's War between the Native American and English residents of New England ushered in several generations of warfare and made the frontier unsafe for settlement. As the price of land rose, men increasingly tried to take ownership of acreage that had been granted previously but had never been laid out and now stood abandoned. Others tried to bring even marginal tracts under cultivation. The result was more conflict, more court cases, and more community strife.

The situation must have been particularly tense for George Walton and his neighbors. There were only 512 acres of land on Great Island, and much of it that was not too rocky or wet to farm was held in common by the town. The 1680 tax ratings for the island listed a total of only 66 acres of arable upland in private ownership. George Walton was the largest landholder, with over 20 acres of that upland and over 100 acres in all. Owning almost a third of all farmland and a fifth of the entire island, property-rich Walton was envied by his neighbors. The next largest holding of farmland was eight acres, and many owned only a half or a quarter of an acre. Land was so valuable that the tax collector even recorded one parcel of just forty square yards.[5]

It is not surprising that Walton and others would argue over the ownership of even small pieces of Great Island, leading some observers to suggest that a bitter property dispute triggered lithobolia. At the beginning of his narrative, Richard Chamberlain stated that the stone-throwing affair arose over a small piece of land that Hannah Jones claimed George Walton had taken from her unjustly. She complained vigorously about the property and repeatedly asserted that Walton would never occupy the land peacefully. The initial onslaught of stone throwing occurred just after Walton had been at the fence gate between his property and that of John Amazeen, a neighbor who was a kinsman of Hannah Jones. Someone had wrung the gate off its hinges and thrown it to the ground. Walton had previously found it in a similar state, and now he had to repair it for a second time. He headed home, only to be caught in the initial barrage of rocks. In an agrarian society where livestock was particularly valuable, having good fences and properly closed gates was critically important. Walton would have seen the destruction of his gate as a very serious matter. The absence of a gate also implied open access to the land, a direct challenge to Walton's ownership and exclusive use of his property.[6]

Several months later on August 3, while the stones were still flying, someone threw the gate off its hinges a third time. John Amazeen deflected the suspicion directed at him by claiming to have heard the gate fall and make a loud noise like a gun. The next day the fence between Walton and Jones was pulled down, and Hannah's cows wandered into Walton's field. When George and his servants went to repair the fence, they suffered a shower of more than forty stones. The attacks seemed to be particularly acute when Walton and his men were working in the field that included the property in dispute with Jones. In addition to the stony assault, many corn stalks were pulled up by the root, and hay mows were thrown into the trees. On September 5, as workers were reaping hay, three sickles were broken "by the force of these lapidiary Instruments of the Devil, as the Sickles were in the Reapers hands, on purpose (it seems) to obstruct their labor." A close look at the lithobolia attacks lends weight to the idea that they had much to do with property—specifically George Walton's field and his dispute with Hannah Jones and her family. So, to find out who perpetrated the lithobolia attack, we need to study Hannah Jones, her family, and her protracted property conflict with George Walton.[7]

Hannah Jones and John Amazeen were members of Thomas Walford's family, a clan beset by property disputes, and not just with George Walton. Despite their disagreement over land, Walford and

Walton had much in common. Both men had settled early in Portsmouth, having left Massachusetts over religious differences with Puritan authorities. Antinomian Walton would later become a Quaker, and Walford belonged to the established Church of England. Both men took exception to established Massachusetts Puritanism, though they stood on the opposite ends of the religious spectrum of their day. Perhaps this helps to explain why these neighbors and their families ended up fighting a bitter property battle for twenty-eight years. In many ways the quarrel typifies the numerous petty differences common among neighbors throughout early New England. In other ways, it was like no other dispute. Not only would it include a stone-throwing devil and cross-accusations of witchcraft, but ultimately it would have to be resolved by the king and his Privy Council—a rare and high distinction indeed for a disagreement between otherwise obscure men living on a small island in a distant colony of the realm.

Thomas and Jane Walford may have arrived in New England in 1623 as a part of a group of planters led by Captain Robert Gorges, the son of Sir Ferdinando Gorges. The Plymouth Colonists and the planters of Massachusetts Bay have tended to get the most attention from historians, but there were also a number of modest efforts to establish settlements along the coast of New England in the 1620s. Some possessed charters to the land while others were outright squatters. Captain Gorges's effort had more legitimacy than most English ventures, for he carried with him a commission from the Council for New England that made him the governor-general of New England. The party included an Anglican minister, who had been given full authority over all churches in New England. Captain Gorges and his settlers took over the recently abandoned settlement at Wessagusset (present-day Weymouth, Massachusetts). This group threatened the political and religious independence of Plymouth colony. As governor-general, Gorges had the authority to rule Plymouth, and to make the settlers worship according to the established Church of England. The Pilgrims' great journey to America to break with the church and worship as they wished could have been all for naught. The threat would soon pass. Sir Ferdinando and the Council for New England had not adequately supplied the colonists, who ran into serious difficulties right from the beginning. Captain Gorges, bred to a life of wealth and comfort in England, soon grew tired of the wild New England frontier. Before long he returned to England, bringing many of the colonists with him.[8]

Several of Gorges's contingent remained in Massachusetts, apparently including Thomas and Jane Walford, who would become the first English settlers of present-day Charlestown. When members of the Winthrop fleet arrived at the mouth of the Mystic River in 1629, they found only the Walfords. On the slope of the Breeds Hill—where the Battle of Bunker Hill would one day be fought—lay the Walford home. It had a thatched roof and was surrounded by a palisade (a fortified fence). Walford had squatted on the lands without proper title, so he lay powerless to halt the flood of settlers. He soon found himself in dispute with the newcomers—not surprising for an Anglican surrounded by Puritans. On May 3, 1631, he was fined forty shillings for contempt of authority and ordered to leave the colony by October 20. Walford paid his fine by killing a wolf, as the colony had recently placed a bounty on these animals, which were attacking English livestock.[9]

Thomas Walford must have been an independent and self-sufficient man, not afraid to strike out on his own. Only a capable diplomat could establish himself as an isolated Englishman living amid the local Native Americans. Trained as a blacksmith, he had to possess a range of skills to build a fortified house with little or no help. He also had to be a woodsman and hunter comfortable ranging the forests of what is now Greater Boston.

When forced out of Massachusetts, the Walfords ventured north to New Hampshire to the young settlement of Strawbery Banke (later renamed Portsmouth). They initially built a house at Sandy Beach (present-day Rye) but by the mid 1630s had moved to Great Island, where they probably became the first English residents of the isle. There they raised their six children: Jeremiah, Jane, Hannah, Elizabeth, Mary, and Martha. By 1649 the Walfords had deeded their Great Island lands to son Jeremiah and daughter Hannah and her husband, Alexander Jones Jr. Jeremiah acquired the old homestead, located at what is now Jerry's Point on the western end of the island (presumably named after Jeremiah Walford). The Joneses received lands on the other side of the island, on what soon became known as Jones Cove. Thomas and Jane Walford then moved to mainland Portsmouth, to a farm near the head of Sagamore Creek.[10]

As a blacksmith, Walford would have been a most welcome and important member of the frontier community. He enjoyed the respect of his Portsmouth neighbors, for at town meeting they sometimes voted him to important offices. In 1653, for example, he served on the committee to lay out lands at Portsmouth plains. The division of the town's common lands to individual townsmen was a difficult job that called for men of wisdom, tact, and diplomacy. The next year, Thomas helped arrange the seating at the meetinghouse—another difficult and important job, since seats were assigned largely on the basis of rank and status within the community. In 1655 his neighbors elected Walford to serve as Portsmouth selectman, a position he would hold twice. As a sign of his respect in the community, in 1666 the town granted him 160 acres—a very large holding in a town that was already beginning to run out of land.[11]

Symptomatic of the problems caused by that land shortage was the fight between the Walfords and George Walton over a small parcel. On New Year's Day 1649, Thomas and Jane Walford deeded to their daughter Hannah Jones four acres of upland and two acres of marsh on Great Island. Hannah and Alexander Jones built their home on Jones Cove, and inland from the shore lay Jones Marsh. At the same time the Walfords gave their homestead on Great Island to their son Jeremiah. This property included several acres of marsh that abutted Jones Marsh. These lands also came with the guarantee of a continued property dispute with neighbor George Walton over the two acres, now called Jones Marsh.[12]

Alexander Jones Jr. was a fisherman working out of the Isles of Shoals, one of the largest and most important fishing stations in New England. He was born about 1616 and may have arrived in New England with his parents, who were early settlers at Great Island. In the male-dominated fishing industry, women were seen as

The Walfords

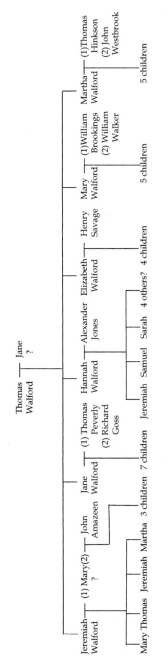

Figure 5.1. The Walfords

a distraction and source of conflict and were prohibited from living on the Isles of Shoals. Most shoals fishermen maintained permanent residences on the mainland, where their wives and families stayed. As it was ten miles from the shoals to Portsmouth and Kittery, these men were early "commuters" frequently forced to be away from their families. Though they lived hard and unenvied lives, fisher folk helped form the backbone of the Piscataqua society and economy. During fishing season, they worked long hours with few days off. They lived with few possessions in modest homes on small parcels of land. On Great Island, the Jones family owned only four acres of upland, with three sheep, two cows, and a hog. In addition to fishing, they farmed their small plot for food, and between fishing seasons they cut timber, harvested hay off marshes, and carried out other activities to make ends meet. To such people living at the margins of society, even a small piece of marsh was a source income and a valued possession.[13]

The tiny Jones Marsh would be the flashpoint of a land debate that would take thirty-six years to resolve. Around 1639 Thomas Walford began to hay the marsh, though he did little to improve it, and he appears to have largely ignored it for some time. So Walford did not object about ten years later when neighbor John Wotton harvested the marsh, piling up two or three small cocks of hay. However, the stacks were so small and the hay of such poor quality that Wotton did not even bother to gather them. John Wotton and George Walton both claimed the land through purchases of property on Muskito Neck, though Walton eventually bought out Wotton's claim. Walton worked hard to improve the value of the land by cutting numerous trees and clearing out the driftwood that had been thrown there by high tides and winter storms. He fenced the area so that the field could be used for planting or grazing livestock. Soon after these improvements had been made, Alexander Jones acquired his claim to the land through his father-in-law. Jones approached local officials about the property dispute, and in December 1652, the Portsmouth town meeting ordered George Walton to remove his fence and return the property to its rightful owner.[14]

Walton ignored the town's command, and the border dispute continued to rage between the two families. In retaliation, Hannah

Jones would tear down sections of the fence and let her cow loose in the marsh, only to have Walton remove the animal and repair the enclosure. Since the town's decision seemed unenforceable, in 1656 Alexander Jones took the matter to the Portsmouth court, which gave him a favorable ruling. In June 1657, George Walton appealed on the grounds that this local court did not have the authority to settle such property disputes. The appeal was deferred to the next Norfolk County Court, to be held in Dover. When the court met, Walton failed to put his arguments in writing or even to summons Jones to present his case, so the Dover Court transferred jurisdiction back to the local court and encouraged Walton to pursue his claim there. In November 1659, the Portsmouth Court finally heard Walton's appeal of the 1656 case and ruled again for Jones, finding Walton responsible for the 10s 3p costs of court. Walton immediately made another appeal to the Norfolk County Court, posting a £10 bond to prosecute the appeal. By this time, tempers between the two families must have been at the boiling point.[15]

Finally, on June 26, 1660, the Norfolk County Court attempted to bring closure to the case, which by this time had dissolved into a tangled mess of charges and countercharges. After hearing all arguments in the case, the court determined to bring all the actions to an end. The court ordered that George Walton and his heirs would have ownership of Jones Marsh, without any disturbance or complaint from the Jones family. In return, Walton would pay Alexander Jones forty shillings to purchase his right to the marsh. Both men were to pay their own costs of court—which must have been mounting by this time. Furthermore, both men were to absorb the costs associated with the other's trespass on the property. Clearly tired of wasting time on this habitual dispute, the court ordered that this would be the final end to the case. The judges, who must surely have believed the issue resolved, would have been shocked to know that the controversy between George Walton and the Walford clan still had another twenty-five years of life![16]

That same year, the death of the Walford's only son, Jeremiah, would embroil the family in another property dispute, making their troubles with George Walton temporarily fade into the background. In the spring of 1660, Jeremiah took ill and died, leaving his widow Mary and four young children: Thomas II, Jeremiah Jr., Mary, and Martha. He left a modest estate of £95, consisting principally of the house and lands on Great Island that his father had deeded him in 1649. The will provided his widow Mary with the use of the entire estate for as long as she remained unmarried. Upon remarriage, she would receive the traditional widow's third of the estate, with the remainder to be divided among the children. The court named Jeremiah's father and Henry Sherborne as executors of the estate.[17]

By 1663, widow Mary Walford had married John Amazeen, a man of unusual background even by the standards of a diverse seaport like Portsmouth. In contemporary documents he is usually referred to as "John the Greek," though sometimes he is styled "John the Italian." This suggests that John was an ethnic Greek, born in one of the Greek maritime enclaves in Italy. According to family tradition, John was a sailor who was shipwrecked in New England. Certainly there were many Greek sailors and other foreign nationals who anchored in Portsmouth and other New England ports in the seventeenth century. Although a varied group of mariners visited the waterfront of Great Island, Amazeen's accent and Mediterranean complexion would have made him stand out in the predominantly English population. Presumably raised in either the Greek Orthodox or Roman Catholic faith, he could not have had an altogether easy time making the transition to the Puritanism of Portsmouth's Reverend Joshua Moody. His designation as "John the Greek" or "John the Italian" suggests that his neighbors did not easily overlook his differences, and he seems to have spent most of his life as an outsider, showing up only occasionally in the town records. The provincial court appointed him constable for Great Island in 1681–82, the first time his neighbors trusted him to hold any municipal office. It had taken him over twenty years to gain this respect, and it was quickly lost: the next year Amazeen admitted to stealing three hats from the warehouse of a Great Island merchant. He must have mended his ways, however, for he was reappointed constable five years later, and in 1691 the town of Portsmouth elected him to the minor office of fence viewer.[18]

Fence viewer was an ironic post for John Amazeen, given that the major controversies in his life were a series of property disputes—one with the town, one with his family, and one with George Walton. The dispute with Portsmouth began in 1667 when one acre of waste land was granted and laid out to Amazeen. It would be the only acre of land the town would ever grant him— another sign of his suspect status in the community. Brazenly, Amazeen fenced in eight to ten acres rather than just one, claiming that the lot layers made this permissible. The selectmen were willing to consider it an honest mistake and decided to give Amazeen two acres of the land, but the rest of his fenced acres had to be turned over to other people to fulfill their grants. Unyielding, Amazeen refused to remove his fences. After several years of impasse, the town took action in 1669. Selectman Phillip Lewis, along with two other men, pulled down the fencing surrounding the disputed land. Amazeen sued them for this action. The jury found for Amazeen and awarded him a miniscule amount of two pence in damages.[19]

Two years later, the town tried to intervene again, and the selectmen sued Amazeen for the property. On the surface, it appears as if it should have been a fairly straightforward case, but the jury again found for Amazeen. The decision surprised the magistrates, who refused to accept the verdict. It was rare for colonial judges to overrule juries, but in this case they stepped in to reverse the verdict. This action brought the controversy to an end, and a 1680 tax valuation lists Amazeen with just two acres of upland, presumably those same two acres the town had agreed to grant him back in 1669.[20]

At the same time that John Amazeen was fighting over land with the town, he was also struggling to resolve a property dispute with his family. The Amazeens had difficulty getting executors Thomas Walford and Henry Sherborne to release to Mary her third of the estate of late husband Jeremiah Walford, per the terms of his will. Perhaps the Walford family and the community did not approve of the Amazeens' marriage, and this was their form of protest. In the summer of 1666, Amazeen took the extreme step of suing the men for his wife's inheritance. The jury found for the Amazeens, ordering the executors to deliver the estate within twenty days. Furthermore, they awarded the Amazeens £45 in damages, and another 18s 6d in costs of court. This was a high award, considering that the widow's third of the estate was itself worth only about £32. The court case and damages created lasting bitterness between the branches of the family.[21]

At least Thomas Walford harbored no ill will toward his grandsons, for as he neared death several months later, he made Jeremiah's two sons his principal heirs. His older grandson, Thomas Walford II, received his grandfather's home and one hundred acres of his farm, complete with orchards, meadow, and even an old mare. The will gave his younger brother, Jeremiah Jr., fifty acres of upland and four acres of marsh. After the remaining bequests and the widow's third, the residue of the estate was to be set aside for young Thomas's education. Hannah Jones's two children must have been envious of their Walford cousins, for all they received was a young sow apiece. With his only son dead, and his grandsons still young boys, Thomas Walford Sr. appointed two respected members of the community to administer his estate. Richard Tucker had been a selectman in 1654, and Henry Sherborne had held that office a number of times. On the surface, they seem to have been good, reliable men for the job. Sherborne must have been a close friend of the family, for he already served as an administrator of Jeremiah Walford's estate. Unfortunately, however, the administrators neglected their duties. Four years after Thomas's death, his widow Jane was forced to go to court to have her lands laid out to her. In 1680, young Jeremiah Walford Jr. complained to the court that the majority of the assets remained in the executor's hands, benefiting them rather than the heirs. By this time, the distribution of the estate had been further complicated by the deaths of Richard Tucker and the chief beneficiary, Thomas Walford II. Matters would soon become even more tangled by the death of the surviving executor, Henry Sherborne.[22]

In 1681, Jeremiah Walford Jr. and his stepfather, John Amazeen, sought to resolve the impasse. As the administrators of

Thomas Walford II's estate, they demanded that Henry Sherborne's heir, John Sherborne Jr., produce the estate papers. They did this on behalf of Jeremiah Jr., who claimed to be the rightful heir of both Thomas Walfords. However, the younger Sherborne refused to comply without an order from the court. In addition to the fight between the two sets of executors, the Walford heirs themselves had a falling out. Jeremiah Jr.'s two sisters petitioned the court for assistance, stating that they believed they had a right to a share of the estate but did not know how to acquire it.[23]

Furthermore, the daughters of Thomas Walford Sr. united to receive their proper share of the estates. On September 7, 1681, Hannah Jones and her three sisters petitioned the court claiming a share of their deceased mother's third. Since their nephew Thomas Walford II died as a minor without a will, the Walford daughters argued that they were the rightful possessors of Thomas II's share of his grandfather's estate. Clearly bitter at their minor bequests, the Walford daughters and granddaughters wanted to see justice served. Their anger was heightened by need, for these women possessed only modest means. Hannah Jones's husband Alexander had died several years before, leaving her a poor widow. Having now dragged on fifteen years, the case threatened to become a poor man's *Bleak House*.[24]

Fortunately, in September 1681, magistrates issued a judgment to resolve the dispute once and for all. The court ruled that the wording of the will indicated that Thomas II should receive possession of his grandfather's inheritance only for the duration of his life. With his death, the estate rightfully passed to the designees for the residue of the estate: Hannah Jones and her sisters. Jeremiah Walford Jr., his sisters, mother, and stepfather John Amazeen had all lost out on the division of the estate. They had to have been bitterly disappointed with the results of this long family struggle. Meanwhile, the victorious Hannah Jones must have been flush with confidence, perhaps so much so that she was even willing to renew the old dispute with George Walton.[25]

Jones and her family would have been wise to leave George Walton alone, for this aggressive man always sought ways to increase his property holdings, even when his claim was not particularly strong. From the time he first purchased land on Great Island, he had been adding acreage, using a constant barrage of lawsuits to further his ends. Walton lived at Muskito Neck when he first moved to the island but soon built a tavern on the waterfront, next to Fort Point, the site of a primitive fortification built in the early 1630s. No sooner was this project complete than he successfully sued the carpenter, Humphrey Chadbourne, for not building the tavern according to the contract specifications. In the spring of 1652, the town granted Walton an additional seven acres near the ordinary. The next year, he was granted an additional strip of thirty feet along the waterfront, next to his house, in order to build a storehouse.[26]

In early 1662, the Portsmouth selectmen noticed that George Walton was building a small house east of his tavern, at Fort Point, and that he was claiming ownership of the entire point. The selectmen were uneasy about development on Fort Point, the most strategic place to fortify and defend Portsmouth and the entire Piscataqua drainage. They demanded that Walton produce evidence of his title to the tract. When he could not do so, they told him to stop construction. At a meeting on May 12, 1662, the selectmen asked Walton to yield the property at Fort Point. He obstinately answered that he would only do so if order by a court of law. The town failed to act for seven years, when the legislature finally ordered the Norfolk County Court to resolve the matter.[27]

The controversy came to a head in the spring of 1669, when Walton took offense at two fish merchants whose crews had built fishing flakes (the drying racks for salted cod) on Fort Point. This was a well accepted use of coastal common lands, but Walton saw the racks as a threat to his ownership claim. The angry Quaker ripped down the flakes, spoiling the codfish in the process. Presumably Walton believed that his bully tactics would win out, as they had against the Walfords, but this time he had picked on the wrong people. The owners of the flakes were James Pendleton and Nathaniel Fryer, prominent men who had far more power and connections than Walton's previous antagonists. Fryer was a merchant and a Portsmouth selectman. Pendleton was captain of the

Portsmouth militia, and the son of Major Brian Pendleton, one of the leading merchants and magistrates in northern New England. Both men were Puritans, and by the late 1660s, they and their allies dominated Portsmouth and New Hampshire politics. Pendleton and Fryer complained to the legislature and sued Walton for trespass and destruction of property. Hearing the case on June 29, 1669, the jury found in favor of Fryer and Pendleton and awarded them twenty shillings in damages. Four days later, the court took up the related case of ownership of Fort Point. After examining the claims of both Walton and the town of Portsmouth, the court found in favor of the town. They gave Walton until the end of August to remove his house from Fort Point or to forfeit ownership of it to the town. Walton moved the house to his property. It became the home of daughter Abishag Walton, who lived there until her death in 1678.[28]

At the same time that Walton was fighting the town over Fort Point, he was also wrangling over their laying out of highways. In 1663 residents built a road across the island, going through much of Walton's property. George protested his loss of land without compensation by digging up the highway in front of his house, making it dangerous to travel. Finally in 1666, the town grudgingly gave Walton a worthless piece of land, a rocky hill next to his home, in consideration of his loss of land to the highway.[29]

George Walton spent much of his time and energy engaged in a series of protracted land disputes. It had taken him fourteen years to secure his title to Muskito Neck. His seven-year effort to take common land at Fort Point suggests he had no compunction against trying to take what might not be his, and he was more than willing to resort to lengthy court cases to gain title. If he did not get his way, he looked to such extralegal methods as destroying the road the town built across his land. Walton was a grasping and quarrelsome man who resorted to whatever means necessary to increase his property. The Puritan settlers of early New England placed a great value on cooperation and neighborliness. If disputes arose, they hoped to mediate them amicably without resorting to the courts. George Walton was neither a Puritan nor a good neighbor, and his aggressiveness and greed helped him become the largest landowner on Great Island and one of the principal property owners in all Portsmouth. Such a man was not going to let widow Hannah Jones get the better of him in a property dispute.

The quarrel between Walton and Jones flared up again during the lithobolia attack. Indeed, George Walton, his family, and at least some observers suspected Goodwife Jones because of the property dispute. Walton laid charges against Jones in court at its June 1682 session and had a bond placed on her to maintain the peace. Only July 4, Goody Jones appealed to the president and Council. She complained of her difficulties with George Walton and his false accusations against her. Walton's horse repeatedly broke into Jones's pasture and caused damage, yet she was afraid to chase it out for fear she would lose her bond for good behavior. She complained of the many other wrongs Walton had done her. In response, the Council ordered that she notify officials if she was injured by Walton while she was under bond. Despite the bond and the close scrutiny that accompanied it, the lithobolia attacks against Walton and his property continued. By August 1682 George Walton was convinced that Hannah Jones was a witch who used supernatural means to carry out the assaults. He confided to a neighbor that "he believed in his heart and conscience that Grandma Jones was a witch, and would say so to his dying day." A property dispute between neighbors had been elevated into a case of witchcraft.[30]

Six

Neighbors and Witches

Until the stones started to fly and George Walton accused Hannah Jones of witchcraft, their property dispute differed little from other land conflicts throughout New England. After years of quarreling over property, it is not surprising Walton would blame Hannah Jones for the attacks. What makes the clash interesting is that he charged Hannah with invoking supernatural forces to press her case. Why did he do this? George's inspiration largely came from Hannah's mother, Jane Walford.

Walton told a neighbor that "Goody Jones and all her generation were accounted witches," implying that not only was Jones a witch, but so too were her mother and sisters. Gossip must have soon reached Jones, for on August 25, 1682 she confronted George. In a heated exchange, Hannah threatened to throw stones at him if he spoke ill of her mother. She then accused the Quaker of being a wizard. Hannah's mother, Jane Walford, had been accused of witchcraft several times. People commonly believed witchcraft passed from mother to daughter, so Walton was not alone in his suspicion that Hannah and her sisters were all witches. Jones chose her words poorly in threatening Walton, for the statement could almost be taken as a confession. Taken together with the fact that the stone throwers remained unseen, the threat was proof enough for Walton and others that supernatural forces were behind the assaults. He chose or pretended to believe this despite the fact that two orchards located only about eighty feet away from the Walton home gave strong-armed assailants excellent cover for an attack.[1]

Over a twenty-one year period, Jane Walford was involved in three court proceedings related to witchcraft. The duration of these court appearances suggests that her neighbors held her under constant suspicion of being in league with the devil; they just lacked the evidence to convict her. When she was first accused of the crime in 1648, the court found her complainant, Elizabeth Row, guilty of slander, and made Row and her husband Nicholas pay a £2 fine, plus the cost of court. In 1656, when seven persons testified against Jane Walford for committing witchcraft, the court took the accusations more seriously.[2]

Susannah Trimmings deposed that on the night of Sunday, March 30, 1656, she and Eliza Barton were walking home to Little Harbor. After they parted, Susannah heard a rustling in the woods and suddenly saw Jane Walford emerge from the darkness, wearing a red waistcoat and petticoat, an old green apron, and a black hat. Jane demanded a pound of cotton. Susannah protested that she had only two pounds and could not spare one. An enraged Walford threatened that she had better lend it to her or something terrible would happen to Trimmings, who immediately felt a bolt of fire hit her on the back. Walford then turned into a cat and vanished.[3]

Susannah's husband testified that she took ill immediately after reaching home. Her back felt like it was on fire, but her legs were numb. She was very sick for several days, and her limbs were still causing her problems when she deposed against Goody Walford over two weeks later. Eliza Barton visited the ailing Susannah and noticed that her face was strangely spotted with several colors and that her eyes appeared to have been scalded. Fortunately for Jane Walford, a neighbor testified that she had been home on the night of the attack, so the alleged meeting could not have taken place. The alibi probably saved Jane from being convicted of witchcraft. Nevertheless, the accusation by Susannah Trimmings prompted others to come forward. As often happened in cases of witchcraft, these other accusers now recalled Jane's suspicious behavior in the past. Nicholas Row recollected back to 1648 when his wife first accused Walford. Soon after the accusation, Row asserted, Walford came to him while he was in bed. She put her hand upon his chest, causing him great pain and rendering him temporarily speechless. She made a similar visit a week later.[4]

John Puddington made a more unusual claim. He said that three years earlier Jane Walford had visited his mother Agnes, and told her that her own husband, Thomas Walford, called her an old witch and accused her of casting a spell on the Walford cattle. John and Agnes Puddington both deposed that in 1656 William Evans's wife came to the Puddington house and spent the night. Just after sunset, the family noticed the appearance of a yellow cat, which followed Mrs. Evans wherever she went. John Puddington fetched his gun and tried to shoot the cat, but the gun misfired. The yellow cat then mysteriously disappeared. The Puddingtons' depositions can be interpreted in several ways. They could imply that Mrs. Evans was also a witch, and that the cat was her familiar (the demonic spirit in animal form that accompanies a witch). Alternatively, they could have suggested that Jane Walford took the form of the cat. Regardless, the Puddington household witnessed what they believed was supernatural activity. They also heard what some might call a confession by Jane Walford, or at the very least, an admission that her husband thought she was in league with Satan.[5]

Even worse, another witness claimed that Jane Walford belonged to a coven of witches who carried out their evil deeds throughout the Piscataqua. Elizabeth Row warned of the presence of three male witches in the community: William Ham, Thomas Turpin, and a third man who should be "nameless, because he should be blameless." The court ignored Trimmings's accusations against these other alleged witches. Certainly no action could be taken against Thomas Turpin, for he had drowned a few years earlier. Obviously Trimmings did not accept the popular notion that witches could not drown. In some instances, authorities would "swim a witch," for they believed that water, the medium of baptism, would reject a witch, preserving her from drowning and proving her guilt.[6]

Trimmings did share the common belief that witches could be helpful as well as harmful; hence her refusal to name the witch who was "blameless." Many cunning folk practiced white magic, that is, magic intended to help people rather than harm them. White magic might be used to find lost items, foretell the future, and even aid the sick. This helpful magic stood in contrast to black witchcraft or maleficium, the magical power to harm. Witchcraft has long had this dual nature, from ancient times to the *Wizard of Oz*, where the Wicked Witch of the West battled Glinda the Good Witch of the North. But a white witch had to invoke satanic forces even when using her powers for good, which is why learned church officials considered even this supposedly harmless practice to be a dangerous heresy worthy of severe punishment. Still, many common folk shared Elizabeth Row's belief that white witches were blameless of any wrongdoing.[7]

These various accusations led the court to continue Jane Walford's case over until its next meeting, when they could investigate the details more fully. Unfortunately, there the trail of evidence ends, for there is no subsequent record of court action against her. Presumably the court dismissed the charges. A cloud of suspicion did remain, however, for in March 1669, the elderly widow brought an action of slander against Dr. Robert Couch for claiming that he could prove Jane was a witch. Couch was a Boston surgeon who sometimes practiced in Portsmouth. In an effort to squelch these recurring accusations once and for all, Jane sued for the immense sum of £1,000 in damages—the modern-day equivalent of a multimillion dollar suit. The judges awarded her a more reasonable £5, plus costs of court. Couch's was the last recorded accusation against Walford, who died a few years later.[8]

Historians have suggested that many witchcraft accusations had their origins in tensions and conflicts among neighbors. Traditional English villages had been largely self-sufficient entities, where people banded together to look after each other. The early modern era was a time of tremendous change. It witnessed the rise of nation states, the evolution of capitalism, and the Protestant Reformation. These political, economic, and religious shifts also led to changing social relationships, where the needs and interests of the individual began to take precedence over the community. People who had customarily relied on the help of fellow villagers were no longer guaranteed this safety net, and all members of society felt some degree of uncertainty as a result. The needy sometimes were forced to endure the sting of refusal when they made a request for charity from a neighbor. Those on the receiving end of the request suffered pangs of guilt over their inability or unwillingness to comply as their parents and grandparents had in the past. The local tensions and conflicts engendered by this situation sometimes resulted in accusations of witchcraft. For example, a poor widow asks her neighbor for some milk. The neighbor denies the request. Traditional bonds were breaking down as communal subsistence farming gave way to individualism and capitalism. People began to look more toward their personal well being rather than that of the community. Still, the neighbor feels guilty, as the two families have lived on adjoining farms for generations. The widow responds in her embarrassment and anger by cursing the neighbor and his cow. When the cow sickens and dies a week later, the neighbor remembers the encounter with the widow and her curse and accuses her of killing the cow through witchcraft.[9]

The initial accusation against Jane Walford would seem to fit this pattern. Susannah Trimmings refused her neighbor's request for some cotton, because she had none to spare. This resulted in an exchange of sharp words. A few days later, as Goodwife Trimmings walked home alone, she may well have thought back to the unpleasant encounter with Walford with a mixture of guilt and anger. The more Trimmings thought of the meeting, the more agitated she became, and soon, she believed she saw Jane's specter threatening her and demanding cotton.

Witchcraft tended to be a "working-class" crime—often related to the curses, threats, charges, and counter charges that would have been heard in poorer neighborhoods. The leading families of a community usually became involved in witchcraft cases only after initial accusations had been made. In most cases, someone of rank had to add their own accusation to have the court take the charges very seriously. This helps to explain why Jane was never convicted. Her accusers—the Trimmings, Puddingtons, Bartons, and Rows—were neighbors from some of the less affluent families in Portsmouth. The Walfords themselves were not particularly well off. When Thomas died in 1666, his estate was appraised at only £75. The value of the estate had been diminished a bit by gifts of property to several of their children; still, it is clear that Thomas and Jane enjoyed only modest wealth.[10]

Jane Walford's antagonists frequently appeared in court, bickering with others over a variety of issues. Nicholas Row was involved in several lawsuits, and not long before his wife, Elizabeth, informed on Jane Walford that she called another woman a whore. Authorities eventually whipped Elizabeth for her slanderous accusations. Likewise, Susannah Trimmings was sued for slander in 1655, a year before she cried out on Jane Walford. Her husband Oliver had previously faced charges of trespass and perjury. In 1651 Edward Barton was accused of beating his wife, Eliza. Perhaps his abuse explains the transient ways of his family, who lived in Salem, Marblehead, and several locations in Portsmouth before finally settling in Cape Porpus. The Bartons and their neighbors the Rows were arguing over a piece of property at the same time they were accusing Jane Walford of witchcraft. Even the most respected of the accusers, Dr. Couch, was known for his loud mouth. Not long after he pointed the finger at Jane, Couch found himself before the court in Boston, apologizing for composing reproachful verses about the town's ministers and the late governor. Overall, Goody Walford's accusers lacked the credibility and standing in society for their charges to be taken very seriously. Rather, their actions seem to be an extension of their habit of slandering their neighbors and enemies. The impartial observer might expect these people to accuse neighbors of witchcraft—which is exactly why the court ignored the complaints.[11]

Such charges were not uncommon, as belief in witchcraft was, and still is, widespread. The practice was first recorded in ancient times, and people are even persecuted for it today. In the 1990s, for example, mobs killed over 500 people suspected of witchcraft in South Africa. The "Great Age" of witchcraft in Europe and America lasted roughly from 1450 to 1750. During this era, approximately 110,000 people were tried for witchcraft and 60,000 sentenced to death. About half of these cases took place within the German states. England and her colonies saw far fewer cases of witchcraft than most other regions of Europe. Still, the practice was common and long-standing. The prosecution of witches came to an official end in England with the passage of the Witchcraft Act of 1735. Nevertheless, in 1944 spiritual medium Helen Duncan was convicted of witchcraft and sentenced to nine months in jail after she uncannily predicted the sinking of a British battleship.[12]

Even in Colonial America, witchcraft extended far beyond Salem. Formal witchcraft proceedings were made in New England against at least 139 people from 1638 to 1697, and others were accused but never formally charged. Historian Carol Karlsen has discovered 344 accusations of witchcraft in colonial New England from 1620 to 1725. A majority of these cases (185) occurred in Essex County in 1692. There were also two smaller outbreaks in Connecticut. In 1662–63, thirteen were accused in Hartford, and in 1692 seven people were accused in Fairfield. Aside from these three episodes, in most New England witchcraft cases only one or two people stood accused. Jane Walford's case was typical—a lone woman accused of the crime by her neighbors. Although the overwhelming majority of cases of witchcraft in America took place in New England, there were instances of it just about everywhere, including New York, Pennsylvania, Virginia, Maryland, and North Carolina. One woman was even executed aboard a ship in transit to Virginia when her fellow passengers came to believe she had used witchcraft to create the tempest that nearly sank their ship. An occasional witchcraft trial even occurred in New Spain and New France. Accusations were made throughout Europe and her colonies, by people of all nationalities and faiths.[13]

Given such a wide range of allegations, it is difficult if not impossible to describe a "typical" witch. Thanks to a steady stream of scholarship in Europe and America, one can now move beyond the idea that all witches were penniless, widowed hags, although this stereotype still does provide a few useful hints. Women did account for about 80 percent of all those accused of witchcraft in early New

England. The overwhelming majority of these victims were middle-aged and older women, often from the lower economic strata of society. Though the stereotype of a witch is an old widow, married women were also vulnerable to charges, for they possessed limited legal status in the English judicial system. Their husbands acted in their stead to buy and sell land, administer estates, file lawsuits, and defend them in court. On the surface it would seem that Jane was not typical here, for her husband Thomas was alive when she was accused of witchcraft in 1648 and 1656. Nevertheless, she was certainly vulnerable. After all, this was the husband who, by her own admission, had called her a witch! At the very least, this would have made it hard for Thomas to defend his wife against charges. That he made such a statement to begin with and that she was willing to repeat it to neighbors are signs of tension and discord in their marriage. In accusing her, Walford signaled that he would not defend his wife against an indictment of witchcraft, and he completely absented himself from the court proceedings. It was Jane's son Jeremiah and not her husband who posted £20 bond for her good behavior in 1656.[14]

Not only did Jane Walford's husband fail to defend her against charges, but his political activities may have led to the allegations against her in the first place. A Portsmouth selectman, Walford was also charged with other important municipal responsibilities during the 1650s. It was a difficult time to hold office in Portsmouth, a town suffering from growing pains. Puritans had been gradually moving north from Massachusetts into New Hampshire, turning the Anglican population into a minority. These newcomers were gaining political power in Portsmouth, and since this group included quite a few prosperous merchants, the Puritan faction began to wield substantial economic influence as well. Their increase in status and power came at the expense of the "Old Planters" like the Walfords and other principally Anglican families who had settled Portsmouth prior to Massachusetts's takeover in 1641. The influx of settlers also led to the town granting more lands to freemen, which in turn gave rise to more tensions and disputes. Walford often found himself standing right in the middle of the conflict, where he undoubtedly made enemies.[15]

In 1653, the town appointed Thomas Walford and three other men to divide and lay out over 360 acres at Portsmouth Plains to individual freemen. The town meeting anticipated the complaints that would arise, asserting that the men would do their best to be fair and warning that no one was to question the results. A total of 39 men received land, with the maximum allotment of 16 ⅔ acres going to Thomas Walford and eight others. Walford's son Jeremiah and his son-in-law Thomas Peverly each received 6 ⁶⁄₇ acres, so the family did quite well, receiving a total of 30 acres. Meanwhile, Oliver Trimmings garnered only the minimum allotment of 3 ⅓ acres. Perhaps the Trimmings's complaints against Jane Walford resulted from ill will toward Thomas over the division. Nicholas Row must have been happy to receive the maximum allotment of 16 ⁶⁄₇ acres, yet he still had land problems of his own. In 1653 the town meeting also gave Nicholas Row permission to mow land formerly hayed by Walford, Thomas Peverly, and neighbor John Puddington. It is possible that Elizabeth Row's accusation of Jane was related to some conflict over this property—especially as John Puddington, another accuser of Jane Walford, was involved. The Rows were also fighting neighbor Edward Barton in a land dispute so bitter that in 1656 Thomas Walford and the other selectmen had to appoint a committee to resolve the differences between the two men. It is probably no coincidence that, less than a month later, Barton's wife Eliza would testify against Jane Walford, or that Elizabeth Row would accuse William Ham, another selectman and Old Planter, of being a witch.[16]

The 1656 accusations against Jane Walford also may have been payback for Thomas's recent role in a controversy over the seating in the meetinghouse. Perhaps a trivial matter to us today, people in early New England cared a great deal about this issue. Pews were assigned based on social rank related particularly to age and wealth. Just as a modern-day bride struggles to determine the proper seating at her wedding reception, committees of freemen in Portsmouth and other towns worked hard to handle the sorting of pews in the meetinghouse. This was a particularly explosive issue in Portsmouth, where the congregation was divided between Anglicans and Puritans.[17]

In 1654 the town meeting appointed Richard Cutts and John Pickering to establish a new seating plan for the meetinghouse. Pickering had arrived in New Hampshire in 1633 as an employee of the Laconia Company. This leader of the Old Planters had risen from a tradesman to become the owner of a sawmill and gristmill. He even donated the land for the meetinghouse. Richard Cutts was one of three wealthy Puritan merchant brothers who had arrived in the Piscataqua in the late 1640s. So, the Old Planter and the Puritan met to determine the seating order, but when they were unable to reach a consensus, the selectmen appointed Thomas Walford to the committee to break the logjam. The seating plan does not survive, but we can assume it pleased Pickering, for Walford was a fellow Anglican and Old Planter. Furthermore, we know that the Puritans were unhappy with the results, for in 1659 they rearranged the seats. After seeing the revised 1659 plan, an infuriated Pickering entered the meeting house and pulled down the papers that directed the congregation to their new pews.[18]

If the spirited debates over the seating plans are any indication, tensions between Anglicans and Puritans were approaching a boiling point in Portsmouth in the 1650s. The accusations against Jane Walford may have had something to do with her being both an Anglican and the wife of one of the leading Old Planters.

Jane Walford was not alone in being accused of witchcraft in April 1656. Most experts of the day believed that witches did not act independently. Rather, they belonged to covens who gathered into small congregations to hold their unholy Sabbath. Witches might come from considerable distance to attend these services. In light of these beliefs, it is not surprising that three Portsmouth men were named along with Walford, or that the accusations would spread beyond the town. In April proceedings would also begin against Eunice Cole, a woman who lived eight miles south of Walford, in Hampton. The Piscataqua region was in the grips of a minor witchcraft outbreak.

The story of Eunice Cole is well known to historians, thanks largely to John Demos's excellent study of her. Still, no scholar has previously linked Eunice and Jane, because the two women are not named together in any of the charges against either of them. Their individual cases seem contained within the bounds of their own communities. Yet, the close proximity of the two women and the remarkable contemporaneity of the first accusations against them suggest some connection. With two women indicted for witchcraft, another possibly implicated, and three men cried out upon, the 1656 Piscataqua outbreak was reasonably large by New England standards.

Eunice Cole would find herself repeatedly accused of familiarity with Satan. When she was first arraigned in 1656, numerous witnesses testified against her, claiming that she had caused the death of an infant, the illness of a man, and harm to livestock. She was also linked to other supernatural acts, including an unexplained loud scraping against the outer wall of a house, the strange behavior of a cat, and her mysterious knowledge of a private conversation.[19]

These complaints—maleficium (harming people and animals), association with a familiar, possession of unexplained knowledge—were typical. Likewise, Goody Cole fit the stereotypical image of a witch. She and her husband, William, were an elderly, poor, childless couple. They had been among the Antinomian settlers of Exeter but had later moved to Hampton. So, like the Anglican Walfords, the Coles were religious outsiders in a region that was becoming increasingly Puritan. From the moment of the Coles' arrival in town there had been contention—perhaps because of their religious beliefs, but also because of their combative, demanding nature. As evidence of the latter, two Hampton women charged Eunice with slander in 1645. Two years later, a violent ruckus erupted over the ownership of a couple of pigs. When the constable came to claim the pigs, the Coles knocked him down and bit his hands. The court admonished Eunice several more times after this unseemly incident. But despite her clashes with the authorities, Cole was not bashful about demanding wood and other forms of public assistance from the selectmen. She was an outspoken troublemaker, a social outcast, and a religious deviant. These characteristics, combined with her poverty, her age, and her childlessness, made her a typical witch (if it is indeed possible to speak of "typical" witch given all the differences among those labeled as such).

The local court took the witchcraft charges seriously and referred her case to the Court of Assistants in Boston.[20]

The records and the verdict for the case before the Assistants do not survive, but the court must have lacked the evidence to convict Eunice Cole and carry out the death sentence, for she was soon back in Hampton. Throughout the 1660s, she remained under suspicion and often ended up in court or in jail. Her situation worsened when her husband died in 1662, leaving her almost destitute. Soon afterward, Widow Cole was accused of signing a pact with the devil. However, for reasons unknown, this indictment was not entered against her until 1673. Perhaps stresses in the community brought the matter to a head, for in 1673 England was at war with the Dutch, and New England's coastal settlements lived in constant fear of attack.[21]

From 1652 to 1674, England and the Netherlands engaged in three brief wars. The conflicts were rooted in an Anglo-Dutch economic rivalry, though the last war, which took place from 1672 to 1674, was also connected with the imperial wars of France's Louis XIV. To some colonial Americans, these recurring hostilities were no more than a distant nuisance. As maritime conflicts fought principally on ships and in ports, however, they were very real threat for coastal New England towns like Hampton and Portsmouth. The Massachusetts General Court took the third Dutch War particularly seriously. On May 7, 1673, it reorganized the soldiers on Great Island and Kittery into a single company of foot soldiers assigned to the fort on Great Island, and instructed "to be ready on all occasions to attend the service thereof for its defense and security." No such orders were issued for lesser coastal towns like Hampton, which were expected to fend for themselves, but in December the General Court did have a ship and a ketch fitted out to defend the colony's coast and vessels. Meanwhile, it prepared to take the offensive, ordering over 600 militia men from throughout the colony to be impressed, armed, and prepared for service against the Dutch.[22]

Less than a month later, on the night of September 10, Great Islanders feared that the Dutch were actually attacking. Fortunately it was a false alarm, triggered by John Davis and his son-in-law John Pennell, visitors from York, Maine. Davis, a magistrate and militia officer who would later serve as deputy president of Maine, was normally a responsible man. Still, he and his son-in-law got carried away in their drinking and soon were in the lead of a group of men playing leap frog and generally making merry. Around midnight, the revelers believed they saw three or four ships entering the mouth of the harbor. In their drunken state, they assumed the Dutch had launched an assault on Portsmouth. They ran around Great Island, banging on doors and spreading panic throughout the sleepy community. One woman testified that the commotion so terrified her family that "her sister was at prayer and her brother was upon his knees." Soon everyone realized it was a false alarm, and the next morning a sheepish Davis apologized to the court and community for his behavior. Gilbert Ferguson, one of the participants called to testify before the court, admitted going to The Anchor, the tavern run by Walton's son-in-law, Edward West, for a quart of sack. He failed to obtain it because West and his family were asleep—though one might presume that, earlier in the night, the Wests' tavern was indeed the source of the drink that led to such trouble.[23]

Though no Massachusetts community suffered direct attack, Dutch privateers did capture Fort Pentagoet, the French stronghold at the mouth of the Penobscot River. The privateers then went on to seize a group of New England trading vessels at the St. John River, including Nicholas Shapleigh's bark, *Trial*, captained by George Walton Jr. So, despite the false alarm on Great Island, residents of towns like Portsmouth and Hampton were not unjustified in their fears of the Dutch.[24]

Amid this Dutch threat, magistrates committed Eunice Cole to jail in April 1673, once more to face trial for witchcraft. The court had had very strong suspicions against her, but the evidence proved insufficient, and again she went free. She was still living in 1680 when Hampton witnessed its last witchcraft accusations. This time, although Eunice Cole was implicated once more, the main charges were laid against other women.[25]

Residents of Hampton may have been anticipating an outbreak of witchcraft or some other disaster in the summer of 1680. The month before the first witchcraft charge, Increase Mather made a record of lightning hitting the Hampton home of Colonel Joseph Smith, killing his mother and injuring his wife, Dorothy, the granddaughter of celebrated Puritan minister John Cotton. Dorothy was also the daughter of Hampton's current minister, Seaborn Cotton. In attacking the family of such prominent divines, God had given a lethal sign of his great displeasure and a warning of punishments to come. The witchcraft accusations that soon followed would have been seen in this light by residents of Hampton.[26]

In 1680 the court laid the principal charge of witchcraft against Rachel Fuller, a young Hampton wife and mother who claimed to have the ability to identify witches. Fuller said she had observed witches, including Eunice Cole, practicing their craft. She had witnessed, among other nefarious activities, "a great row" at Henry Robie's tavern, where a boarder had been pulled out of bed by witches who, "with an enchanted bridle did intend to lead a jaunt." Soon Fuller herself was accused of causing the death of a fifteen-month-old boy. Ironically, it was counter magic that led suspicion to fall on this self-proclaimed witch finder. Foreman Henry Robie and his jury of inquest found that Fuller had murdered the infant through witchcraft.[27]

On another occasion, Fuller had urged the family of the afflicted boy to lay bays of laurel under the threshold of the house to keep witches out. But after the family followed her instructions, Fuller implicated herself by trying to squeeze through the side of the threshold that did not have laurels under it. After she got in the house, she appeared uncomfortable, staring at the doorway where the bays lay. Just as counter magic had cast suspicion on Elizabeth Morse, so too did it incriminate Rachel Fuller. Eunice Cole would also face charges, as would a third Hampton woman. While many people believed the women to be in league with the devil, the judges had to set them free for lack of proof.[28]

These events in Hampton can surely be considered precursors of the lithobolia attacks on Great Island two years later. Henry Robie, the Hampton magistrate whose tavern was the alleged scene of the Hampton witches' romp, was a business partner of George Walton. His younger brother Samuel lived on Great Island and was Walton's son-in-law. George Walton knew Eunice Cole from the days when they were both living in Exeter. Certainly the Walton clan would have heard of the accusations against the Hampton witches and would have been on the lookout for more.

So, when the unexplained attacks on George Walton's property persisted, the conditions were in place for him to begin to look for a supernatural cause. That witches inflicted harm through maleficium was a commonly held belief. Sometimes the damage they did was to individuals, as when Susannah Trimmings took ill and Nicholas Row suffered great pain after their encounters with Jane Walford. At other times, the evils were directed toward property. Witches killed livestock, damaged crops, caused ship-sinking storms, and carried out a range of other crimes against property and prosperity. Often it was real estate rather than personal possessions that lay at stake. Inheritance struggles between widows and stepchildren, for example, or the property-line disputes between neighbors often fueled charges of witchcraft. If nothing else, the lengthy clashes between the Waltons and the Walfords demonstrate that such conflicts could take years to work their way through the complex court system—and sometimes justice was still not served even then.

Salem is the best known example of witchcraft accusations stemming partly from a property dispute. In their classic study, *Salem Possessed*, Paul Boyer and Stephen Nissenbaum describe the community tensions and factionalism that were a major influence in the witchcraft outbreak of 1692. Much of the trouble came from the Putnams of Salem Village. Thomas Putnam Jr. and his family were the leading accusers. The clan had been on the losing end of a nasty legal battle with Thomas's younger half-brother, Joseph Putnam, who had inherited the largest share of the estate. In 1692, the dispute had only recently been settled in Joseph's favor, and Thomas's fortunes had begun to decline. At the same time, Joseph's favorable marriage and his rise to both economic and political prominence in the village made him the envy of his older half-siblings. According to Boyer and Nissenbaum, Thomas and his family believed that witchcraft lay at the roots of their problems, and this is what led them to charge so many people. Interestingly, one of the accused was Rebecca Nurse, whose family had been involved in a protracted property dispute with the Putnams back in the 1670s.[29]

In her study of New England witchcraft cases outside Salem, Carol Karlsen has noted that accusations were often closely related to property holding, particularly disputes over inheritance. The same is true elsewhere. European historians frequently point to the 1324–25 case of Dame Alice Kyteler in Kilkenny, Ireland, as an important early instance of witchcraft. Her maleficium allegedly included the murder of several husbands whose wealth and property Kyteler hoped to gain; the accusations were made by jealous stepchildren and in-laws who believed themselves to be the rightful heirs. Church authorities also accused Alice and her associates of holding nighttime meetings to renounce Christianity and make sacrifices to demons. Here we can see the beginning of the concepts of the witches' coven and witches' Sabbath. The Kyteler case is one of the first to combine the general public's image of the evil, harmful witch with learned authorities' fear of heretical devil-worship. Most scholars see the union of these two concepts as a main cause of the so-called Great Age of Witch Hunts.[30]

As a common man, George Walton probably did not concern himself with the scholarly assertions of satanic heresy. Instead, he just wanted an explanation for—and an end to—the lithobolia attacks. Once he focused the blame on Hannah Jones, Walton had to seek a supernatural accomplice, for it would have been clear to the tavern owner that a lone elderly woman could not mount the repeated assaults. She would have been physically incapable of making the kind of furious, clandestine attack described by Richard Chamberlain. If his observations are even close to accurate, it would have taken an all-star baseball pitching staff to hurl the barrage of missiles at the Waltons and their property. Moreover, it is particularly unlikely that the aged woman could have pursued Walton five miles upriver, continuing the attack on the Walton farmstead at Herrods Cove on Great Bay. But rather than give up his suspicion of the widow, Walton assumed that she enlisted the devil's aid to carry out the mischief.

A witchcraft accusation against Jones was the easy path for Walton, for the alternative would have implicated members of his own household. Chamberlain's account takes particular care to note that, during the attacks, stones were thrown through the tavern windows from the inside, and also that some objects had disappeared from inside the inn. It was far easier, or at least less painful, to accuse a long-standing adversary of working with the devil than to suspect members of his own troubled household.

If George Walton gave his household serious consideration, he would have realized that several people there had motives to carry out an attack against the master of the house. The servants would have headed the suspect list. George Walton had a long history of treating his servants badly, and it is quite possible that the crew working in the tavern in 1682 resented him. Certainly William Agawam would have been most unhappy. The young Native American had tried to free himself several years earlier, only to have the court order him to serve Walton until his (Agawam's) twenty-fourth birthday. In addition to unhappy servants like Agawam the many young grandchildren in the house could have raised suspicions. In the few years before lithobolia, George and Alice Walton had lost four children and three sons-in-law, leaving nine young orphans. Many of these grandchildren would have lived and worked at the tavern. Although such personal loss was far more common in the seventeenth century than today, the Waltons found themselves in a most unusual situation. It must have been difficult for all to cope, and some of the children may have lashed out at their grandparents or simply enjoyed a bit of mischief as a way to relieve their sorrow.

Grandson John West had been apprenticed to another man, but after his conviction for theft from his mother's trunk, he still would have had both access to the tavern and ample reason to hate his grandfather. For it must have been George Walton who, as administrator of the estate, uncovered the robbery when going through his late daughter's possessions. He could have quietly made his grandson and daughter-in-law return the missing money, but instead he had them charged and convicted of robbery, thus forcing them to pay heavy damages and suffer considerable embarrassment. Stone throwing may have been John West's revenge.

Alternatively, it is possible that George Walton never believed himself to be under supernatural attack at all. For even if he had suspected angry neighbors, he was savvy enough to recognize a charge of witchcraft as a solid legal tactic. As Mary Beth Norton has suggested, the witchcraft accusation was Walton's ultimate weapon against Jones in their endless property dispute. It might be seen as the seventeenth-century equivalent of "playing the race card." Walton may have cynically made his accusation against Hannah Jones as a calculated legal move to win his dispute with her. Perhaps Hannah Jones realized this, prompting her counter charge that Walton was himself a wizard. Anyone who had heard of the Morse case knew that, although the Morses had brought the original charges, it was Elizabeth Morse who was ultimately convicted of witchcraft. So, there was recent precedent for the suggestion the supposed victim of witchcraft was actually the perpetrator.[31]

In addition, it certainly would not have been the first time that someone made a charge of witchcraft for purely personal ends. Take the celebrated case of Anne Gunter. In 1605, the twenty-year-old English girl became well known for fits and contortions that showed all the signs of demonic possession or witchcraft. Eventually Anne confessed to no less a personage than King James I that her father had encouraged and aided her in simulating bewitchment in order to gain the upper hand in his feud with the family of Elizabeth Gregory, the leader of a group of three women Anne had accused. The Gunters had carefully constructed their deception to make it convincing. In addition to Gregory, Anne had also cried out on a woman reputed to be a witch and on the woman's illegitimate daughter. By combing them with accusations against these "usual" suspects, Gunter gave increased credibility to her charges against Gregory.[32]

We will never know for sure whether George Walton truly believed that he was beset by witches or merely made these charges to win his property dispute. But everything we know about the man suggests that he would not have been above this kind of subterfuge. As modern observers, we also know that witchcraft does not exist outside of Wicca, the modern-day naturalistic religion whose followers claim no harmful supernatural powers. Lacking supernatural ability, Hannah Jones would have needed considerable help to carry out the attacks. Moreover, it would have been particularly foolhardy for an aged, poor widow whose freedom depended on a bond for good behavior to go out of her way to provoke a cantankerous old foe like George Walton after many years of uneasy peace.

So, while generations have pointed to Hannah Jones as the culprit, a close look at the evidence suggests her innocence; and even if she was responsible for lithobolia, most of the work would have had to be done by others. In fact, Hannah may have been framed by neighbors, perhaps even by her own nephew Jeremiah Walford. At any rate, there is no shortage of possible suspects other than Jones, for in the summer of 1682, most of the residents of Great Island had very good reason to throw stones at George Walton.

Seven

Great Island's Great Matter

In December 1663, Great Island cobbler Thomas Parker drunkenly lashed out at Portsmouth authorities while at a neighbor's home. Reverend Joshua Moody was an ungodly and wicked man, a whore and a "lubber more fit for the plow tayel then for a pulpit." He defamed four Portsmouth merchants as bastards and cheaters, and encouraged them to take their rightful place in hell with the devil. Authorities soon found Parker guilty of reviling speech and drunkenness. They sentenced him to receive fifteen lashes and an hour in the stocks unless he paid substantial fines.[1]

Parker's scandalous speech is indicative of the tensions and troubles that divided Portsmouth on many occasions during this era. The 1650s and 1660s saw repeated conflict between the Old Planters and the Puritans. Parker belonged to the Old Planter faction, for he questioned the fitness of Harvard-trained Reverend Moody. The calling of this ardent Puritan from Newbury, Massachusetts, to Portsmouth in 1658 signaled the growing political and spiritual power of the Bay Colony in Portsmouth.

All the other men threatened by Parker were both civic leaders and Puritan merchants, so he undoubtedly disliked the men for their politics as well as their religious views. He also felt threatened by their economic power. Parker complained that Brian Pendleton owed him fourteen pence. Nathaniel Fryer owed Parker two shillings, but insisted the cobbler pay him cash for bread. So, the lines of division in Portsmouth ran between Puritans and Anglicans, early settlers and new arrivals, successful merchants and struggling townsmen. There were also deep geographical divides, for Portsmouth was really a series of neighborhoods rather than a unified town. These conflicts created an evolving series of factions that came together and dissolved again, depending upon the particular issue at stake. An Anglican might disagree with his Puritan neighbor about the choice of minister, but the two would completely concur that the new meetinghouse ought to be constructed close to them. It was just such an argument over the meetinghouse that would elevate the level of animosity toward George Walton in the summer of 1682 and eventually culminate in lithobolia.

Although lithobolia was a remarkable event, virtually every early New England town suffered from at least some of the social tensions Portsmouth faced. The general public still tends to view early New England as a peaceful place, the home of democracy and religious freedom. While the settlers who founded many of these towns envisioned them to be utopias, the reality was far different, as many historians have demonstrated. The Puritans of Massachusetts Bay founded a theocracy, not a democracy. Yes, the communities were run by town meetings, but only the adult, property-holding, male church members could attend. Freedom of religion began and ended with the freedom to join the orthodox Puritan church. Would-be settlers who envisioned even a slightly different interpretation of Scripture, such as John Wheelwright or Roger Williams, faced ejection from the colony. A generation of historians has produced individual case studies of seventeenth-century New England towns, mostly focusing on Massachusetts Bay, and concluded that virtually all were ridden with conflict. The title of Roger Thompson's study of early Watertown, *Divided We Stand*, says it all. Discord and dissent wracked the typical community. The most impressive accomplishment of early Watertown, one of the original six townships of Massachusetts Bay and part of John Winthrop's "city upon a hill," was probably its ability to avoid falling into complete anarchy amid its frequent conflicts.[2]

As was the case in Portsmouth, religion was often at the root of the disagreements. The most famous example of this was in Boston, where the Antinomian controversy at its height threatened to split the town in two. In addition to questions of orthodoxy, personal preferences over the choice of ministers could also lead to bitter disputes. In 1640, for example, townsmen in Portsmouth's neighbor Dover nearly took up arms during a dispute over the appointment of a new minister. Between 1672 and 1689, Salem Village hired four different religious leaders, as factions within the community struggled bitterly to control the governance of the parish and the hiring of its ministers. Paul Boyer and Steven Nissenbaum have convincingly demonstrated the link between these problems and the onset of witchcraft in 1692.

In Massachusetts Bay, religious disagreements also had political implications. Only men who owned property and were members of the church had the status of freemen—that is, citizens who could vote in town meeting and hold office. This meant that non–church members usually did not receive land, since the town had authority to grant or deny it, and thus found it hard to survive in the community. The rules were not as strict in Portsmouth. When Massachusetts extended authority to New Hampshire, authorities agreed to allow considerable latitude in worship and church membership in a colony that was then largely Anglican. So, having Anglicans, Puritans, Antinomians, and even the occasional Quaker together as freemen was the norm in New Hampshire in the mid-seventeenth century. This made it different from the rest of the Bay Colony, where orthodoxy was enforced and Puritan patriarchs controlled religious affairs, town meetings, and the division of common lands.

Although ownership of real estate would become a particularly contentious issue in many instances, communities initially had more land than they could possibly use. As Philip Greven has demonstrated in his classic study of Andover, Massachusetts, the eighteen families who founded the community in 1642 had thousands of acres—enough land for the current settlers, and several generations to come. The planters of Andover initially settled only a small part of their township, placing their homesteads side by side on small house lots. The village was surrounded by several large agricultural fields, which were worked in common. Early Andover replicated the open-field villages popular since the Middle Ages in many regions of England. This close settlement in what is called a "nuclear village" emphasized neighborliness and cooperation and fit well with the Puritan ideal of community. John Winthrop's utopian city upon a hill was meant to be a place where Puritans could live harmoniously in close proximity to one another. Unfortunately, this would prove to be an elusive ideal. As its founders were joined by a second generation as well as newcomers, Andover soon apportioned most of the town's extensive unclaimed acreage to these new citizens. By 1662, a total of forty house lots had been laid out in Andover, and the lion's share of the remaining land in town had been divided among the families owning these homes. Thanks to four allotments (or divisions) of common land, even the most modest freeman in Andover presided over 122 acres, while some community leaders owned more than 600 acres. These divisions must have brought a sense of security to settlers, particularly those who had owned little or no land in England. But the situation would also result in community strife.[3]

As soon as freemen received large divisions of land far from Andover's village, many of them began to move away and build farmsteads on their holdings. Despite warnings and even fines from the town government, by the 1680s close to half of the families had moved out of the village and onto these far-flung lands. Some saw this as a breakdown of the communal ideal of the village, a threat to the city upon a hill and the Puritan experiment. The sizable land divisions also gave the freemen extensive control over the town and even over their families. Although the first generation of settlers could clear and use only a portion of their vast holdings, Philip Greven has demonstrated that these men maintained control over the entirety of the land, delaying the transfer of usage and ownership rights to sons and daughters eager to marry and establish their own households on the unused acres. Andover's patri-

archs wielded considerable power over their children, often forcing
the second generation to defer marriage in order to continue to
work for their fathers. This must have led to considerable tension
between the generations.[4]

As common land was divided and town residents relocated,
other kinds of problems often arose. In 1636 the town of Dedham,
Massachusetts, was founded by about thirty families. The General
Court granted them a huge township of nearly 200 square miles,
stretching from Watertown on the northern end to what would become the Rhode Island border on the south. Like Andover, Dedham was meant to be a Puritan utopia, yet from the beginning it
was too large to exist as a single community. By 1673, the towns of
Medfield and Wrentham had been carved out of the original grant
and settled by families from Dedham. These were amicable part-
ings, but in the coming decades conflicts would arise over the se-
cession of towns from Dedham. The main argument given by
residents in these outlying villages was that they were too far away
from the main settlement to attend Sunday worship or perform
other civic duties. They would ask for the right to establish their
own minister, and inevitably, to incorporate their own town. Often
in Dedham, and in other locales, the parent town balked at such requests, though typically the outlying districts eventually won the
bitter struggles that would ensue. The boundaries of the original
Dedham grant now include all or part of thirteen different Massachusetts towns.[5]

Portsmouth was not unique in its problems, though the community's unusual diversity meant that the tensions ran deeper there
than in many other places, and helps to explain the frustrations of
Thomas Parker and others. As a resident of Great Island, the cobbler's outbursts may have also been a symptom of tensions between
island and mainland residents of Portsmouth, as the islanders were
in the middle of an ongoing effort to incorporate as an independent town. Much of this long drama would be played out in the
summer of 1682, simultaneous with the lithobolia attacks. The
push for independence had as much to do with religion as with politics, for Great Island was a hub of religious activity and controversy at the time. If it was a property dispute that originally sparked

lithobolia, it was local politics and religious controversy that added fuel to the fire.

The town of Portsmouth as originally bounded made for an unwieldy community that covered many miles of land. Few roads existed in the region, so most settlers built their homes near their principal means of travel and communication: navigable water. Since Portsmouth had miles of water frontage, settlers were truly scattered. There were at least five foci of settlement in Portsmouth: Greenland (east of the town of Hampton), Strawbery Banke (the area between Fresh Creek and Salt Creek), Sagamore Creek, Little Harbor (including Seavey's Creek, Odiorne's Point, and Sandy Beach), and Great Island. Today this territory comprises all or part of seven distinct townships: Portsmouth, Great Island, Rye, Newington, Greenland, Stratham, and North Hampton. The simple factor of distance made it difficult to keep these communities, with their diverse interests and needs, together as a single town.[6]

The different sections of Portsmouth generally managed to get along until 1667, when it came time to select the site of a meetinghouse. The Massachusetts General Court had to intervene to resolve this contentious debate, appointing a commission to arbitrate the issue. This commission concluded that the best spot for a meetinghouse was on the south side of Salt Creek, near Pickering's mill. The site itself was not a center of settlement, but it was the location on the mainland most convenient for Great Island residents to reach. As such, it was a compromise that made no one happy.[7]

The residents of Great Island felt particularly burdened by the choice, for they had to sail as much as two miles through the narrow and often treacherous mouth of the Piscataqua River to reach the site. The trip was extremely difficult if not impossible in harsh winter weather. After having made the trek for over two decades, in 1679 the residents of Great Island petitioned the Massachusetts General Court for permission to hire their own minister. The petition, which stressed the difficult passage to the mainland, seemed entirely reasonable. In fighting the tides and the winds, it pointed out, men were working harder on the day of rest than any other day of the week. The petitioners further argued that in abandoning the island on the Sabbath, they were leaving their homes open to robbery or destruction by fire. They were also leaving the fort on Great Island, the key defensive point for the whole Piscataqua region, without enough men to defend it should the settlement be attacked. The legislature responded by telling the petitioners to present their request to their own town meeting first. If they received the approval of the freemen of Portsmouth, then the legislature would take up the matter. At the next town meeting, in September 1679, residents of Great Island made a motion proposing they be organized as a separate parish. In response, the town meeting appointed a committee to meet the representatives of Great Island to resolve the matter.[8]

In the ensuing negotiations, the Great Islanders requested that they be freed of their obligation to contribute to the support of Portsmouth's minister, Joshua Moody. They would divide Portsmouth into two parishes—Great Island, and the mainland—each with its own minister supported by taxes raised locally. The Great Islanders even conceded that the arrangement did not have to be permanent. They would be willing to reunite with the rest of Portsmouth as soon as a bridge could be built from the island to the mainland. The island was certainly close enough to the mainland, and also to Blunt's Island, which abutted the mainland, for a bridge to be feasible. In 1671 the town had even authorized the construction of one, if private investors willing to fund the venture could be found. Presumably, this effort had been made at the behest of Great Islanders, with the Sabbath services in mind. However, nothing ever came of it.[9]

The sides were able to agree on these terms, but they had more difficulty with the issue of the town's outstanding debts. Collecting taxes to pay Reverend Moody had been a long-standing problem, and many townsmen were in substantial arrears. As early as 1673, the town had ordered the arrest of constables who were behind schedule in collecting the rates (or taxes). The redoubled efforts were fruitless, however, for the next year the selectmen proposed that they effectively clear the books, remitting the rates assigned to all the former constables who had failed in their attempts to collect. The town meeting refused to approve this motion and instead ordered the selectmen to use whatever means they could to recover monies due from the discharged constables. The struggle over rates must have grown even worse by the late 1670s. King Philip's War had proved very costly and the General Court had required all towns to raise extra rates to cover the expenses.[10]

Initially, the Great Islanders agreed to remain part of Reverend Moody's church for one more year, during which time they would collect the delinquent taxes required to satisfy their share of the town debt. In return, the townsmen would allow Great Island to create its own parish and hire its own minister. A day after reaching the accord, however, the mainlanders reconsidered and ended up repudiating the agreement. What they proposed instead was that Great Island would be free to create a new parish only when all town debts were satisfied—including many accounts for mainlanders that had not been settled in years. Given that the neighborhood constables had not been able to collect these rates, and that many residents of the mainland opposed separation, the Great Island residents doubted that they would be able to do so. The petitioners reported back to the General Court, asking them to intervene. In October 1679, the Court granted the Great Islanders permission to form a parish once the terms of the original agreement had been fulfilled. If the islanders' back taxes could be collected, they would have their own parish in the fall of 1680.[11]

On the brink of achieving their long-standing goals of building a meetinghouse and hiring a minister, the Great Islanders' efforts would be completely frustrated in early 1680 when Massachusetts lost its authority over the territory and New Hampshire became a royal colony. The islanders would have to begin their quest all over again. In the spring of 1682, they petitioned the president and Council of New Hampshire for permission to hire a minister. They asked that they be allowed to do this either as a parish of Portsmouth, or as an independent town. On May 2, 1682, the Council ordered the selectmen of Portsmouth to hold a town meeting on the matter and report back to them. On June 6, just two days before the first lithobolia attack on the Walton tavern, the selectmen reported that an agitated town had met and that the majority did not favor a new parish. Although things looked bad after this response, the fate of Great Island's petition remained formally undecided throughout the lithobolia incident.[12]

Until the June 6 meeting, Great Islanders must have assumed they would succeed in their efforts to create their own parish. After all, they had already been granted permission to do just that several years earlier. They may even have had their minister picked out. In the summer of 1682, "Mr. Woodbridge, a Minister," was present on Great Island to witness several episodes of lithobolia and even to be hit by a rock himself. The minister was almost certainly Reverend Timothy Woodbridge, a member of an important family of divines. Timothy was the son of Reverend John Woodbridge, the former minister of Newbury, and the nephew of Reverend Benjamin Woodbridge, the first graduate of Harvard College. Timothy's brothers Benjamin and John were both ministers as well. The boy's mother, Mercy, came from an even more prominent family, for she was the daughter of Massachusetts Governor Thomas Dudley.[13]

Timothy Woodridge graduated from Harvard in 1675 and took his second degree from the college in 1678. Presumably, he had come to the Piscataqua through the efforts of his sister Dorothy, who was married to Nathaniel Fryer, a leading merchant of Great Island. As a recent Harvard graduate from a prominent family of ministers, Timothy would have been most welcome. From the surviving evidence, it is unclear if he was hired to serve on Great Island or across the river at Kittery Point. Both communities needed a minister, and Timothy appears to have been involved in the affairs of both places. By 1683, however, he had moved on, accepting a position as minister for Hartford, Connecticut. He would later serve as a founding trustee of Yale College.[14]

Perhaps the actions of the New Hampshire Council inspired Woodbridge's departure, for in the fall of 1682 the Council ultimately ruled against Great Island's petition. The island would not become a town for another decade. Only a handful of documents survive regarding Great Island's separation efforts, so it is difficult to trace the exact course of events and the impact of this controversy. Still, looking closely at those few records and taking into account the timing of events does provide some insight. The 1679

Great Island petition itself is particularly important, for in addition to listing the practical motive for separation, it expresses the Great Islanders' concern for maintaining a godly society and claims that only about one third of the population of the island regularly attended the Sabbath on the mainland. Many of the island's children had never heard a sermon. Great Island was the home to many sailors and fishermen, and the port of call for others. These groups included numerous ungodly men, who used the long distance to the meeting house as an excuse to avoid worship and instead go to private houses to drink and profane the Sabbath. Residents feared that, unless they had their own meetinghouse and minister, they would descend into heathenism.[15]

No doubt the Great Islanders had George Walton and his family in mind when they raised concerns about preserving a moral and devout society. With the death of his daughter Matha and her husband Edward West, Walton resumed operating the family tavern and brew house. Also, while his residence technically remained a private home, he used it to run an inn, providing meals and rooms to guests such as Richard Chamberlain. At the time, there was only one other tavern on Great Island, so the petitioners surely would have seen the Waltons as at least partially responsible for the unruly behavior on Great Island. The island was a unique part of Portsmouth, in that no other community relied so heavily on the sea for its survival. Elsewhere fishing and seafaring mixed with a substantial amount of husbandry to make up the local economy, but in 1680, there were just seventy-six sheep, thirty-seven cows, and twenty-nine pigs on Great Island. For a population of perhaps three hundred people, there were only fifty-eight acres of upland for farming—not enough for the island to provide for itself, let alone the many ships that docked at one of its eleven wharves. Thus, Great Island was an overwhelmingly maritime community, made up principally of sailors and fishermen. It also included a fort, which came with a garrison of young soldiers. Not exactly the backbone of Puritan society, the sailors, soldiers, and fishermen who populated the island were dangerously prone to falling into blasphemy.[16]

In their 1682 response to the governor and Council, the Portsmouth selectmen implied that not all islanders supported the separation measure. Rather, the four petitioners who resided on Great Island were "gentlemen . . . who *call themselves* persons unanimously chosen by the inhabitants for that end." Were there people who did not want parish status, or were the townsmen just posturing? A look at the identity of the petitioners does raise skepticism about how representative they were of the interests of all Great Islanders. Nathaniel Fryer was a leading merchant of the Piscataqua. Married to Dorothy Woodbridge (who was the daughter of a leading Puritan minister, and granddaughter of the late Massachusetts Governor Thomas Dudley) Fryer held impeccable Puritan credentials. Two of Fryer's sons-in-law and fellow merchants, Robert Elliot and John Hinkes, also signed the petition. The fourth signatory, George Jaffrey, was also a member of Portsmouth's Puritan merchant faction. Jaffrey was actually hit by a stone during the lithobolia attack, though it probably was meant for his companion, Puritan minister Timothy Woodbridge, the brother of Dorothy Woodbridge Fryer. The Portsmouth selectmen surely had reason for their suspicions about the petition. It appears these men may have hoped to find a position for their kinsman and friend Reverend Woodbridge who had recently moved to the Piscataqua. It is unlikely that Quaker George Walton would give his consent to this Puritan petition.[17]

A wealthy man such as Walton may have also opposed the measure because it would come with the threat of higher taxes. As long as Great Island remained a part of Portsmouth, the islanders' tax burden was shared with the townsmen—including the many prosperous merchants on the mainland. If Great Island were to become its own town, however, the costs of supporting a minister would have to be borne by far fewer people. Furthermore there would be the expense of building a new meetinghouse. As the largest landholder on Great Island, George Walton was certain to see a significant increase in his taxes to support the new minister—inevitably a Puritan cleric with whom he would have no desire to worship. It is easy to believe that the Quakers of Great Island, led by George Walton, would have opposed separation from Portsmouth, as the selectmen's statement intimates. And it is just as easy to understand why neighbors of the Waltons might have retaliated by pelting the family with stones.

Even if the Waltons had not operated a tavern and an inn or formally opposed separation, their Quaker faith alone would have made their neighbors perceive them as intractable obstacles to the creation of a godly community. Not only were the Waltons prominent members of the Society of Friends, but Great Island was a major center of Quaker activity in colonial America. In 1675, Quaker missionary William Edmundson spent considerable time on Great Island and attended several Quaker meetings there. Leaving his horse on the island, he made several visits to the Kittery home of Quaker Nicholas Shapleigh and also held a large Quaker meeting in Dover. He then returned to Great Island to participate in one last religious gathering before leaving the region. George and Alice Walton are not mentioned by name in the accounts of Edmundson's time on Great Island, but a weary Quaker traveler in search of a place to stay and to tend to the needs of his horse almost certainly would have lodged at the Walton tavern. The Waltons may even have hosted the Great Island Quaker meetings, as taverns were often used for large public gatherings. Thus, the attempt to erect a meetinghouse on Great Island and shore up Puritan orthodoxy there was in part a response to the Waltons and Quaker activity on the island.[18]

The timing of events in June 1682 confirms that islanders viewed the Waltons as hindrances to the forming of a godly community. It is no coincidence that the lithobolia began just two days after attendees at a heated Portsmouth town meeting voted against supporting Great Island's application for separation. Returning to a theme raised in the 1679 appeal to the General Court, the 1682 petition noted the concern for those who profaned the Lord's Day by staying home. If there was opposition to the measure, it would most likely have come from the island's Quakers, for they had nothing to gain by the establishment of a church on the island. In fact, they had something to lose, since the distance to meeting would have served as a convenient excuse for the Waltons and other Great Island Quakers to miss services held by those whose religious beliefs they did not share.[19]

If the rest of the Great Islanders could not hire a minister to fight the profanity threatening their community, they could at least, some probably reasoned, make trouble for the most profane tavern and family on the island by assaulting them with a hail of stones.

In 1681, Richard Waldron had succeeded the late John Cutts as president of the Council of New Hampshire. The appointment of this prominent Quaker-hater to the highest office in the colony created a permissive atmosphere in which people could attack the Waltons with little fear of legal consequences. By 1682 there had already been a substantial history of animosity and violence between Puritans and the Society of Friends (better known as Quakers) in both old and New England. The Quakers emerged in England in the 1650s after Parliament granted religious toleration to all Protestants. In the early part of the decade, they developed in northern England under the leadership of George Fox. In opposition to the Puritans, Fox did not believe in the predestination of a small group of saints. Preaching a democratic vision that was truly radical for its day, the Quakers denied the importance of ministers and church hierarchy. Rather, all were equal, and all could be saved. They believed in direct revelation from God, accessed by looking within and seeing the inner light.[20]

The social turmoil following the execution of Charles I and the overthrow of the Church of England gave birth to numerous sects opposed to mainstream Protestantism and often to the social, political, and economic restraints of hierarchical society. Some, such as the Fifth Monarchists and the Muggletonians, believed that the execution of Charles had paved the way for the second coming of Christ and the establishment of the Kingdom of Jesus. The Seekers considered all churches to be corrupt, withdrawing from religion institutions to await the coming of Christ and his apostles, who would establish the one true church. Although the Seekers and the Muggletonians were peaceful, the Fifth Monarchists called for the overthrow of political leaders to hasten the return of Christ. The Ranters took the logic of predestination to its extreme. If God had already determined who would and would not go to heaven, all could do as they wished in life. They avoided organized religion and the Bible, and openly swore, drank, and practiced free love.

Today it is hard to believe that the Quakers, a group renowned for their egalitarianism and pacifism, could have been seen as a radical threat. However, in the seventeenth century, a time dominated by hierarchy, their religious and social views posed a serious challenge to civil order. Moreover, the early Quakers were not pacifists. Indeed, many of them joined Fifth Monarchists and Baptists in a military revolt against the newly restored King Charles II in London in 1661. The uprising, led by Fifth Monarchist Thomas Venner, was quickly put down, and it was only in its aftermath that Quakers adopted pacifism, in part to protect those among them suspected of supporting the coup.[21]

Even before the first Quaker missionaries arrived in Boston in 1656, New Englanders saw the faith as a serious threat. Massachusetts Bay had struggled for almost two decades to establish a Puritan orthodoxy. The colony had withstood religious controversies over Roger Williams, the Antinomians, and others. Bay Colony magistrates looked on in horror at the growth of the radical sects in England.

So concerned were officials that they called for a day of fasting in June 1656 to strengthen the church and its ordinances. Less than a month later, the first two Quakers arrived in Boston, to be soon followed by eight more. Authorities quickly deported these missionaries before they could spread their faith, and the General Court soon passed laws forbidding Quakers to enter the colony. But these prohibitions seemed only to encourage them, for over the next three years several dozen more Quakers managed to land in Massachusetts. Finally, in desperation, the General Court ordered that all Quakers who returned to the colony after banishment would be hanged. Upon hearing of the new law, several missionaries deliberately set out to test it. Between 1659 and 1661, four Quakers were executed in Massachusetts.[22]

Officials showed great reluctance to enforce this law, preferring that the missionaries would simply leave and thereby end what many Puritans viewed as a major threat to peace and order in the colony. The court itself also seemed to lose its stomach for such terrible business, moderating its earlier decree by passing the Cart and Whip Act in 1661. Now Quakers entering the colony would simply be tied to a cart and whipped through the streets of the towns as they were escorted out of the colony. Even as Massachusetts authorities were struggling with Quaker missionaries, however, a growing number of residents were beginning to adopt the faith. By 1657, a Quaker movement had begun in Salem, and within four years more than fifty residents had been "convinced" (or converted to Quakerism), despite the threat of persecution. The uneasy peace that finally emerged was punctuated by symbolic acts of civil disobedience, such as the Friends' refusal to remove their hats in court or the defiant act of walking naked through the streets. The refusal to tip or remove one's hat—a traditional sign of respect for authority—symbolized the Quakers' egalitarian sentiments. The removal of clothes was meant to evoke the spiritual nakedness of those unconvinced of Quaker beliefs.[23]

Puritans considered Quaker meetings to be a dangerous antithesis of their own services. Puritan ministers led their congregation in a well-ordered service, focused around reading and interpreting the Bible. Everything about the event stressed the control of the wealthy and devout men of the community. A rigid seating plan reinforced this hierarchy, with men and women seated separately, and everyone assigned seats based on their social rank and age. Quaker meetings had no structure. There was no minister leading the congregation, and no reading of scripture. People sat where they liked, and any man or woman could speak when the spirit moved them.

In 1662 five Quaker missionaries arrived in Dover, New Hampshire. George Preston and Edward Wharton were members of the small Quaker community in Salem, while Mary Tompkins, Alice Ambrose, and Anna Coleman came from England. Despite the threat of legal persecution, they met with some success. At the invitation of Major Nicholas Shapleigh, the group soon crossed the river to York County, where they visited for some time. Although Maine was then a part of Massachusetts, citizens there enjoyed considerably more religious freedom than they did south of the Piscataqua. Symbolic of this toleration was the fact that Major Shapleigh, one of the most important magistrates in the county, felt at liberty to host the missionaries. The three women among them soon tired of their safety, and in the late fall of 1662, they re-crossed the Piscataqua to seek more converts in New Hampshire.[24]

This time, the women met with firm legal opposition. Richard Waldron, the magistrate of Dover, arrested the women and convicted them of being Quakers, sentencing them to be punished according to the Cart and Whip Act. On December 22, he ordered the women stripped to the waist and tied to the tail of a cart, which would drive them out of Massachusetts Bay. In each of the eleven towns on the road between Dover and Boston, the women were to be whipped up to ten stripes each. The sentence was carried out in Dover and Hampton, where the women were forced to walk through deep snow on a cold winter day. In Salisbury, however, Walter Barefoot mercifully intervened to stop the proceedings. Barefoot, a political opponent of Waldron and the Puritans, was also a doctor, and he attended to the women's medical needs. The women then retreated to Kittery to Major Shapleigh's to recover, but the zealous missionaries soon returned to Dover. Here they again received severe punishment. Tompkins was beaten, while Ambrose was dragged through the snow and set in the stocks. Coleman fell into the river trying to get away from the constables and nearly froze to death after being denied proper shelter.[25]

Despite the harsh treatment received by these and subsequent missionaries, a few converts were made in New Hampshire, and a substantial number of Kittery and Berwick residents adopted the faith, including Nicholas Shapleigh, the major of the county militia. He and other Quakers also served as county judges and in other important public offices. In this way, Quakerism began to pose as much a political as a religious threat to Massachusetts Bay. In 1663 when Shapleigh and two other Quakers held the majority of seats among the Kittery selectmen, Massachusetts took the extreme measure of removing them from power by disenfranchising them. Shapleigh and the others left no account of why they converted to Quakerism. However, this political aspect cannot be overlooked, as most of these men were supporters of the Gorges and Mason families—Royalists who opposed Massachusetts.[26]

Major Shapleigh also happened to be a friend of George and Alice Walton, and he must have been concerned when he learned in early 1664 that the court had convicted them of being Quakers. This was not a case of merely absenting themselves from Puritan worship. The Waltons dangerously engaged in religious debate with Portsmouth officials. One exchange between the Waltons and Portsmouth magistrate Major Brian Pendleton was recorded by William Sewel in his 1728 *History of the Rise, Increase and Progress of the Christian People called Quakers.*

> Bryan Pembleton was ask'd by George Walton, and his wife Alice, who was reputed one of the most godly Women thereabout, What anointing was which the Apostle John exhorted the Saints unto in the Day: But what a wicked Man this Pembleton was, may appear by the abominable Answer he gave, viz. That John was either a Fool or a Madman, or else he did not know what he said. And blasphemous in a very high Degree was what he said to the Question, What was the Light which shone about Paul? For his Answer was, It was the Light of the Devil for ought he did know.[27]

Sewel's description of the debate between the Waltons and Pendleton should not be taken at face value. After all, it was a secondhand account first published in Low Dutch over fifty years after the fact by a Quaker enthusiast. Still, the very inclusion of such a debate in a major Quaker history affirms the significance of the Waltons as outspoken Quaker leaders. Whatever exact words they might have uttered in the debate, Pendleton and other Puritan officials of Portsmouth must have considered them a serious threat to the religious and social stability of the community.

The Waltons came to pose an even greater threat when their daughter Dorcas married Shapleigh's nephew, Samuel Treworgy. Now the family was allied to a fellow Quaker who was one of the wealthiest and most influential men in the region. The new connections brought important political and economic opportunities for the Waltons. Samuel Treworgy's sister Lucy was married to Humphrey Chadbourne, a prominent sawmill owner and merchant. Brother John was a Kittery merchant who had been appointed governor of Newfoundland by Oliver Cromwell. Mother Katherine Shapleigh Treworgy had been widowed at a young age and then married Edward Hilton, sawmill owner and merchant of Exeter. Collectively, the Hiltons, Treworgys, and Shapleighs were among the wealthiest families of the Piscataqua. Their ownership of a network of sawmills, their extensive business contacts, and the high offices they held brought them amazing wealth for early New England.[28]

Though they were stronger in Kittery, Quakers maintained a presence in New Hampshire as well. The most prominent Quaker in the colony was Captain Christopher Hussey. Hussey had been one of the first settlers of Hampton—the son-in-law of the town's first minister. He served repeatedly as selectman, town clerk, town meeting moderator, and representative to the General Court. In April 1674, Hussey and his son John were admonished for being Quakers. Still, five years later he was appointed to the New Hampshire Council, the governing body of the colony. Thus, Hussey was one of the men responsible for deciding the fate of Great Island's separation petition in 1682. At the opposite end of the political spectrum lay shadowy characters like the Waltons and the Furbushes, whose behavior seemed to threaten the social order. William Furbush, who converted to Quakerism in Dover in 1662, was prosecuted in 1674 for getting Indians drunk. In 1679, he was fined for abusing the constable, whom his wife Rebecca was convicted of striking. In 1683, husband and wife were both fined for speaking against the government.[29]

In addition to believing that most Quakers were lawbreakers like the Furbushes and the Waltons, outsiders sometimes suspected Quakers of holding mystical beliefs that linked their religion to witchcraft. There were a number of aspects of Quakerism that made it stand out. Opponents of the faith claimed that Quakers must have used charms and potions to attract so many converts. Such claims not only filled the English popular press of the mid-seventeenth century; leading English ministers made similar arguments as well, one going so far as to implicate Quaker leader George Fox as a sorcerer. The "quaking"—the trances and fits of religious ecstasy that gave the faith its popular name—was seen by members of the sect as evidence of saintliness, but it is easy to understand how opponents could view the fits as evidence of demonic possession. As late as 1691, Reverend Richard Baxter wrote that when the Quakers began meeting in England "their Societies began like Witches, with Quaking, and Vomiting, and Infecting others." Baxter's contemporary Increase Mather believed Quakers to be deluded by Satan. His son Cotton Mather complained that one of the Goodwin children of Boston to be afflicted by witchcraft in 1688 could read only Quaker tracts, implying that the witches preferred Quaker books.[30]

Some English Quakers were accused of witchcraft as part of a general effort to demonize the faith. In New England, Quakers themselves tended to avoid such charges, but their kin and their associates often did fall under suspicion. Several historians have suggested that the Essex County witch trials were part of a Puritan counteroffensive against the Quakers. Another prominent element of that attack was a tract campaign. The first publication, written by Portsmouth's Reverend Joshua Moody and two other divines in 1690, suggested that the gravest threat to Puritan New England came from the heresy of Quakerism, "the particular plague of this age . . . this great Choak-weed of the Christian and Protestant Religion, taking root in the borders of New England." One can picture a man of such opinions actively encouraging, or at least passively tolerating, his parishioners' stoning of the Waltons and their tavern.[31]

In addition to facing legal charges of witchcraft, Quakers also found themselves under considerable threat of violence. In England, numerous minor riots and lesser acts were aimed at Quakers during the Civil War era. David Underdown has suggested that all ranks of society feared the Quakers, each for its own reasons. Leaders of Puritan England and New England saw the Quakers as a threat to order, morality, and Puritan dominance. The working-class residents who carried out most of the aggression against the Quakers feared them because of the way the sect's egalitarianism challenged patriarchal order. Also, Quaker unwillingness to support the local church made them a threat to the harmony of a co-operative community.[32]

In New England, official persecutions by the General Court and the county courts were so common that local Puritans probably saw less need for informal, extra-legal violence against Quakers. No mass riots and only a few incidents of any kind are recorded, which makes the outbreaks of group violence against Quakers that did occur all the more notable. In April 1682, a group of Salem boys threw stones at Thomas Maule, a leading Salem Quaker. Maule was in his barn at the time, and the stone throwers taunted him to come out so they could beat him. The affair soon escalated into a scuffle when one of the boys struck Maule several times and pushed him onto the ground while swearing at him. Another youngster grabbed Maule by the throat, while two girls called Maule an Irish whore-master. Somehow Maule managed to lock one of the boys into his barn, repeatedly striking the lad's sister when she tried to free him. Several days later the boys got their revenge, cutting down the apple trees in Maule's orchard. At the root of the incident was a long-standing dispute between Maule and his neighbors, who alleged that he beat his indentured Irish maid (hence the reference to Maule as an Irish whoremaster).[33]

Several months later Maule would be present at another stoning—the lithobolia attack on Great Island. On Friday night, June 28, he was at the Walton's tavern as part of an impressive gathering of prominent Quakers from throughout the colonies. The dignitaries included Samuel Jennings, the governor of West Jersey; Walter Clark, the deputy governor of Rhode Island; and Christopher Hussey's son and daughter-in-law. Oliver Hooten, a Barbados merchant, held no political office, but as the son of the late Elizabeth Hooten, he would have been an honored guest. Elizabeth had been George Fox's first convert and the first Quaker woman to become a missionary. Quite possibly the Waltons were hosting the yearly New England meeting, a week-long gathering that brought together leading Friends from across the region every June to discuss church organization and policy. If not the actual yearly meeting, presumably the distinguished guests had come from that meeting to discuss Quaker affairs in the Piscataqua. Perhaps they had come specifically in response to the news of the attack on the Walton tavern.[34]

The group signed a deposition drawn up by Richard Chamberlain testifying that they had witnessed a supernatural stoning of Walton's tavern. Exactly why Maule believed it to be a supernatural attack is hard to understand. After all, he was all too familiar with neighborly disputes that spilled over into violence, including stone-throwing, against Quakers. Great Islanders must have viewed the large meeting of prominent Friends from throughout the English colonies—unprecedented in New Hampshire—with suspicion and hostility, and they undoubtedly gave vent to these feelings by launching the lively lithobolia attack.

This disturbing Quaker presence was not the only spiritual threat the Great Islanders were facing in the summer of 1682, for Baptists had also arrived in the region. Just across the narrow mouth of the Piscataqua River from Great Island lay Kittery Point—closer to Great Island, in fact, than the residents' own church on the mainland at Strawbery Banke. The Puritan islanders would have been deeply concerned by the early 1682 establishment of a Baptist congregation so close by. The previous year, fourteen Kittery residents had accepted baptism and joined the Baptist church at Boston, the Baptist congregation nearest to Portsmouth. Like the Quakers, many of these Baptists were prominent members of society. The group's minister, William Scriven, was married to Bridget Cutts, a niece of the late president of New Hampshire, John Cutts. The sizable Cutts clan was made of wealthy merchants counted among the elite of Piscataqua society; several of these joined the Baptists, including Bridget and her mother, whose second husband was the elderly Captain Francis Champernowne, a close ally of the Shapleigh family and a leader of the Royalist faction in Maine and New Hampshire. The Kittery Baptists had other radical ties as well. One parishioner was the sister-in-law of the Muggletonian Leader brothers, the men who had established the Great Works sawmill upriver in Berwick in the 1650s.[35]

The Baptists posed a threat to both Great Islanders and mainland Portsmouth residents. The islanders might have found it faster to travel to Kittery for Baptist services than to go to their own Puritan church on the mainland. On the mainland, even Reverend Moody's congregation was affected, losing to the Baptist newcomers William Scriven, who previously would sail across the Piscataqua to Portsmouth to attend Moody's church. Moody and the other church leaders no doubt feared that other parishioners might follow Scriven's lead and convert to the Baptist faith. It is no wonder that the Great Islanders immediately petitioned the Council to establish a separate parish. They were truly concerned about the spread of blasphemy.[36]

Baptists were poorly understood in the seventeenth century. Rather than referring to a single organized faith, the term "Baptist" was applied to several groups holding diverse beliefs. Initially, Puritans labeled Baptists eccentric Protestant fanatics—avatars of the sixteenth-century Anabaptists of Munster, the polygamous radicals who led a violent revolt against their government. By the midseventeenth century, however, it was clear that, while English Baptists believed in rebaptism or full immersion of adults, they were not wild-eyed rebels bent on overthrowing society. Still, they were considered dangerous and often lumped with Levellers, Ranters, Quakers, and the other groups that emerged out of the radicalism of the English Civil War. In truth, their belief in adult Baptism and adult-only membership in the church excepted, Baptists differed little in their convictions from mainstream New England Puritans. Still, their distinctive practice seemed to place them on the slippery slope of heresy, signaling the presence of religious radicals in the making. Consequently, Massachusetts Puritans made repeated efforts to stamp out the Baptist threat in the seventeenth century, treating the early Baptists almost as severely as they treated the Quakers.[37]

In the spring of 1682 Maine authorities jailed William Scriven for his Baptist beliefs, and for holding Baptist services in his home and elsewhere on the Lord's Day. The magistrate's prosecution efforts were aided by Reverend Woodbridge, who engaged Scriven in a long conversation to draw out his Baptist views. In June 1682, Scriven was ordered to give bond for his good behavior, and he promised to leave the province. Fortunately for the Baptist leader, the Bay Colony then abruptly stopped persecuting his faith, in response to rising fears that the king might revoke the colony's charter. The crown had many complaints with the government of

Massachusetts, and one of them was its lack of religious toleration. So, Scriven and his followers remained in Kittery. Several years later they would migrate to South Carolina, founding the Southern Baptist movement.[38]

Thus, several religious tensions were all coming to a head in the spring and summer of 1682. Residents of Great Island had been attempting to form their own parish for decades, and after having come so close to realizing this goal several times in the past, their frustration must have been mounting. The continued presence of the Quakers and the new challenge from the Baptists posed direct threats to their faith and their efforts to establish their church. They must have assumed that the New Hampshire Council would approve their application; after all, Massachusetts had granted them permission to separate just two years earlier. But things were not to be so easy this time. The town fathers of Portsmouth opposed the measure, and so the effort stalled. This led some devout Great Islanders to take out their frustration on the Waltons, the family whose presence seemed to mock their desire to maintain a godly community. So the stones flew all summer long. The names of the culprits will probably never be known. The active participants were no doubt joined by who others just silently observed the attacks and refused to implicate the guilty. As we will see, however, it was not just the pious residents of Great Island whose dislike of the Waltons was strong enough to inspire an attack. Most of New Hampshire, in fact, had excellent reason in 1682 to be angry with the family.

Eight

The Mason Family
Stakes Its Claim

"You have been to Mr. Mason for a confirmation of your lands, for which I will smoke you over the coals." Thus Major Richard Waldron threatened one New Hampshire man in 1665, when the King's Commissioners visited the colony and threatened to take it away from Massachusetts and to put it under control either of the king or the Mason family. Waldron angrily told another settler, "You are one of those that petition for kingly government. You shall have a king, and I will be your king." This was no idle threat—Waldron was powerful and connected man who would later run the colony, albeit briefly. His ally, Richard Martin, warned others "that neither the King nor Mason has any more right to the land in New England than Robin Hood." These heated words hint at the deep animosity and bitter political disagreements that not only helped to fuel the lithobolia outbreak on Great Island but repeatedly threatened to tear New Hampshire apart during the seventeenth century. The roots of the conflict ran all the way back to the founding of New Hampshire and Maine by Captain John Mason and Sir Ferdinando Gorges several decades earlier. Though he was not there for the colony's creation, George

Walton did get caught in the middle of disputes with origins that far in the past. Indeed, lithobolia is directly linked to the Mason family's long-standing struggle for control of New Hampshire, as a consideration of the beginnings of the colony will reveal. The unseen hand behind the lithobolia attack on the Walton tavern can serve as an apt symbol of the Mason family, the inconspicuous force that would dominate New Hampshire's politics throughout the seventeenth century.[1]

New Hampshire was established as a proprietary colony, initially claimed by one man, Captain John Mason. As such, her fate rested largely on the interests and fortunes of Mason and his family. Mason's untimely death and the irregular attention paid to the colony by his heirs meant that early New Hampshire lacked political stability. In contrast, Massachusetts Bay, was founded as a joint-stock company, with many different shareholders to help order, plant, and rule. Much more successful than her neighbor to the north, it often intruded into New Hampshire's politics. For a time, in fact, the Bay Colony usurped New Hampshire's very sovereignty.

John Mason and his family remain controversial figures in New Hampshire to this day. Some historians consider them visionaries, while others view them as villains. It is hard to see through the rhetoric to a clear picture of what the Masons were like, or even what they actually accomplished. Unfortunately, most of the descriptions of their ventures were made after the fact, in depositions, claims, and petitions made to serve as evidence in court or to bolster political arguments. Consequently, even many of the supposedly factual documents detailing the Mason family's efforts to establish New Hampshire are not beyond the possibility of taint. Gorges and Mason believed that their ventures would strengthen England, the Anglican Church, and the monarchy, but what was most important to both was turning a substantial profit. For several decades, many English explorers and promoters, including Gorges, were aware that the coasts of Maine and New Hampshire had rich fishing grounds. Seasonal fishermen had successfully been venturing to the region since the early 1610s, and by 1622 Gorges had established a small year-round fishing station at Damariscove Island, off the mid-coastal region of Maine. Mason also knew the value of a rich fishing ground, especially a largely untapped one that did not have to be shared with the French and Basques, as in Newfoundland.[2]

Early explorers of the region had raved about the economic potential of northern New England. Virginia's Captain John Smith had spent the summer of 1614 on its coast, and he immediately became a strong promoter of the area, publishing *A Description of New England* in 1616. Smith is credited with giving the region the name of New England. He pointed out that, in addition to the superabundance of fish, the territory also contained a wealth of lumber and furs, as well as Native Americans hungry for English trade goods. Smith even experimented with gardening and found the ground exceedingly fertile. It was reports like his that drove Mason and Gorges to try repeatedly to establish colonies on this segment of the Atlantic rim.

Captain John Mason and Sir Ferdinando Gorges belonged to that group of Englishmen who looked to America in the early seventeenth century as the key to the prosperity of both their families and their growing nation. Gorges never ventured to the New World, but he had been a promoter of early explorations and a principal investor in the Popham (or Sagadahoc) Colony. This venture, established on the Kennebec River in present-day Maine, lasted less than a year after its founding in 1607, but rather than becoming discouraged by the failure, Gorges soon involved himself in other projects in the region. One of his associates in these efforts was Captain John Mason.

Unlike Gorges, Mason had practical experience as a naval officer and explorer. In 1610, when he was only twenty-four, King James I entrusted Mason to command a small naval expedition to put down a rebellion in the Hebrides Islands. In 1616, the proprietors of Cuper's Cove colony in Newfoundland appointed him governor, an office he held until 1621. He surveyed the island and eventually published the first map and description of Newfoundland. With Gorges's encouragement, the Crown established the Council for New England in 1620, making the body responsible for establishing and governing all lands in America from the fortieth to forty-eighth parallels (i.e., from present-day Pennsylvania to New-foundland). Since Ferdinando Gorges was president of the Council and John Mason was secretary, it is not surprising that each was the recipient of a number of land grants. The tracts they received, and others allocated by the Crown in the 1620s and 1630s, often over-lapped and conflicted, creating the confusing landscape that would trigger a series of court cases in New Hampshire until the mid-eighteenth century.[3]

In March 1622, the Council for New England granted Mason all lands between the Naumkeag River (in present-day Salem, Massachusetts) and the Merrimac River. Later that year, the Council granted Mason and Gorges all the territory between the Merrimac and the Kennebec Rivers, a region known as the Province of Maine. Before the end of 1622, the Council would issue over a dozen formal patents throughout their territory to a range of Englishmen.[4]

One of these patentees, David Thompson, became the first European settler of the Piscataqua. In 1623, he established a small settlement at Pannaway or Little Harbor, at present-day Odiorne's Point in Rye, New Hampshire. Although the trading venture failed in 1626, Thompsons employee Edward Hilton established his own fishing operation nearby. Edward, a fishmonger from London, was joined by his brother William, who had been living in Massachusetts at Plymouth. Within a year or two the Hilton brothers had abandoned the mouth of the river to establish themselves upriver at what would become known as Hilton Point, in present-day Dover. Having chosen a location that was both fertile and a strategic spot for the fur trade, they soon prospered.[5]

Meanwhile, Gorges and Mason did little with their holdings. Ferdinando's son Robert Gorges received the appointment of gov-ernor-general of New England in 1623. He established a colony at Wessagusset (present-day Weymouth, Massachusetts) but aban-doned the venture within a year to return to England. Gorges and Mason soon put their colonizing schemes aside to help England fight wars against Spain and then France. As the long-standing captain of the fortress in Plymouth, England, Gorges had the re-sponsibility of protecting this strategic post. The Lord High Admiral, the Duke of Buckingham, appointed Mason as commissary general for the 1625 expedition against the Spanish port of Cadiz. The next year, Buckingham promoted Mason to the demanding job of treasurer and paymaster for all the English forces involved in the wars. These high offices demonstrate that Mason and Gorges were powerful figures and staunch supporters of the Stuart monarchy. Indeed, the Duke of Buckingham, a royal favorite, was staying as a guest in Mason's Portsmouth home in 1628 when he was assassinated by an intruder. This was one of the most famous murders in English history, yet James I did not hold Mason in any way accountable, continuing to appoint him to high office and bestow on him royal favors.[6]

When England's wars came to an end in 1629, Mason and Gorges refocused their efforts on New England. They reorganized their holdings and divided the patent at the Piscataqua, with Gorges taking ownership of a much reduced Province of Maine. The Council for New England issued new bounds for Gorges's province and gave Mason a patent for the Province of New Hampshire, named after the captain's home county in England. But the efforts of the two men would be hampered by the continuing stream of patents issued by the Council, as well as by the Crown's approval of the Massachusetts Bay Company charter in 1629. The latter established the Bay Colony's northern border three miles north of the Merrimac River, effectively extinguishing Mason's claim to the land between the Naumkeag and Merrimac Rivers.[7]

Despite these setbacks, Mason and Gorges remained unfazed. In 1631, the Council of New England gave two patents to the Laconia Company for lands along the Piscataqua River. Mason and Gorges headed this eight-merchant partnership designed to profit from the fur trade and other New England exports. The Laconia Company equipped a substantial expedition to harvest the resources of the Piscataqua. One settlement was established at the mouth of the river, taking over the Thompson plantation at Odiorne Point. A mansion house and extensive farm were also developed at Strawbery Banke. This area, the core of the community soon renamed Portsmouth, would gradually evolve into the commercial and political center of the colony. Also at the mouth of the river on Great Island, several buildings were erected, including a modest fort armed with several cannon. A fur trading post was established upriver as well. Mason and his fellow stockholders invested heavily in equipment, hoping to sustain the profitability of their venture for as long as possible. They encouraged numerous settlers to participate in fishing, lumbering, agriculture, and other enterprises. Soon an orderly colony was beginning to arise along the Piscataqua.[8]

The Laconia proprietors developed their holdings south of the Piscataqua jointly, but they divided some lands to the north. John Mason was granted a tract of land upriver at Newichawannock (present day South Berwick, Maine). Here colonists constructed a fortified trading post and the first gravity-powered sawmill in New England. Unfortunately, starting colonies in the seventeenth century was an expensive and risky proposition. Few companies ever turned a profit, and those that did often took years to do so. By 1634, the Laconia Company was deeply in debt.

The company's financial difficulties stood in marked contrast to the prosperity of Massachusetts Bay. The rapid success of this colony had brought it under the close scrutiny of English officials, including Mason and Gorges. Since the initial formation of Massachusetts, Gorges had fought against it. Not only did its charter exclude it from the authority of the Council for New England, but its Puritanism threatened Gorges's vision of a New England loyal to the Anglican Church. After repeated efforts by Gorges, the Privy Council in 1633 established a special Commission for Regulating Plantations, headed by William Laud, to look into the governance and charter of Massachusetts. Laud was Bishop of London and a fierce opponent of Puritanism. Later that year he would become Archbishop of Canterbury, the religious leader of the entire Church of England. He would use this post to further attack Puritanism and enforce orthodoxy.[9]

In 1635, Gorges and Mason initiated their own attack against Massachusetts Bay when they helped dissolve the Council for New England. With the termination of the Council, the entire region returned to direct royal authority. Gorges then successfully lobbied to be appointed as governor-general of New England, with Mason as his vice-admiral. In theory, this gave them governance over Massachusetts Bay and all the settlements of New England. Meanwhile, the Crown initiated proceedings to revoke Massachusetts Bay's charter. When the Council for New England was dissolved, the members divided its territory, with the intent that each member would have his tract formally patented by the king. Gorges would eventually receive a grant for the Province of Maine, but Mason would not live long enough to lobby for a patent for New Hampshire.[10]

In the fall of 1635, Mason and Ferdinando Gorges prepared to sail to New England to exercise their new authority and oversee their plantations. A new vessel was built in preparation for the voyage. Unfortunately, however, Captain Mason died in early December 1635, never making it to New Hampshire. Sir Ferdinando's plans to cross the Atlantic also fell through unexpectedly when the new ship broke up just after its launching, foiling his efforts to bring down Massachusetts. Had he succeeded, the history of New England and America would have been very different. The Puritans' city upon a hill would have come to an abrupt end, and New England would have been an Anglican colony loyal to the Crown.

Gorges would remain somewhat active after this failure, finally gaining a royal patent for the Province of Maine in 1639 and sending over a series of governors to run the colony. Financially weakened by the loss of his new ship, and becoming increasingly drawn into the events that would lead to Civil War in England, the aged knight would never again pose as serious a threat to Massachusetts as he did in 1635. However, his family, along with the Masons, did remain embroiled in a recurring struggle with Massachusetts Bay for control of northern New England for the next forty years.

When he died in 1635, John Mason's properties in New England were optimistically appraised at £10,000. Over a period of thirteen years, he had either issued or received numerous patents that led to hopeless confusion. Some grants superseded earlier ones, and some conflicted with grants to other groups. A close examination indicates that at the time of his death he actually owned only three-eighths of the bankrupt Laconia Company and its holdings. Mason did not have individual title to any property in New

Hampshire. Ironically, the only New World property this so-called proprietor of New Hampshire personally owned was the Newichawannock tract, across the Piscataqua River in Maine. Thanks to his involvement in the Council for New England, he did hold a claim of sorts to New Hampshire; without a royal patent, however, that claim was absolutely meaningless.

Nevertheless, as the primary stockholder of the Laconia Company and chief promoter of the colony, John Mason was indeed the driving influence behind New Hampshire. His death at age forty-nine left the future of the Piscataqua settlements very much up in the air. Mason's will made clear his desire that his family pursue his ambitions, stipulating that the income from 1,000 acres of land in the colony be set aside for the maintenance of a minister, and from another thousand acres to establish a free grammar school to educate the colony's youth. Mason's heirs were his widow, Ann, their daughter, Ann Mason Tufton, and their infant grandsons, Robert and John Tufton. By terms of the will, Robert and John would ultimately inherit the colony if they adopted the Mason surname. Only Robert lived to maturity, and as Robert Tufton Mason, he eventually assumed the family's claim to New Hampshire.

The family interests remained in the hands of widow Ann Mason until her grandsons came of age, and she did little to honor the wishes of her late husband. After Captain John's death, approximately one hundred settlers waited for word from Ann. They sat in a precarious state. Most of the colonists lived west of the Piscataqua on land that had been held by the Laconia Company; now, however, the bankrupt enterprise existed only on paper. Furthermore, the dissolution of the Council for New England meant that the Mason family had little real authority, despite their involvement in six different grants since the early 1620s. Ann never even pursued the legal patent to New Hampshire that would have given her the right to rule. She did lease out the sawmill and property at Newichawannock, though these territories were within Maine, not New Hampshire. By this time, the Mason family had spent a fortune, with no profits to show for it, so Ann walked away from the project, leaving the employees to shift for themselves. By this time, political upheaval was threatening England, and the English Civil

Wars would soon take over the country. Even if the Masons had wanted to maintain the colony, it would have been difficult to do so through the turbulent 1640s. Left to their own devices, Mason's former employees cashed in on his abandoned investments. Within a few years, these men had taken over the family's land and possessions and used them as the foundation of their own prosperity. In the coming decades, this untidy and informal division of the Mason and Laconia holdings would repeatedly return to haunt the former servants and their descendants.

Although the colonists were able to rapidly digest the Mason and Laconia assets, their efforts to replace Mason's governance did not proceed as smoothly. Initially, the settlers at Portsmouth and Dover organized themselves into self-governing bodies. When John Wheelwright arrived in 1638, there was no central authority to ask for permission to settle, so he and his followers simply purchased the land from the local Indians and wrote their own compact to govern themselves. Massachusetts Bay officials noted with relief the collapse of the Laconia Company and death of Mason, and they followed with great interest the developments taking shape in New Hampshire's power vacuum. In 1638 the Massachusetts General Court authorized townsmen in Newbury to establish a new settlement to the north at Winnecunnet—soon to be known as Hampton. Winnecunnet lay beyond Massachusetts Bay's northern boundary three miles north of the Merrimac River, but at the time there was no one in a position to raise any formal opposition. The next year, representatives from Dover proposed to the Massachusetts General Court that their settlement also join the Bay Colony.

Dover had good reason to seek to place itself under Massachusetts authority, for the settlement had been torn by dissension and strife ever since its founding. In its brief life, the community had gone through several ministers from a variety of different faiths. In 1633, a Puritan minister named William Leverich had arrived in Dover, but he left several years later complaining of a lack of support. George Burdett briefly preached in the community, then departed in a storm of controversy over his radical views, which included the practice of "free love." In 1638, Hansard Knollys, a religious radical, was welcomed as Dover's new minister by Captain John Underhill, an Antinomian leader who had fled Massachusetts to become the leader of Dover for a brief time. Knollys's beliefs proved too extreme, and parishioners forced him to yield the pulpit to Thomas Lakeham in 1640. In the circus atmosphere that followed, Knollys excommunicated Lakeham for unchastity and other moral vices—only to be found in bed with his maid the very next night! Amid this confusion, the leading Puritan settlers of the area pushed for the stability that Massachusetts could bring to the community. In 1641, the Dover patentees gave jurisdiction over the town to Massachusetts.

Though Dover contained a mixture of Anglicans, Puritans, and even Antinomians, Portsmouth seems to have been initially dominated by members of the Church of England. In 1640, settlers selected Anglican priest Richard Gibson to be their minister. The next year, the Massachusetts legislature, known as the General Court, ordered that the Piscataqua settlements be brought under Massachusetts jurisdiction. There is no surviving evidence that Portsmouth citizens were consulted on this matter, though only Reverend Gibson seems to have raised any objections. He openly protested the Massachusetts takeover and later attempted to spark a revolt against the Bay Colony. After Massachusetts brought him up on charges for his rabble-rousing, the priest prudently returned to England before he could be prosecuted.

Exeter, the sole remaining holdout town, finally yielded to Massachusetts in 1643, but only after the General Court guaranteed the civil rights of all New Hampshire freemen, including those who did not belong the Puritan church. Having won this concession, which was not granted anywhere else in the Bay Colony, the townsmen decided that the increase in political stability would outweigh the religious disadvantages that joining the colony might bring. Massachusetts's conquest of New Hampshire was now complete, and with the Civil War under way in England, it would be some time before her rule would be challenged. The Bay Colony tried to legitimize its expansion by exploring the Merrimac River and stretching the interpretation of her northern bounds, specified in her charter as three miles north of the Merrimac. Conveniently, the source of the Merrimac River was at Lake Winnepausaukee, well north of the mouth of the river. When an easterly line was drawn three miles north of the headwaters of the river, it led to Casco Bay—giving Massachusetts a tenuous claim not just to New Hampshire but to the Province of Maine as well. In the 1650s, when Maine fell into disorder after the death of her proprietor, Sir Ferdinando Gorges, Massachusetts would assert this claim to take over the province. Cromwell and the Puritan Parliament—allies of Massachusetts—were ruling England at the time, so the aspirations of the Puritan Commonwealth continued to grow unchecked.[11]

Despite the considerable political obstacles, however, the Mason family and several other Laconia Company investors made periodic attempts to reassert their claims in the region. John Littlebury had invested £300 in the Laconia Company, and he came to New Hampshire around 1649 to try to recover his money. He laid claim to the Isles of Shoals and took possession of the Laconia Company's house and land at Little Harbor. For twenty years Littlebury would wage a struggle for his properties, finally giving up his claims in 1669 in return for £200 from the Massachusetts General Court, money he needed to settle his debts and pay for his passage back to London. In 1651, Joseph Mason, a kinsman of Captain Mason, came to New Hampshire as the family's agent, taking up residence at Little Harbor. He began legal proceedings to reclaim the Mason sawmill and lands at Newichawannock, but his efforts were unsuccessful. When widow Ann Mason died in 1655, the family holdings were firmly in the possession of her grandson, Robert Tufton Mason, but they were now of dubious value. A few years later, Joseph Mason stepped down as the family agent, having accomplished very little.[12]

The Masons were not the only family to be caught up in legal wrangling over New Hampshire property. The family's questionable claim to the colony directly contradicted claims asserted by others over certain tracts in the region, and this led to protracted court battles. One such battle erupted when George Walton purchased his one hundred acres on Great Island. The story begins in 1637, when Francis Mathews purchased a one-thousand-year lease to the one hundred acres at Muskito Neck from the agents of the John Mason, the late proprietor of New Hampshire. Mathews was to hold the property in escrow for John Heard, an arrangement in keeping with Mason's vision of New Hampshire as a feudal property in which all land would be rented from the Mason family. In 1646, Mathews sold his right to Muskito Neck to John Wotton, a Portsmouth man. Apparently there had been a disagreement between Heard and Mathews over the ownership of Muskito Neck, for in 1649 Heard sold the same property to George Walton, who promptly took possession of it. Wotton and Walton immediately clashed over the land. On September 30, 1651, John Wotton unsuccessfully sued George Walton for trespassing onto his land and cutting £20 worth of timber.[13]

Wotton had far more serious legal problems to resolve than his conflict with Walton. The court repeatedly ordered him to return to Plymouth, England, where he had abandoned his wife almost twenty years before. He finally did return in June 1653, leasing Muskito Neck to his attorney, Richard Tucker, before he left. George Walton tried to take advantage of Wotton's absence, suing him for ruining a corn field. Walton won the case, but not before Wotton died back in England. Around the same time, Walton also had a suit against John Heard for selling him the unsecured title to Muskito Neck, though they soon reached a settlement, with Heard apparently reimbursing Walton part of the purchase price. In 1657, Wotton's long-suffering widow sold her interest in Muskito Neck to Richard Tucker. That same year, Tucker sold his house on Great Island to George Walton; in 1664, he deeded his interest in Muskito Neck to Walton. Fourteen years and many complex lawsuits after his initial purchase, Walton must have thought that undisputed title to Muskito Neck was finally his. This would only be the first of many disputes George Walton would fight over his properties.[14]

The fate of some of Walton's land claims would ultimately depend on the Mason family's efforts to gain ownership of New Hampshire, and finally a political change in England would give the Masons reason for hope. The death of the Lord Protector Oliver Cromwell led to the restoration of the Stuart monarchy in

1660. Massachusetts no longer had strong political allies ruling England, and the new king, Charles II, was much more likely to favor an Anglican family like the Masons who had been loyal supporters of the monarchy. Emboldened by the restoration of Charles II, young and ambitious Robert Tufton Mason expanded his claims. In the past the family had fought to receive their proper due as shareholders of the Laconia Company. Now, Robert wanted to assert the full proprietary rights that had been the goal of his grandfather, John Mason. In 1661, Robert Mason petitioned the Crown to be appointed governor-general of New Hampshire. He claimed that he should be recognized as the sole proprietor of the colony because of his grandfather's patents and huge outlays of cash in New Hampshire. He further argued that Massachusetts had illegally usurped the land. The Crown largely ignored these claims, though in 1664, Charles II did dispatch a royal commission to New England to investigate the state of the region.[15]

Robert Mason seized on the opportunity this presented. Before the royal commission left England, Mason granted power of attorney to commission member George Cartwright to settle his (Mason's) title to New Hampshire, offering Cartwright the post of governor should he succeed. He also empowered commissioner Richard Nichols to grant lands in his name. When Nichols arrived in New Hampshire, he appointed Nicholas Shapleigh as his deputy. Such powerful incentives to two of its five members predisposed the commission to support Mason's claims.

When the commission met in Portsmouth in July 1665, there was a tremendous amount of tension and division within the colony. Two different factions submitted separate petitions to the commissioners. The first, made up of thirty-two Portsmouth townsmen, petitioned the Crown for royal protection, complaining that their town leaders favored Massachusetts and Puritanism, and requested that a royal government replace Massachusetts's rule. A second petition, signed by sixty-one men from all over the colony, asked that New Hampshire be united with Maine in a new royal colony.[16]

The different petitions hint at the conflicting loyalties of New Hampshire residents, some of whom supported the Crown and others of whom inclined toward Massachusetts. Puritans had been

Figure 8.1. Mason's Patent and the Province of Maine. In calling New Hampshire "Mason's Patent," the author of the anonymous 1653 Province of Mayne Map demonstrates his support for the Mason family's claim. Courtesy of the Maine State Archives (Baxter Rare Map 84).

moving north into New Hampshire in increasing numbers, eventually turning the Anglican population into a minority. Throughout the 1650s and 1660s, the newcomers' political power in Portsmouth grew steadily, as did their economic influence, particularly since their group included a large number of merchants. Their increased status and power in the community came at the expense of the Old Planters—the largely Anglican families who had settled Portsmouth prior to 1641. Much to their displeasure, these Old Planters found themselves being gradually eased out of political and military office.

In the first 1665 petition, the thirty-two Portsmouth residents complained about the Puritans who had come to dominate the town. "For several years past," the petition reads, "they have been kept under the Massachusetts Government by an usurped power, whose laws are derogatory to the laws of England, under which power five or six of the richest men of the parish have ruled and ordered all offices both civil and military at their pleasures . . . and none durst make opposition for fear of great fines or long imprisonment." They have "denied in our public meeting the Common Prayer, Sacraments, and decent burial of the dead . . . and also denied us the benefit of freemen." Imploring the commissioners to protect them and redress their grievances, they specifically named their oppressors: Reverend Moody, Richard Cutts, John Cutts, Nathaniel Fryer, Brian Pendleton, and Elias Stileman.[17]

A mixed lot, the men who openly challenged Puritan authority in this way signed the petition for a variety of reasons. Many were like John Pickering—Old Planters who were angered to see their Anglican services replaced by Puritanism. Others were loath to see their political and military authority eclipsed, or to find themselves at the economic mercy of the relative newcomers to Portsmouth. George Walton and his sons-in-law, Edward West and Samuel Robie, also signed the petition. As Quakers who felt oppressed by Massachusetts authorities, they had excellent reason to favor a royal authority likely to be more tolerant of their faith.

Petitioning the royal commission did not immediately achieve all the Mason family's goals, but it did cast enough doubt on Massachusetts's authority over New Hampshire for Charles II to summon agents from the Bay Colony to London. This request caused considerable consternation in Boston. Some authorities argued that to disobey a royal command would be foolhardy, while others feared that the powers of royal prerogative would be used to strip Massachusetts of her charter. In the end, the General Court voted not to send the agents. Fortunately for Massachusetts, Charles and his ministers would be kept busy in the next decade fighting two wars against the Dutch. Only in the late 1670s would English officials again turn their attention to Massachusetts.

In the meantime, Robert Mason continued to push his interests, petitioning the Crown and its various commissions at every available opportunity. Meanwhile, in 1667 he authorized Nicholas Shapleigh, the Kittery merchant (and kinsman of the Walton family), to grant land in Mason's name. The grants made by Shapleigh, as well as those made earlier by Richard Nichols, were all invalidated by local courts. In 1669, John Littlebury wrote to the governor of Massachusetts to express his alarm that "George Walton the Quaker" had been involved in Joseph Mason's sale of land at Little Harbor. Presumably, Walton was associated with these ventures through his connections to Shapleigh. Littlebury's reference to "George Walton the Quaker" suggests his religious allegiance, as much as his political loyalties, was perceived as a threat to the community and the colony.[18]

In 1675 Robert Mason and the heirs of Sir Ferdinando Gorges formally requested that the Lords of Trade recognize their proprietary rights to New Hampshire and Maine. Their petition, combined with other complaints and Massachusetts's previous unwillingness to send agents to England, finally spurred the Crown into action. In 1676, the Lords of Trade ruled that the claims of the Mason and Gorges families would be heard and that Massachusetts must send agents to London to represent the colony. At the suggestion of Robert Mason, his cousin Edward Randolph received the job of delivering the news to Boston. The Lords of Trade also instructed Edward to study the New England colonies and report his findings to them. This would be the beginning of Randolph's long career as an imperial watchdog in New England.[19]

In 1677 the Lord Chief Justices ruled on the case, awarding governance of Maine to the Gorges family based on the 1639 charter for the Province of Maine. The Mason claim was not so clear. Although John Mason had petitioned for a charter in 1635, the Crown had never approved this request. The Lords ruled that the Council for New England had the authority to grant land to Mason, but not to grant governance to him or to anyone else. The power of government remained with the Crown. As for the Mason and Gorges land-ownership claims, the Lord Chief Justices ruled that any determination had to be made in New England, in the presence of Mason's and Gorges's tenants. This meant that Mason would have to press his land claims in New Hampshire, where he was sure to face a hostile reaction and an unfavorable verdict.

Mason realized that he had no chance to win a suit in the New Hampshire courts unless he could curb the power of Massachusetts and the pro-Massachusetts faction in the Piscataqua. In the dozen years since the petitions to the royal commission, many of the Old Planters had died, and the number of Puritans loyal to Massachusetts among New Hampshire's population had risen sharply. Furthermore, even Royalists in New Hampshire were unlikely to support the Mason family when doing so meant risking the title to the very lands they lived upon.

So Mason and Randolph set about attacking Massachusetts before the Lords of Trade, building a case to revoke the Bay Colony's charter. Mason and Ferdinando Gorges (grandson of Sir Ferdinando) also petitioned for the union of Maine and New Hampshire into a single royal colony. They went so far as offering to surrender their claims of governance of their colonies if a new royal government were formed to rule over their lands. But the offer was to no avail, and in 1678 Gorges gave up his efforts and sold his claim to Maine to the agents of Massachusetts. This was a huge victory for the Bay Colony, and the loss of a key ally for Mason. In a way, however, it proved to be the very undoing of Massachusetts because it raised the Lords of Trades' suspicions about the Bay Colony and prompted them to listen more sympathetically when Mason and Randolph renewed their attacks. This time, they would decide to make New Hampshire a royal colony and begin proceedings to vacate Massachusetts Bay's charter.

In July 1679 the Privy Council reached a compromise on the Lords of Trades' recommendation to make New Hampshire a royal colony. They would support the establishment of a royal colony, which would protect the Mason claims. In return, Mason agreed to forfeit all right to quitrents (annual rents to be paid on all lands) before 1678 and to limit his quitrents to a maximum of 2.5 percent of assessed value annually. He would make out titles to settlers to arrange for their future rents, and he would work with a newly established New Hampshire Council to seek a peaceful resolution to his claims. The Council, under President John Cutts, would serve as the governing body of the colony.

Why would the Lords of Trade, the Privy Council, and the king affirm Mason's rights of ownership, when the Lord Chief justices had been unwilling to do so? Randolph's reports made it clear that Massachusetts's power in the region had to be curbed. The most effective way to do this was to establish a strong royal colony on Massachusetts's border. No doubt Mason's strenuous efforts, combined with his family's steadfast loyalty to the Crown, also factored into the decision.

Edward Randolph personally delivered the new commission to New Hampshire in December 1679. News of Mason's victory did not go over well with the locals, a strong majority of whom supported Massachusetts Bay and did not want to leave its jurisdiction. Most of the Old Planters had largely died off, replaced by a growing population of Puritans. Whereas thirty-two Portsmouth residents had signed the petition against Massachusetts in 1665, fifty-six men signed a 1677 petition in support of the Bay Colony. Many residents of New Hampshire had migrated from Massachusetts since it annexed the region, and their discontent with the new governance plan took many forms. As John Demos has suggested, the outbreak of witchcraft in the summer of 1680 in Hampton was certainly related to New Hampshire's recent break with Massachusetts and the concomitant renewal of the Mason family claim. The tensions in the community, which was founded by Massachusetts Puritans and situated just across the border from the Bay Colony, must have been particularly high after the old ties were severed. Even non-Puritans had little reason to look forward to paying Robert Mason a rent on land they believed was rightfully theirs. Many of the members of the newly appointed New Hampshire Council were so displeased with the new arrangement that they almost refused their appointment. Their consolation was the opportunity to use their office to oppose Mason and Randolph.[20]

When Randolph arrived in Portsmouth, he came armed with his new appointment as Customs Collector of New England and a determination to bring New Hampshire and all of New England into conformity with the Navigation Acts—a series of laws passed by Parliament to secure the trade of England's colonies. The initial acts of 1650 and 1651 barred foreign ships from entering the colonies, and further specified that all goods traded to England had to be shipped to her in either English vessels or ships from the nation where the goods had been produced. In 1660, another Navigation Act insisted that all trade to the colonies had to be by English ships with English captains and crews that were at least three-fourths English. Furthermore, certain goods—including sugar, cotton, ginger, tobacco, and indigo—could not be shipped outside of the Empire. Essentially, this meant that all foreign goods destined from the colonies had to be shipped first to England.

British authorities established the Navigation Acts as a part of a colonial system for the emerging British Empire. The mother country developed colonies to harvest natural resources, and also to create markets for English manufactured goods. Parliament passed the first Navigation Acts when it realized that the growing Dutch merchant marine was threatening to take over much of the colonial trade. The later acts were meant to further safeguard this system; however, the Crown lacked the extensive bureaucracy and navy necessary to enforce them. Enforcement was particularly lax in New England, where a growing mercantile fleet imported and exported goods throughout the American colonies, the Caribbean, and continental Europe in addition to England. Much of the trade with other nations was illegal, and even legal commerce tended to go on without the required paperwork and tariffs. If the New Hampshire Council accepted English authority, it would mean they would have to abide by the trade restrictions, taxes, and paperwork required by the Empire but contrary to the commercial interests that dominated the Council. So, they vigorously opposed the plan.

First, the Council told Randolph that, because it did not recognize him as customs commissioner, he had no right to seize even those vessels that appeared to be in violation of the Navigation Acts. Regardless, Deputy Customs Collector Walter Barefoot seized a series of vessels in 1680 and 1681, sparking well organized opposition. When Randolph seized the vessel of a Portsmouth merchant in 1681, the owner successfully sued for illegal seizure. The Council forced Randolph to apologize and pay £5 in damages. Other ship owners would follow a similar legal strategy, suing Randolph and Barefoot for trespass and damages. It was open season on the Customs Collector. One did not even need to own a ship to sue him: When Randolph broke open the door to Obediah Morse's Great Island house in search of smuggled goods, Morse sued for damages.[21]

Later, in March 1680, the Council took action after Barefoot posted the customs regulations on Great Island. They ordered him to return his commission to Randolph and imprisoned him until he paid a £10 fine. The Council then appointed Richard Martin as the colony's Customs Collector. The appointment of this merchant, Council Member, and Treasurer of the Colony ensured that the acts would be ignored. When Barefoot persisted in his efforts to enforce them, he was reprimanded and fined by the courts again.[22]

Soon Randolph and Barefoot had allies in their fight. In December 1680, Robert Mason himself arrived in Portsmouth. The same ship delivered Richard Chamberlain, who had been appointed as Secretary of the New Hampshire Council. Chamberlain had been trained in law at Gray's Inn at the Inns of Court in London and was expected to create a new legal code for the colony. Randolph had carefully chosen him for the task. Not only was the forty-eight-year-old an accomplished lawyer called to the bar in 1659, he was also an old school chum of Randolph's from Gray's Inn. It is quite possible that he also knew Randolph's kinsman, Mason. If not, the two appear to have become friends during their long sea passage together. So, Chamberlain was appointed not just to aid the Council members, but to actively spy on them, reporting on their activity to Randolph and Mason.[23]

For their part, President Cutts and his Council focused their energy on defeating Robert Mason's land claims and Edward Randolph's effort to build an effective royal government. Exercising their power of appointment for judges, justices of the peace, militia officers, and even three members of the Council, they appointed prominent Puritans to these offices, ensuring Mason a tough opposition to his efforts. The Crown instructed Cutts and the Council to pass a set of laws for the new royal colony, with the help of an elected assembly. The commission indicated that the assembly should be elected by the populace but did not spell out the suffrage requirements. As a result, the Council itself selected the voters, thus guaranteeing the creation of a like-minded assembly. The Crown anticipated that the legal code would be drawn from the set of English laws recently brought by Richard Chamberlain and that the Council would draw on his legal experience of the new Secretary to the Council.[24]

Chamberlain would quickly find his advice and his set of laws ignored. Instead of turning to him, the Council and Assembly frequently looked for guidance from Reverend Joshua Moody, the Puritan supporter of Massachusetts Bay. Chamberlain objected to Moody's presence before the Council, but to no effect. The attorney appears to have developed a real animosity toward Moody, whom he referred to as "their archbishop" in his private correspondence.[25] The laws adopted by the Council show the influence of Moody and the Puritans. The criminal and civil codes were modeled on the laws of Massachusetts Bay and Plymouth rather than English precedent. The assembly agreed to these laws, despite the continued opposition of Chamberlain, who pointed out the laws were contrary to those of England and hence in conflict with the commission itself.[26]

Even as they fought Randolph and the Navigation Acts, the Council was also engaged in an ongoing struggle against Robert Mason's efforts to assert his land claims. In the newly passed civil code, the Council assumed the final authority to rule on disputed property titles, thus ensuring Mason's defeat. Once he arrived in Portsmouth, Mason hired agents and advertised his willingness to grant titles for a fee to existing landholders. At this point, there was some division within the Council. Some moderates led by President Cutts wanted to negotiate a settlement with the would-be proprietor, while Richard Waldron's faction opposed any conciliation. Cutts's death made Waldron the acting president and ended any hope of a compromise. The Council refused to accept Mason's title as proprietor and rejected his land claims. Mason then issued a summons, under his own name, to the president and Council to appear before the king in three months. An infuriated Council issued a warrant for Mason's arrest, leading Mason to flee to England in May 1680.[27]

Once safely in England, Mason began a crusade against the New Hampshire Council. He petitioned the Lords of Trade for a new government in the colony, one that would truly enforce royal authority, including its recognition of his land claims. In his petition he attacked the Council for its pro-Massachusetts bias and for usurping his own legitimate authority. He asked that all land grants issued under Massachusetts jurisdiction be declared void, and that those who opposed him be summonsed for trial before the Privy Council. This self-serving bombast was supported by extensive correspondence from Randolph and Chamberlain, as well as a copy of New Hampshire's flawed new legal codes. The New Hampshire Council wrote the Crown to defend itself and to expose Mason.[28]

On December 23, 1681, the Lords of Trade presented Mason with an early Christmas present, expressing their dissatisfaction with the proposed New Hampshire legal codes and urging the king to reject them all. Furthermore, "since the people of New Hampshire have taken upon them to dispose of and confirm lands to themselves," the Lords ordered these laws to be set aside and reserved for the king the right to determine land titles. Protesting the extra-legal character of the colony's proceedings, they encouraged the king to send a royal governor to enforce law and order.[29]

By late January 1682, the king had accepted the advice of the Lords of Trade and had appointed Edward Cranfield to settle the difficulties in the colony. Though his official title was lieutenant governor, he functioned essentially as the governor of the colony. A month later, the Lords of Trade had prepared a draft of Cranfield's commission and instructions. The governor would have strong powers, including the authority to veto the legislation of the Council and Assembly. Cranfield would also have the ability to remove councilors and replace them with his supporters, to choose his own deputy governor, to create courts and appoint justices, and to suspend the Assembly if necessary. On the advice of Robert Mason, Richard Waldron and Richard Martin were suspended from the

Council for misbehavior, though Cranfield could reinstate them if he saw fit. Robert Mason, already on the Council, was also given the authority to appoint two Council members; he chose his allies Richard Chamberlain and Walter Barefoot. While Cranfield's commission focused attention on the Council and urged him to seek their advice, it also made clear that he was free to act without their consent.[30]

Cranfield's commission was finalized in March but not approved by the king until May. By June, its contents were well known in New England, where they caused considerable consternation. On June 14, Edward Randolph wrote to the Earl of Clarendon complaining that, through friends at court or perhaps even bribery, his opponents had copies of official papers, including Cranfield's instructions. How long they had known the details about the new governor is unclear, but given that Randolph seems to have been made aware of the issue when he appeared before the General Court on June 9, there is every reason to believe that Portsmouth residents would have known about Cranfield's commission and instructions prior to the outbreak of lithobolia on the evening of June 11. All New Englanders were concerned by the strong display of royal authority. New Hampshire had essentially lost self-government to the forces of Stuart royal prerogative. Other colonies feared they might be next.[31]

The citizenry of New Hampshire had very real reasons to be worried, for Robert Mason had made sure that the expansion of royal authority would come with a favorable resolution of his land claims. His commission empowered Governor Cranfield to settle the bitter, longstanding disputes between Mason and New Hampshire landholders. Cranfield's commission itself made no secret of how the new governor would rule. The specific details of Mason's claim to the colony were included in the governor's commission. Mason cut two deals to secure this favorable and profitable outcome. First, he surrendered one-fifth of all quitrents, fines, and revenues to the king. Next, he offered the governor an annual salary of £150 a year, to be collected out of the quitrents. Cranfield's huge financial incentive guaranteed his loyalty to Mason, regardless of the merits of his case.[32]

Robert Mason seemed so close to achieving his goal of establishing himself as proprietor that it is hard to believe his family's
struggle for New Hampshire would continue another sixty years
and ultimately end in defeat. Nathaniel Hawthorne may have
drawn inspiration for the Pyncheon family of the *House of Seven
Gables* from the Masons. Both families are caught up in fruitless
and seemingly endless quests to validate an ancient patent to
lands in northern New England. The novel also features a character named Matthew Maule, an alleged wizard. Hawthorne
named him after Thomas Maule, the Salem Quaker, outspoken
critic of the Essex County witch trials, and witness to lithobolia
on Great Island.[33]

You did not have to be a wizard like Matthew Maule to predict
stormy times for New Hampshire in the summer of 1682. A new
royal governor was preparing to sail for Portsmouth with a commission that would severely restrict the liberties of all residents.
They faced loss of title to their lands and the imposition of
quitrents. Further financial hardship loomed in the enforcement of
the Navigation Acts. Colonists also feared for their religious freedoms, for it was reported that Cranfield would be accompanied by
an Anglican priest. The overwhelming majority of the citizenry
stood opposed to Cranfield and Mason and their allies.

Royalist supporters of the Mason family were a distinct minority in New Hampshire, but George Walton was one of them. Indeed, the Walton tavern was the symbolic headquarters of the
pro-Mason faction. Walton, Nicholas Shapleigh, and other Quakers supported the would-be proprietor in the hopes that a royal
government would prove more tolerant of their faith. Their small
circle grew even smaller, however, when Major Shapleigh died in a
freak accident on April 29, 1682, killed by a falling mast at the
launching of a new ship in Kittery. As a wealthy merchant and
holder of high military and civil office, his death would certainly
have been a blow to the Quaker community and the Mason family
efforts. It is probably not a coincidence that the lithobolia attack on
the tavern began only a little over a month after Shapleigh's death.
Had he been alive, it is doubtful that anyone would have dared to
carry out such an assault, the Waltons' unpopularity notwithstand-

ing. If they had, Shapleigh surely would have brought the business to a speedy end.

Presumably it was Walton's ties to Shapleigh and Royalist views that led Richard Chamberlain to board at the Walton Tavern. By June 1682, news of the hated Chamberlain's appointment to the new Council would have become known, making him an even more reviled figure. Other unpopular royal officials visited the tavern during the lithobolia attack as well. In late June 1682, Edward Randolph went to Portsmouth looking for ships trying to avoid the Navigation Acts. He was foiled by the Council-appointed customs collector, who refused to let Randolph see his books. During this unproductive stay in Portsmouth, Randolph boarded at the Walton tavern, in the room next to Chamberlain. It is quite possible that he had stayed in the tavern during his earlier visits to Portsmouth as well. Another Mason supporter, the would-be Deputy Customs Collector Walter Barefoot, was a neighbor of the Waltons and frequenter of the tavern. A contrary character, Barefoot had many enemies dating back to long before his customs appointment. This Anglican, who had interceded to stop the whippings of the three Quaker women in 1662, was also present during several of the lithobolia attacks.[34]

On July 1, during Randolph's unsuccessful customs visit, Richard Chamberlain noted that rocks flew at him as he stood on the porch of Barefoot's house. That night, a violent lithobolia attack struck the tavern, with not only rocks flying, but also a porringer hitting a maid's head and a clothes iron hitting the wall adjacent to the rooms where he and Edward Randolph were staying. This attack was probably triggered by Randolph's presence and his efforts to enforce the Navigation Acts. Chamberlain himself was targeted more than once—a fact that he seemed to overlook, though it is obvious from his own account of the proceedings. On many occasions, rocks were thrown at the door and wall of Chamberlain's room, often waking him in the middle of the night. In the initial attack, a huge stone narrowly missed his head. Another time he was hit on the thigh, and another on the calf. In one particularly violent attack, Chamberlain was eating dinner when a stone broke the window nearby, sending some small shards of glass flying into his face. Later that night, Chamberlain was hit by twenty or thirty small stones, an attack that did make him feel he had been deliberately targeted.[35]

In addition to prominent Mason supporters like Chamberlain and Randolph, Robert Mason might have resided at the tavern on at least one occasion, namely during his stay in Portsmouth from December 1680 to May 1681. Mason did not purchase a house, and it makes sense that he would have sought accommodations at an establishment friendly to his cause. With or without Mason's presence, however, the Walton tavern would have been viewed as the center of opposition to Waldron and the Council. Not only was it a profane Quaker tavern, but also the residence of the hated Richard Chamberlain, the sometime residence of Edward Randolph, and a business frequented by Walter Barefoot. Here, conveniently gathered under one roof, were most of the enemies of Puritan New Hampshire. A bull's eye might as well have been painted on the tavern door.

Certainly Chamberlain, the Waltons, and these other allies of Mason were all targets of the stone-throwing devil. The Mason family's campaign explains the attack on the tavern and also clarifies why no one would admit to participating in the assault or observing the assailants. Complaints against the Waltons, Chamberlain, and Randolph were so common that a great many locals may have thrown stones at one time or another. At the very least, there must have been a conspiracy of silence among the Walton's enemies, for many of them had to have witnessed the attacks.

Jeremiah Walford Jr. probably led the stone-throwing conspiracy. This nephew of Hannah Jones was also a neighbor of George Walton. In the summer of 1682 Walton and Walford were engaged in a property dispute completely unrelated to Hannah's quarrel, but closely tied to the Mason family and their land claims. On April 22, 1681, George Walton bought several properties from Robert Mason, who had demanded that all residents of New Hampshire purchase title to their holdings from him, in acknowledgement of his rights as proprietor. Though they risked losing their land, very few New Hampshire men followed these instructions. Walton did, however, and he received Mason's confirmation for both his holdings on Great Island and the lands occupied by Shadrach Walton at Herrod's Point, on Great Bay. Ever the political opportunist, Walton saw the Mason claim as a chance to gain more land, so he also purchased title from Mason to Walford lands at Little Harbor on Great Island, as well as to forty acres on the mainland at Long Reach. If Robert Mason did reside at the Walton tavern during his stay in the colony, he might have settled his bill before leaving the colony by giving land to George Walton.[36]

Jeremiah Walford Jr. occupied the Little Harbor lands Walton now claimed, and he and his step-father, John Amazeen, refused to yield them without a fight. It is quite likely that these men, rather than Hannah Jones, were the prime culprits behind lithobolia. The breaking of gates and tearing down of fences seems like the kind of retaliation angry neighbors embroiled in a property dispute might resort to. They also could have cut down the corn and scattered the haycocks—though one wonders if these were not the actions of Ferdinando Huff, retaliation for George Walton Jr.'s theft of hay from his fields at Cape Porpus several years earlier. Precisely identifying the culprits must remain a guessing game. However, it does seem almost certain that an aged woman could not have done this demanding physical work by herself. Even if the attacks had begun at her behest, she certainly would have stopped them once she was placed under bond of good behavior—a bond she could not afford to lose.

Jeremiah Walford Jr. must have smiled quietly when Aunt Hannah was accused of witchcraft. He may even have taken measures to frame her for the crime. After all, just the previous September he had lost a protracted legal battle to her and his other aunts over his brother's estate. Jeremiah Jr. clearly held a grudge over this dispute, for in 1686 he sued Jones, trying to recover her share of the estate. After the Portsmouth Court found in favor of Jones, Walford even appealed to the court in Boston.[37]

Just as Jeremiah was unyielding with his aunt, he stubbornly fought on for years against George Walton. One day in early December 1682, the lithobolia outbreak had passed and George Walton must have been thinking that his troubles were behind him as he and four workers went out to the disputed Little Harbor lands and set about cutting wood. Jeremiah soon arrived and forbade the men to cut any more trees. Two days later, the lumbering crew returned to the woodlot, only to be met by a group of men including Walford and his stepfather, John Amazeen, who was constable of Portsmouth. They had a warrant from magistrate Elias Stileman to arrest the cutting party and to bring them before the magistrate. Stileman ordered the Walton crew to cease cutting and hauling wood or face a £5 fine apiece, granting Amazeen and Walford rights to the wood instead. Several days later, a Walton servant spotted in John Amazeen's yard logs that he (the servant) had personally cut.[38]

At the next county court, in February 1683, George Walton sued Jeremiah Walford and John Amazeen for trespass for their actions the previous December. The jury found for Walford and Amazeen. Richard Chamberlain complained that the jury based their decision on their own self-interest rather than the merits of the case, for the entire jury held land under similar threat from Mason. Walton appealed the decision to the King in Council, jointly posting with Robert Mason and Walter Barefoot a substantial bond of £200 to be forfeited should the royal body affirm the judgment. Mason bankrolled this appeal as a test case, hoping to determine whether or not his property titles and land-granting authority would be recognized. Walton gave Edward Randolph the power of attorney to prosecute the case in England. On October 24, 1683, the King in Council referred the case to the Lords of Plantations for examination and report. In November, the Lords of Plantations summonsed Robert Wadleigh, the attorney for Walford and Amazeen, to answer Walton's appeal. Accordingly, the Lords of Plantations set January 8, 1684, as the date to hear Randolph's appeal for Walton. Wadleigh was in attendance, but Randolph did not show up. When Randolph missed a second appearance on January 9, the Lords of Trade recommended dismissal of Walton's appeal and the affirmation of the judgment of the New Hampshire court. Although the actual document is lost, all evidence indicates that the King in Council accepted this recommendation and formally dismissed Walton's appeal.[39]

Edward Randolph's specific whereabouts at this time are unknown, though he was certainly in England. Why did he fail to pursue the appeal, when Mason had finally achieved a longstanding goal of getting a property case before English justices—men who were much more likely to agree with him than the residents of New Hampshire? It may be that Wadleigh outmaneuvered Randolph. Wadleigh asked for a speedy hearing of the case, perhaps because he hoped Randolph would not learn of the appeal, or knew that Randolph was elsewhere in England and could not monitor the case. Alternatively, it may be that by late 1683, Mason and Governor Cranfield had changed their tactics. By this time, Cranfield had assumed full control of the colony, having removed all opposition from the New Hampshire Council and handpicked the judges and juries. Once Cranfield had the courts under his control, Mason could at long last bring his property cases to trial within the colony, no longer needing to go to London to achieve a favorable audience.[40]

Regardless of the reason, after more than thirty years, the bitter Walford-Walton property dispute had finally reached a conclusion. It was a double victory for Jeremiah Walford. Not only did he safeguard the title to his lands, he had also managed to deflect all blame for lithobolia onto Aunt Hannah Jones. It certainly was no coincidence that the last action of the stone-throwing devil on Great Island was to take George Walton's axes, thus preventing him from cutting down any more trees on the land in dispute with Jeremiah. The story of the stone-throwing devil had come to an end—or it would have, had the supernatural actions been confined to Great Island. Amazingly, though, lithobolia had already spread to other communities. Two new outbreaks began soon after the stones first flew at the Walton tavern.

Nine

The Spread of Lithobolia

Itself inspired by a case that took place miles away—the demonic possession of the Morse family home—the lithobolia attack on the Walton tavern spawned similar incidents beyond Great Island. Two copycat attacks took place later that same year, one in Maine and another in Connecticut. Increase Mather noted all three of these New England incidents in *Illustrious Providences* and pondered the connections between them. "It is observable, that at the same time in three houses in three several towns should be molested by demons, as has now been related." Since witchcraft spread from one community to the next only rarely—usually during major outbreaks, such as Salem—these tricks of the stone-throwing devil certainly merit a closer look.[1]

On June 11, 1682, the first stone flew on Great Island. Remarkably, sometime that same month a similar incident took place nearby in the Berwick district of Kittery, Maine. The community sat on the banks of the Salmon Falls River, a fifteen-mile sail upriver from Portsmouth and home to Antonio and Mary Fortado. One evening, Mary heard a strange voice outside her house but could find no one there. Later, while standing at the door, she received a blow to the eye from an unseen attacker. Mary reported that, after this initial attack, the house had been peaceful for two or three days when a large stone dropped down the chimney and into the house. When she went to grab the rock it had disappeared. Then a frying pan hanging in the chimney began to clang so loudly that it could be heard over a quarter of a mile away. Whoever or whatever was behind these actions remained invisible.[2]

Soon, however, the Fortados did catch a glimpse of one of the malevolent spirits while canoeing across the Salmon Falls River. They saw the freshly shaved head of a man in the water, and two or three feet away, his white, cat-like tail. No body joining the head and tail was visible. On their return passage, the specter followed them but disappeared when they reached land. The physical attacks at their home resumed a day or two later, more terrible than before. Mary was standing in the yard of her house when a large flying stone struck her on the head. She then retreated into the house and reported she "was bitten on both arms black and blue and one of her breasts scratched; the impressions of the teeth being like man's teeth were plainly seen by many."[3]

After this the terrified family abandoned their home to live with neighbors across the river. Here another spirit troubled Mary. She beheld an apparition of "a Woman clothed with a green safeguard, a short, blue cloak, and a white cap." This figure threatened to strike her with a burning stick. The next day, the same figure—this time, dressed in white—tormented her again. It appeared to laugh but produced no sound. After having spent the winter away, in March 1683 the Fortados returned home. When Antonio first entered his house, he heard the footsteps of someone walking upstairs in the bedroom chamber, even seeing the floor boards buckle as if under the invisible man's weight. Antonio went upstairs to see who it was, but no one was there. The Fortados hastily left their home and resumed their stay with their neighbors. Antonio did return to the homestead regularly to plant and tend his corn crop. One day he discovered that something had torn down a long section of his log fence. What appeared to be cattle hooves clearly marked the field between almost every row of corn, yet not a cow was seen, and there was absolutely no damage done to the corn, as would be expected if large and hungry livestock had been loose. The hoof prints must have come from something else. Increase Mather left the answer to his reader's imagination, though surely many would have thought Antonio saw the cloven hooves of the devil.[4]

Antonio Fortado was an unusual man by early Maine standards, a Portuguese immigrant from Fayal in the Azores. In this he was similar to John Amazeen, a sailor from a distant land who found a new home in America. Since the early 1640s, New England merchants had carried on extensive commerce in the Azores, as a part of the so-called triangular trade, the backbone of the colonial New England economy. New Englanders shipped wood products, fish, and other foodstuffs in return for wine and sugar. Much of these tropical goods were then sold in Europe for return cargos of manufactured products needed by the colonies. Fortado first appeared in the local records in 1673, but no surviving documents indicate when he arrived in the Piscataqua or why he decided to stay. Regardless, his nationality and his faith would have made him a suspicious character.

Though he was not an active Catholic, Fortado would have been born and raised one, which immediately would have distinguished him from almost all of his neighbors. He was not a practicing Catholic, but he would have been viewed as one anyway because of his nationality. The only other Portuguese resident of the region was Dr. Anthony Lamy. Unfortunately the doctor did not give the Portuguese the best of local reputations. In 1673 he fled Maine when he was charged with poisoning to death one of his patients out of lust for the man's young wife. At a time when strangers like John "the Greek" and Anthony "the Portyngayl" were recognized by their nationality, Antonio Fortado must have been viewed with suspicion.[5]

Seventeenth-century Englishmen had a fear and hatred of Catholics, thanks in part to the exposure in 1605 of the Gunpowder Plot, an effort by a small group of Catholic extremists to blow up the houses of Parliament. This animosity was bolstered by the fact that England's leading political foes were the Catholic nations of Spain and France. The Popish plot of 1678 spread fear across England as well, when two Anglicans fabricated a wild story that Catholics were plotting to assassinate Charles II and put his

Catholic brother on the throne. In the national panic that ensued, numerous English Catholics were arrested, and twenty-four were convicted and executed for treason. Thanks to this deadly hoax, Catholic resentment ran particularly high at the time of the attack on the Fortado home.[6]

But any suspicions about Antonio Fortado's moral character would have been confirmed already in 1673, when Fortado and eighteen-year-old Mary Start were charged with fornication. They pled guilty and were given the choice of each paying a fine of £5 or receiving ten lashes with a whip. Their choice is unknown, but given their reduced financial circumstances, they may have been forced to submit to the whipping. The couple soon wed.[7]

If Antonio was one of the more unusual settlers in the Piscataqua, his wife Mary was much more typical. She was the daughter of Edward Start, one of many English fishermen who migrated to northern New England in the seventeenth century. Edward was born in Brixham, Devon, in 1614, and married Wilmot Lamsytt there in 1645. A little over a year later, their first child, Thomas, was born, soon followed by daughter Sarah. Located on Tor Bay, Brixham and its neighboring towns were significant English fishing ports and the home of numerous early Maine immigrants, including the Shapleighs. By 1650, the Start family had migrated to Agamenticus (later Gorgeana and now York), where daughters Elizabeth and Mary would be born. The Starts soon bought the Agamenticus home and house lot of Thomas Venner, who had returned to England and would eventually be executed for leading a rebellion of the Fifth Monarchists, Baptists, and Quakers against King Charles.[8]

Though the Starts bought their home from this religious extremist, there is absolutely no evidence that they shared his views. On the other hand, until it became a part of Massachusetts, Agamenticus was known as a town where people of a wide range of faiths were tolerated—a place of refuge for those forced to flee Puritan Massachusetts. The community was the capital of Sir Ferdinando Gorges's Province of Maine. The aged knight saw his colony as a stronghold of Anglican and royal authority. The first Anglican chapel in New England was built there in 1635, and in

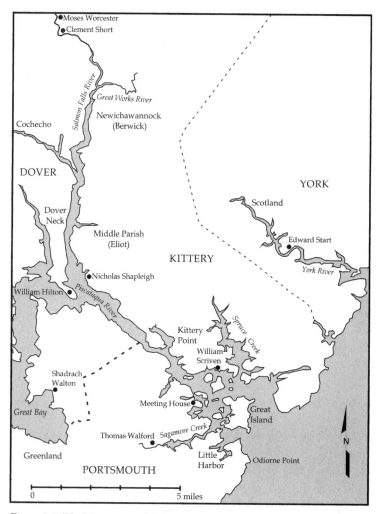

Figure 9.1. The Piscataqua and Salmon Falls Rivers. Drawing by the author.

1641, Gorges obtained a royal charter for the City of Gorgeana—
the first step to making it the home of an Anglican bishop and
cathedral. Despite these lofty goals, the reality turned out to be
far different. Agamenticus went through a quick succession of
ministers of dubious talents and wide-ranging beliefs. Most of the

West Country fishermen who migrated to York and other Maine settlements tended to be Anglican, though some could be irregular in their worship, particularly if it interfered with the busy and hard life of harvesting codfish. Thomas Morton, the Anglican nemesis of the Puritans, lived his final years in exile in Agamenticus, after having been deported repeatedly from Massachusetts. In a 1643 entry in his journal, Massachusetts Governor John Winthrop poked fun at what he saw as a small and irreligious settlement: "They ran a different course from us both in their ministry and civil administration, for they had lately made Acomenticus (a poor village) a corporation and had made a taylor their mayor, and had entertained one Hull, an excommunicated person and very contentious, for their minister."[9]

Agamenticus would have been the last place a Puritan family arriving in 1650 would have chosen to settle. The great Puritan migration to New England ended in 1642 with the outbreak of the English Civil War. By 1650, the king had been executed, and the Puritans had taken over the Commonwealth. It is unthinkable that a Puritan would leave England at this time, especially to go live in an Anglican-Royalist stronghold. Furthermore, it is highly unlikely that a God-fearing Puritan family would have let their teenage daughter marry a Portuguese Catholic. We may presume the Starts were at least nominally loyal to the Church of England and migrated for economic opportunity, not for religion.

Overall, the Starts lived a quiet life. Though some fishermen were often brought before the magistrates for their rowdy behavior, Edward appeared in court only as a member of a grand jury. He was a hard worker, for when he died in 1671, his probate inventory totaled £167—a sound estate far larger than most fishermen's. His property included five head of cattle, six pigs, and even a horse—a rare status symbol in a region with few passable roads.[10]

By the time the final estate division was ordered by the court on March 11, 1674, Mary had wed Antonio Fortado. Though Edward's estate had been substantial, when the division came, there was not much left for the girls. After accounting for debts as well as the deaths of a cow and a steer the three girls were left with £16 each—a very modest sum with which to begin their married lives. Despite the relative success of their father, Edward Start's daughters would have to work hard to achieve their own prosperity.[11]

In seventeenth-century New England, there was always opportunity for poor couples like the Fortados who were willing to risk life on the frontier. So Mary and her two sisters would become neighbors along the Salmon Falls River in Berwick—the most remote corner of settlement in southern Maine. Sister Sarah and her husband, Henry Wright, were the first to reside there, receiving a fifty-acre grant from the town of Kittery in 1671. Henry worked for Roger Plaisted, one of the owners of the Salmon Falls sawmill. Sister Elizabeth married Moses Worcester soon after his 1674 purchase of 200 acres at Salmon Falls. Worcester had been raised in Salisbury, Massachusetts, where his father, William, was the minister. Mary was probably the last sister to move to Berwick. There is no record of Antonio and Mary owning land there. It is most likely that they rented from other family members, or possible that they purchased land from them and the deed was lost during subsequent events that would destroy many court records.[12]

Berwick was a remote and thinly settled outpost, a vastly different world from the busy wharves and crowded house lots of Great Island. Life in Berwick revolved around the lumber industry; its first mill was built in 1634—one of the first sawmills, if not the very first, built in New England. The saw mills were large operations that required much capital, equipment, and manpower. In addition to mill workers, lumberjacks, and associated blacksmiths and carpenters, numerous teams of oxen had to be trained and harnessed to haul the logs. Some particularly large trees were harvested for ships masts—a complicated but profitable enterprise. In addition to these skilled workers, a substantial farming operation was necessary to feed them and their livestock. One of the owners of the Salmon Falls mill was the Boston merchant and magistrate Samuel Sewall, who recorded a 1687 business trip to the area in his diary. Sewall was particularly excited when he observed the felling and hauling of a ship's mast of about twenty-eight inches in diameter. It took about thirty-six pair of oxen to haul the log out of the swamp where it was felled. "'Twas a very notable site," he exclaimed in his diary. Five years later, he would be one of the judges at the Salem witchcraft trials.[13]

New England Puritans considered Maine to be an irreligious place where Quakers, Anglicans, and godless Englishmen lived near "heathen" Indians and French "papists." Berwick had all of these, and then some. Although much reduced by European disease, a small Native American community continued to inhabit the Salmon Falls River into the 1670s. In the later seventeenth century, New Englanders increasingly came to see such Native American neighbors as allies of the Pope. By the mid-seventeenth century, French Jesuit missionaries began to have limited success converting some of the Wabanki peoples of northern New England to Catholicism. This was little or no improvement from their "heathen" state, one that many English settlers considered to be nothing more than devil worship. In the early 1670s, the local Indian leader Mr. Rowls, lamented having sold most of his tribal lands to English settlers, for there were few places left Berwick for the Wabanki to reside. Nevertheless, there were enough still living close by to keep a trading post or two in operation.

Quakers posed another threat to Puritan orthodoxy, for Kittery was a Quaker stronghold, and a majority of its fifteen Quaker families lived in the Berwick district. Even the Puritans of Berwick shared great sympathy for Friends, as they were tied to them by kinship as well as business. For example, Humphrey Chadbourne was the leading merchant and Puritan politician of Berwick. His sister and neighbor was a Quaker, and Humphrey's son married into a local Quaker family as well. Furthermore, his business partner was his wife's uncle, the Quaker Nicholas Shapleigh, which made him kin by marriage to the Waltons. In 1662, when Massachusetts purged Quakers from positions of leadership in Kittery, Chadbourne replaced Shapleigh as a judge for the county court, thus assuring the continued protection of family interests. The two men understood that in the politically conflicted Province of Maine, family loyalties were far more important than religion.[14]

Making Berwick stand out all the more was its significant population of Scots Presbyterians, who had arrived in New England in the 1650s as prisoners of war. They had been part of a

Figure 9.2. Berwick and vicinity in a detail from the John Scott, Map of
Piscataqua River in New England, ca. 1665, Maine State Archives. Scott's
imagery of mountains and wild beasts punctuate the map's depiction of Berwick as a
thin line of settlement on the edge of the wilderness.

Scottish rebellion against the English that Cromwell had ruth-
lessly put down. The English captured thousands of Scots at the
Battles of Dunbar (1650) and Worcester (1651). After Dunbar,
5,000 Scots prisoners were marched south and imprisoned in
Durham Cathedral, where they were forced to live under truly
horrible conditions. Half were dead within a few months, and the
survivors were shipped to the Americas to serve as laborers. One
hundred and fifty were sent to New England, sold into indentured servitude for a term of seven years with the proceeds going
to pay for their forced passage. Many of the Scots ended up as
workers in the early industrial efforts, some at the ironworks in
Saugus and others in the sawmills and lumbering operations of
Maine and New Hampshire—demanding jobs that would have
been difficult and expensive to fill with free labor.[15]

At the end of their terms of indenture, the Scots were stuck in New England. They had no money to pay for their passage home and no idea of what sort of reception they would receive from English authorities should they even try. They had to leave their families behind and make the best of a new life in a strange land. Many Scots remained in Berwick, and others gravitated there. At least eighteen Scotsmen settled in the community. By this time, the men were experts in the lumbering business. Furthermore, as relative latecomers to New England, they could acquire land only at the edge of English settlement. Presumably, the community was named Berwick in reference to these settlers. The town of Berwick-on-Tweed lay in the extreme north of England, on the Scots borderlands. Thirty miles north of the Tweed River lay the small Scottish port of North Berwick, close to the site of the Battle of Dunbar. So Berwick was a perfect name for a town at the extreme northern limit of English colonial settlement, full of Scots captured at Dunbar.[16]

Although the Province of Maine was a part of the Massachusetts Bay Colony, the Scots, Quakers, Indians, and others gave Kittery a distinct character, far removed from that of a Puritan stronghold. Ministers were hard to come by in the community, and when they did come, they were not always promptly paid. Some of the residents were rather profane. For example, in 1671, the court admonished a group of Scotsmen and their wives for using profane speech, particularly for invoking the devil. In 1675, the court cracked down on the wayward residents of Kittery. A total of twenty-one residents (many of them Quakers) were charged with being absent from public worship. The court further presented the Selectmen of Kittery for failing to provide a proper education and the teaching of the catechism to their youth. By 1682, Berwick had secured the services of a minister, John Emerson, a 1675 graduate from Harvard. (His classmate was Timothy Woodbridge, the minister who witnessed the lithobolia attack on the Walton tavern.) Emerson helped secure Mary Fortado's account of events in her house for Increase Mather.[17]

Mather and Emerson must have considered Berwick a very likely place to find Satan. It perched at the margins of the English civilization bordering on lands occupied by Native Americans and French Jesuit priests. Even within Berwick, the English Puritans were a minority in a population that included many Quakers and Scots Presbyterians, in addition to other outsiders such as the Fortados. The very name of Berwick was suggestive, for North Berwick had been the scene of one of the largest and most spectacular witch trials in Scottish history. Therefore, it is not surprising that Mather included the strange events at the Fortado household in the chapter on "Things Preternatural," alongside the attacks on the Morses, the Waltons, and others.

The Fortados knew otherwise, for a close reading of the story indicates that the attacks covered up a serious case of domestic abuse. Mary said she was hit repeatedly with stones, although witnesses saw not the attacks themselves but only their results: bruises, swelling, and scratch marks on her head, arms, and a breast, and even human bite marks on her arms. Mather indicated that Mary alone was the target of Satan's fury; no one else was hurt. Unlike the events on Great Island, which were observed by many members of the community, the attack on the Fortado home was witnessed only by Antonio and Mary. Even more suspicious, the afflictions stopped when the Fortados abandoned their house to live with friends. Of course Antonio would not dare beat his wife while under the watchful eye of his neighbors. Increase Mather himself appeared a bit skeptical about Mary's assertion of supernatural assault, writing that she was "striken on her head (*as she judged*) with a stone."[18]

Domestic abuse in seventeenth-century New England was a well-known phenomenon. As rulers of their families, husbands were given wide latitude to physically punish their wives. Only in extreme cases were they brought up on charges. Such cases were often seen as joint failures. The husband had used excessive punishment and not governed his wife properly, and the wife had failed to submit to him. One of the very few cases tried in Maine in the seventeenth century was in Mary Fortado's family. In 1697, the court convicted her brother-in-law, Moses Worcester, of beating his wife on the Sabbath. Worcester was a tough frontier man renowned for his ability to fight the Wabanaki. His nickname of "Old Contrary" may suggest his prowess in fighting, as well as his difficult nature.[19]

Unfortunately, Mather's account, taken from Mary Fortado's "own mouth" gives a very vague starting date for the attacks, claiming that they began "In June 1682 (the day forgotten)." But it seems likely that Mary invented her story out of details taken from the Walton case, which would mean that the incident could have started no earlier than late June—i.e., after the assaults on the Walton tavern had already begun. One can imagine what happened: Mary is spotted with a black eye by a neighbor soon after the initial attack. The neighbor asks what happened. Shamed and afraid of her husband, she quickly thinks of a way to cover up his abuse. All of Berwick has been abuzz with the news of the stone-throwing devil on Great Island, so she announces that she has been attacked by the same demon. Unfortunately, once she concocts this story she receives more blows to the head, bite marks on the arm, and scratches on her breasts. Only she and her husband know who the actual demon is.

With Antonio's complicity, Mary crafted a convincing story to deflect any suspicion away from her husband and suggested links to the devil of Great Island. Apparitions were seen in the river and in their neighbor's house—but only by the Fortados. Their fences were destroyed and something trod through their fields imitating the damage to the Walton's fences and crops, but only Antonio observed the destruction. Mary further sold the community on her supernatural affliction by using countermagic. Mather described her placement of boughs of evergreen around the house to prevent the activity of evil spirits. As long as they remained green, she was free of torment, but once they withered, Mary's torments returned. This traditional form of countermagic had been employed just two years earlier in Hampton, New Hampshire, so its use would have been readily understood by neighbors.[20]

Finally, there was the subtle description of the specter who threatened to strike Mary with a burning stick while she was staying at her neighbors. She described the apparition as "a Woman clothed with a green safeguard, a short, blue cloak, and a white cap." Particularly notable is the safeguard, an outer skirt or petticoat worn by a woman to protect her skirt when she was riding. Safeguards and cloaks were so closely associated with women riding horses that it was standard for stage direction in Elizabethan and Stuart drama to call for them to indicate a woman on a journey—usually on horseback. (Interestingly, one play that includes such stage directions is *The Merry Devil of Edmonton*.)[21]

Mary's careful description clearly implied a supernatural assailant who had traveled some distance to torment her. A logical but unspoken assumption was that a witch had suspended her assault on the Walton tavern and traveled upriver to terrorize another victim. One wonders if Hannah Jones owned a green safeguard and a blue cloak.

Unfortunately, Increase Mather's published narrative of events at the Fortados ends abruptly without describing how the situation was resolved. In late October 1683, he did receive a letter from Joshua Moody that updated events in Berwick. It is unclear if Mather had already completed the soon-to-be-published manuscript of *Illustrious Providences*, or if he simply did not consider the news to be worthy of inclusion. Moody informed him that "There are sundry reports among us of new things that seem to bee matters of witchcraft." The Portsmouth minister thought the reports were "to bee little heeded," so he had not traveled upriver to investigate for himself. However, he had heard of one recent event too troubling to be overlooked—the so-called "monstrous birth" of a child to the Plaisted family of Salmon Falls. Reverend Moody went into extreme detail describing the severely disfigured baby girl.

Frome the waste downward it was like another child and a female.
Above the waste all effective or misplaced.
The Head extraordinary large & no skull or Bone in it.
The face as big as a womans face.
It had no right Arm, but somwhat like a Teat, some say like a
    finger where the Arm should have come out.
The left Arm extraordinary long, the hand reaching down to the
    knee.
No Nose, but somwhat like nosethrills, and those in the
    forehead.
The two eies upon the two cheeks.
No mouth, but a little Hole & (if I mistake not) misplaced also.
The eares, one under the chin, the other at the top or near the
    top of the head.

A very short neck.
Somwhat on the Breast like a Kidney.
The Belly seemed as if it had been ript open, & the Bowells
    were out & eithr by one side, or on the Back.[22]

A monstrous birth was a bad omen indeed. In the seventeenth century, people often viewed extreme and unusual birth defects as a sign of the devil's work—as if Satan himself had impregnated the mother. There had been two famous cases in Massachusetts—both in 1638, and both involving the Antinomian leader Anne Hutchinson. In February 1638, Mary Dyer gave birth to a stillborn infant. Dyer, a follower of Anne Hutchinson, was aided in the delivery by Hutchinson and other female friends and relatives. During labor but still several hours before delivery, the birthing bed shook violently, and the baby died in the womb. This was followed by a horrifying smell that caused most of the women to vomit and purge their bowels. Some of the women and their children were also overcome with convulsions. Then, the child was delivered, complete with horns, claws, scales, and other ghastly abnormalities. Winthrop clearly considered Dyer and Hutchinson to be witches delivering Satan's offspring. The shaking of the bed, the foul odor, vomiting, convulsions, and the monster itself all pointed to this conclusion. Later that year, after Hutchinson, Dyer and other Antinomians had been exiled to Rhode Island, Anne Hutchinson had a miscarriage, and Governor John Winthrop and others claimed it too was a monstrous birth.[23]

Winthrop used these incidents as a further argument against Hutchinson's Antinomian beliefs and threat to the male hierarchy of Massachusetts Bay. Mary Dyer was never accused of witchcraft, but her subsequent conversion to Quakerism would have been seen by many as proof of her allegiance to the devil. In 1660, she would be executed by Massachusetts when she repeatedly returned to the Bay Colony in open defiance of its anti-Quaker law.[24]

So, when Joshua Moody described a monstrous birth in Berwick, people were alarmed. The event reinforced the fear of Satan that had grown out of the lithobolia attacks on Great Island and at Salmon Falls. The devil had been set loose in the fertile ground of Piscataqua—a borderland of Puritanism where Quakers, Baptists, Native Americans, Anglicans, and the occasional Catholic threatened the souls of the godly.

❦ ❧ ❦

That lithobolia immediately spread upriver from Portsmouth to Berwick in the summer of 1682 is noteworthy. Even more remarkable, however, is that another copycat incident occurred later the same year over 150 miles away in Hartford, Connecticut, in the home of Nicholas Desborough. In 1636, Puritan Minister Thomas Hooker led one hundred settlers from Cambridge, Massachusetts, overland to the Connecticut River. Here they established Hartford, the first English settlement in what would eventually become the colony in Connecticut. Twenty-two-year-old Nicholas Desborough was among those settlers. He had migrated to Massachusetts Bay from Saffron Walden, a prosperous center of the wool industry in Essex, England. Desborough is a rare English surname, with all branches originating in Essex and neighboring Cambridgeshire. This means that Nicholas was at least a distant kinsman of John Desborough, the brother-in-law of Oliver Cromwell and one of the governors-general of England during the Protectorate.[25]

Nicholas Desborough would also serve as a soldier. Like all men under age sixty, he joined the militia, and the year after arriving in Hartford, he fought in the Pequot War. As European fur traders and settlers moved into the Connecticut River Valley in the 1630s, they quickly came into conflict with the Native American inhabitants of the region, the Pequots. In 1634, Dutch traders murdered a Pequot chief, leading to reprisals and escalating violence. In August 1636, Massachusetts Bay launched a military expedition against the Pequots. The following spring, the tribe retaliated by raiding the new settlement at Wethersfield, killing nine English settlers and destroying a great deal of property. This attack would give the English the justification to launch a large-scale expedition against the Pequots. There can be little doubt that the English sought a war of extermination, intending to eliminate the Pequots and open Connecticut to widespread English colonization. Nicholas Desborough became a member of a substantial army that surprised the Pequots' principal stronghold, killing hundreds of Indians, including many unarmed women and children. The attack broke the power of the Pequots, and the relict Native population would stand powerless to prevent Desborough and hundreds of other Englishmen from spreading their settlements throughout the Connecticut River Valley.[26]

Hartford soon divided the so-called "Soldier's Field" into house lots for Desborough and twenty-eight other veterans. Desborough and most of his neighbors received modest half-acre lots—enough for a home, a barn and some outbuildings, an orchard and a kitchen garden, but not much more. His home was on the northern end of the Soldier's Field, at the edge of settlement. Beyond the house lay the Cow Pasture and the other fields and meadows where Desborough and his neighbors grew their crops and pastured their livestock. Desborough was a furniture maker who worked in a sixteen foot by sixteen foot shop he built on the side of the road, next to his house.[27]

In early 1640, Nicholas wed Mary, the sister of his next-door neighbor, John Bronson. Just before her marriage, the court charged her with committing "wanton dalliances and self pollution" with three young men. Perhaps her nuptials were an effort by her brother to quickly marry her off before she got into more serious trouble. Although this was a less than ideal start to their life together, the Desboroughs were law-abiding citizens who subsequently avoided controversy. The family quietly raised four daughters, and Nicholas became a respected member of the community. From 1647 to 1669, he was elected once as a surveyor of highways and four times as a surveyor of chimneys.[28]

After Mary's death, Nicholas wed Elizabeth Strickland, a Hartford widow with five children of her own. They would live together from their marriage in 1669 until Nicholas's death in 1683. His probate inventory, made in August 1683, provides a snapshot of the Desborough household, for it lists and appraises everything he owned. It suggests a fairly typical household for the day. Nicholas left an estate valued at £210, meaning that he was slightly wealthier than the average Connecticut man at the time. Almost two-thirds of his wealth came from his property and livestock: the house, barn, outhouses, and orchard, seven and a half acres of pasture and fields, a horse, two cows, and three pigs. Furnishings were sparse, which was typical of seventeenth-century homes, even a furniture maker's. Four beds and a trundle bed attested to the sizable family that had once lived in the home. The only other furniture was a chest, two tables, six chairs, and a bench. The Desboroughs' possessions evoke a world of few belongings, much hard work, and little leisure time. The only items that suggest a break from the routine of work are a Bible and some other books, though these Puritans surely considered the Bible to be a spiritual necessity.[29]

The children grew up and gradually left the home to establish their own families. By the late 1670s, only Elizabeth's son Joseph remained. At the time he was in his mid-twenties. Then, a series of tragedies struck the family. First, Elizabeth's daughter and namesake died, leaving a very young daughter, also named Elizabeth. Rather than being raised by her father, John Andrews, little Elizabeth Andrews came to live with the Desboroughs. A chest filled with her late mother's clothes came with her. On the morning of May 17, 1682, Elizabeth was sent to fetch water from the Desboroughs' pond, where she was later found floating, dead. A coroner's jury uncovered no evidence of foul play and ruled that Elizabeth Andrews simply fell in and drowned.[30]

John Andrews soon claimed ownership of the trunk of clothes that had belonged to Elizabeth's mother. Nicholas Desborough believed that he should keep the clothes, in payment for his looking after the child for more than three years. The two men failed to come to an agreement, and Desborough considered the matter throughout the summer and sought advice on what to do. Finally, in late August or early September 1682, he informed John Andrews of his decision—he would keep his late stepdaughter's chest and possessions until he was forced to surrender them.[31]

Increase Mather described the events that followed in *Illustrious Providences,* drawing on an account he received from Reverend John Russell of Hadley, Massachusetts, upriver from Hartford.

Several days after Desborough's confrontation with Andrews, he "was strangely molested by stones, pieces of earth, cobs of Indian corn," and other items. Soon both Desborough and stepson Joseph Strickland were under attack night and day, assaulted in their home and working in the fields, the objects coming from an unseen hand. Sometimes the assailants struck in an open field where there was a clear line of sight for a quarter of a mile. When Nicholas was at home, the objects would fly through the doors and windows, and when these were shut, they would come down the chimney. The attacks took place whenever Nicholas was home but never when his wife was alone in the house. The attacks went on for two full months until November, when Desborough's barn burned down with his corn harvest inside, causing him a considerable financial loss. For several days afterward, the stones disappeared, only to resume flying for another month. In December 1682, the Hartford Court finally ruled over the disputed trunk of clothes, giving them to John Andrews. The day following the court decision, two or three more stones fell on Desborough's hat, and after that, the violence finally ended. While Mather acknowledged the argument over the chest when describing the events at the Desborough house, he nevertheless held the devil responsible for the incident.[32]

To the modern observer, it seems quite clear that John Andrews undertook the clandestine attacks in retaliation for Desborough's refusal to surrender the trunk. As at the Walton tavern, stealth and perhaps conspiracy rather than supernatural forces must account for the invisibility of the assaults. There are similarities between the Great Island and Hartford incidents. A property dispute (in this case personal property) led to resentment, which resulted in a stoning. The drowning death of a young child in both families is an eerie coincidence. Another parallel is the presence of Native American servants in both stories. Nicholas Desborough first believed the attacks were the work of a neighbor's Indian servant who Desborough saw on his property the day the lithobolia began. Yet, the neighbor provided an alibi for his servant, saying that he was far away from Desborough's that day. Though there are no direct links between these outbreaks, the similarities point to larger connections. Witchcraft accusations often stemmed from property disputes. Petty disagreements could escalate due to other tensions, such as the unexpected death of young children, and the presence of Native Americans and other outsiders in the neighborhood.[33]

The bitter dispute between Desborough and Andrews may have been tied to the old man's indebtedness. Nicholas's 1683 probate inventory records a total of £81 owed to thirty-nine men. In contrast, only two men owed his estate money, and the total amount due was just seven shillings and six pence—about the value of a chamber pot. It was unusual for anyone, particularly a tradesman of modest means, to have owed so much to so many creditors. The debts exceeded the value of his house, barn, and house lot. How he had come so deeply into debt is unclear. Mather indicated that the barn fire in 1682 had caused Desborough financial hardship, but £81 far exceeded the value of a barn—even one filled with a harvest and tools. Furthermore, it appears that the debt had been growing for many years.

In 1669, the court had appointed Nicholas the administrator of the estate of the deceased husband of his new bride, Elizabeth Strickland Desborough. He was to give each of his stepchildren their £5 portion of the estate when they came of age. By 1683 the Strickland boys were all in their thirties, yet Ephraim was owed £5, Jonathan was owed £5 and 5 shillings and Joseph Strickland was Desborough's leading creditor, being owed almost £13. Desborough had never given these stepsons their inheritance. Five pounds was not an immense sum in 1683. It was approximately the value of a cow and a couple of hogs, or perhaps an acre of pasture land. Still, owing that much or more to each of his stepsons was probably enough to disturb the family harmony. And as if that were not bad enough, he was also in debt to perhaps a quarter of the other men in town.

Desborough's difficult financial circumstances explain his heated struggle with John Andrews. Nicholas insisted on keeping his late stepdaughter's trunk of clothes because he needed any windfall he could find to help cover his debts. Meanwhile, Andrews must have known that Desborough's financial state would make it difficult to get anything from him. Presumably, he resented the fact that his brothers-in-law had not received their inheritance. It is quite possible that his late wife had never received hers either, though Andrews was not on the 1683 list of creditors. Perhaps authorities awarded Andrews his late wife's clothes in lieu of her £5 inheritance.

Regardless, Desborough's status as debtor made him a target. As the leading debt holder, Joseph Strickland may have looked the other way when his brother-in-law launched an attack. Surely there were many other creditors who would merely have chuckled rather than report Andrews to authorities had they caught him in the act. Strickland and other debt holders must have realized their slim chance of being paid, so they may have thrown a rock or two themselves. Even the court magistrates seemed pessimistic about the prospect of Desborough's debts being paid. In December 1683, when authorities granted administration of Desborough's estate to Joseph Strickland, it instructed him to "pay debts out of the personal estate so far and as soon as he can."[34]

❦ ⚜ ❦

Increase Mather thought enough of the cases in Hartford, Portsmouth, and Berwick to consider them together. Portsmouth was an active port, and news spread rapidly from it. At the time, Piscataqua merchants owned twenty-eight vessels, with a total burden of 406 tons. The June 23 attack on the Walton tavern was observed by a group of visiting Quaker dignitaries, including the governor of West New Jersey, the deputy governor of Rhode Island, and merchants from Salem, Philadelphia, and Barbados. These elites were important members of communication networks in early New England.[35]

Certainly, after June 23, the news of lithobolia would have quickly spread throughout New England, reaching as far as Philadelphia or even Barbados. Word could have reached Hartford via any one of several intermediaries. Though it is located well inland, the Connecticut River made Hartford an active port that sent ships to trade in Barbados, Jamaica, St. Christopher's,

Salt Tortuga, and other Caribbean islands. Hartford also participated in the coastal trade of New England, so her ships would have carried letters from and to her residents, enabling them to receive recent news from across the region. There were even some personal ties between the Hartford region and Portsmouth—most notably through the Woodbridge family. Reverend Timothy Woodbridge was in residence in Great Island or Kittery in 1682 and 1683. He witnessed lithobolia and once was even hit by a rock. By the fall of 1683, he had moved on to become the new minister at Hartford. He may have been in correspondence with people in Hartford for some time, and it is likely that any letters he sent would have contained local news as well as negotiations over his new post. Even if Woodbridge had not confided such matters to Hartford citizens, he surely would have related the mysterious events to his family. Brother John Woodbridge served as minister at Wethersfield, Connecticut, the town immediately downriver from Hartford, and word of lithobolia may have reached several people in the Hartford area via his correspondence with his brother.[36]

Other links between the Piscataqua and Hartford remain more deeply hidden, as in the case of Mary Love Wyllys. In 1682, Mary and her first husband William Love were neighbors of the Fortados in Berwick. In 1688, after William's death, she married Samuel Wyllys of Hartford. This second marriage, so far away from her home, was unusual. It hints that Wyllys, a prosperous merchant, may have been a visitor or at least in communication with the Salmon Falls region well before marrying Mary. In the 1640s, the Wyllys family had been among the shareholders in the Dover, New Hampshire, patent, and it is possible that they maintained an interest in the area despite their residence in Hartford. It is altogether clear that word of lithobolia could have reached Hartford by July 1682 via several different avenues—for example, the communications of Timothy Woodbridge or the reports of visiting Quakers and other local residents—in plenty of time for the story to inspire John Andrews to attack Nicholas Desborough.[37]

The campaign against the Desborough house was the last of Increase Mather's supernatural coincidences for 1682. However, these incidents would not be the end of lithobolia, or of witchcraft, in New England. In the summer of 1692, at least a few stones would fly during the Salem witchcraft outbreak—reinforcing other links between the stone-throwing devil of 1682 and the more famous events of a decade later.

Ten

Ɑ❧Ɑ❧Ɑ❧Ɑ❧Ɑ❧Ɑ❧Ɑ

To Salem

Let's consider a tale of witchcraft in early New England. Amidst local religious and political disputes—and under dark clouds of political uncertainty that cover an entire colony—a community demands the right to form its own township and to call its own minister. The players include Quakers as well as Native American household servants and even a stone-throwing devil. The case is influenced by prior accusations of witchcraft, and the infection quickly spreads. Although this describes the lithobolia attacks on Great Island it also fits the infamous Salem or Essex County witchcraft outbreak that occurred ten years later, in 1692.

In many respects, Salem is a unique event in the annals of American history. More people were accused and executed in this outbreak than all the other cases of New England witchcraft combined. Over 150 people faced charges, 19 were executed, 1 was pressed to death, and 5 died in jail. Such events dwarf those on Great Island, where just two people—George Walton and Hannah Jones—exchanged accusations, and no formal trials took place. One even wonders if either of the litigants believed their own charges, or just used them to gain legal advantage in their decades-old property dispute.

Despite these differences, however, Great Island in 1682 and Salem Village in 1692 had much in common, and these similarities provide insights into the nature of witchcraft in early New England. Both communities found themselves on the losing end of struggles to break off from their parent towns in the hopes of hiring their own ministers and forming their own local churches. An effort to maintain Puritan orthodoxy and carry out moral reformation was critical to both campaigns. Also, Great Island and Salem Village both had to cope with colony-wide political change and uncertainty. New Hampshire in 1682 and Massachusetts in 1692 fell under the jurisdiction of newly formed governments and charters. Both episodes began while the colonies awaited the arrival of a new governor. Cultural and religious outsiders—including Indian servants in the Parris as well as the Walton household—appear in both stories. Additionally, both cases of witchcraft spread beyond their places of origin—a rarity in early New England.

Although the best-known events of Salem witchcraft trials are the spectral attacks on a group of girls, incidents of lithobolia were also noted. In 1692, the Brown family heard strange creatures crying on the roof and stones hitting their Reading, Massachusetts, home. After an apparent ten-year hiatus, the stone-throwing devil had struck again. Sarah Cole, from the town of Lynn, was held responsible for the stone-throwing, the supernatural sounds on the roof, and a serious illness that afflicted the Brown family.[1]

Others would testify against Cole with a variety of reasons. Her own husband blamed her for the supernatural happenings at their house, including the appearance of strange cats and dogs as well as a ball of fire. Additionally, "as he was at prayer in his family," he "heard something like a great thing flung against the house & on a sudden it was at him & struck him on the head & on one of his sides, and almost beat the breath out of his body." Brown was so afraid that for the next three nights he did not want to stay in his home. Cole was fortunate that the accusations came late in the Salem outbreak, for otherwise she too might have faced execution.[2]

Gloucester, located north of Reading and Salem Village, also witnessed lithobolia and other strange happenings. Throughout the summer of 1692, residents reported seeing French soldiers.

Gloucester Minister John Emerson also noted that the occupants of one garrison house heard "a Noise, as if men were throwing Stones against the Barn." Soon the Englishmen saw three soldiers run off into the woods. No witchcraft accusations resulted from these occurrences, but by the end of the year, Emerson had concluded that the enemy soldiers and stone-throwers must be phantoms rather than real men, for they always disappeared quickly without firing their guns. Emerson would have heard of similar specters and stone-throwing demons from his nephew and namesake. The younger Reverend John Emerson had been minister in Berwick in the 1680s and had helped gather the account of the strange happenings in the Fortado household for Increase Mather.[3]

Today we recognize the 1692 outbreak as a major event in American history. When it began to unfold in the early months of 1692, however, it would have been viewed in Salem Village as just the most recent manifestation of the supernatural, essentially no different from the mysterious happenings of the previous decade, including the Morse case and the lithobolia outbreaks of 1682. These incidents had become common knowledge, thanks in part to the publication of Mather's *Illustrious Providences*. So, when trying to understand their own situation, residents of Salem Village and surrounding communities would have reflected back on the Walton tavern and the Fortado and Desborough households. In fact, some would need no reminder from Mather's book, for there were a surprising number of people connected to the Essex County outbreak who had first encountered "satanic" activity on Great Island or in Berwick in 1682. Historians have recently stressed the failing war effort against the Native Americans and their French allies along the New Hampshire and Maine frontiers as a key cause of the Essex County epidemic. People's knowledge and fear of that dangerous frontier would have included the supernatural events at the Walton tavern and the Fortado homestead.

Salem was in no way a copycat incident of Great Island, but what happened there and on the northern frontier clearly influenced the events of 1692. Furthermore, parallels and direct connections between Salem Village and Great Island are striking. An analysis of these can help explain some aspects of witchcraft in early New England. The investigation begins with a brief summary of events in the Essex County outbreak.

❦ ⚜ ❦

In the early months of 1692, bizarre things began to occur in the household of Samuel Parris, the minister of Salem Village. Parris's nine-year-old daughter, Betty, and his eleven-year-old niece started to complain that they were afflicted by the specters of witches who caused them extreme pain and threatened to take their lives if they did not sign Satan's book. At the end of February, the girls named their tormentors, and authorities arrested three women for witchcraft. One of the accused was Tituba, the Indian slave of the Parris family. She confessed to witchcraft and suggested that a large coven of witches was at work in the region. Fueled by this confession, the number of afflictions and accusations grew rapidly, as more specters began distressing a growing circle of people. By the time the newly appointed Governor Phips arrived in Massachusetts in May, the region was facing a major outbreak of witchcraft. Phips quickly designated a special court, the Court of Oyer and Terminer, to deal with the matter.

The accusations continued to mount, even as witches were tried and executed. The charges soon spread throughout Essex County and adjoining towns. Officials even traveled to Maine to arrest George Burroughs, a former Salem Village minister. By the end of August, Burroughs and eighteen others had been executed and over a hundred more people stood accused. As the execution of a minister attests, the accusations went up the social ladder to include leading citizens whose devoutness and innocence seemed beyond question to many observers. Amid mounting opposition, Governor Phips finally abolished the Court of Oyer and Terminer in late October after his own wife was accused. A new court would meet in early 1693 to deal with the remaining cases. Refusing to accept spectral evidence, the court rapidly dismissed the cases and emptied the jails of alleged witches—even those who had confessed to the crime. The largest and most lethal witchcraft episode in American history was over.

First settled in 1626, Salem was not only one of the oldest townships in New England, but also one of the largest in square mileage. In the 1630s and 1640s, newcomers settled in the distant parts of town and soon began to push for their independence. In 1643, Wenham was the first town to secede, followed in succession by Manchester (1645), Marblehead (1648), and Beverly (1668). The loss of these communities led to a growing concern among many Salem residents, particularly those who inhabited the busy and prosperous area around the harbor, which was known as Salem Town. They feared further loss of tax revenues, as well as loss of control over the rural farmlands that helped to feed their growing urban population. When another area, known as Salem Farms or Salem Village, sought its independence, the residents of Salem Town refused to assent.[4]

Salem Village began a protracted struggle for independence in the 1660s. In 1672, after several failed efforts, the General Court stepped in to pressure the town to make some concession. The town agreed to let Salem Village hire their own minister, and to release them from paying taxes to support the Salem Town church. The village would remain a part of Salem and would pay all other taxes paid by the other residents of the town. The General Court instructed the villagers to elect five members to a committee each year to oversee the minister and raise the money to pay him. It would take eighty more years before Salem Village would leave what was essentially parish status and become the town of Danvers.[5]

Such dramas were played out repeatedly in early New England. Soon after colonists established communities, growing populations moved to outskirts increasingly distant from the initial center of settlement and far from the established church. This process inevitably led to efforts to gain independence from the parent township. Salem Village and Great Island stand out not because they tried to gain their independence, but because their efforts failed, leading to growing tension and conflict that found no suitable outlet or resolution. Salem Village lacked any official political status or power. Essentially, it was a stillborn town—desiring autonomy but unable to achieve it. This quickly led to turmoil.[6]

One might have thought that Salem Village's struggle for independence might have led to unity in the community, but any agreement among the residents quickly evaporated after achieving parish status. Villagers repeatedly argued over the choice of minister and his salary. The community went through a succession of three ministers—James Bayley, George Burroughs, Deodat Lawson—from 1672 to 1689, before inviting Reverend Samuel Parris to serve in the role. All four men would be the focus of discontent and conflict. As each were attacked and defended by different factions, Salem Village reached levels of conflict well above most other communities. Boyer and Nissenbaum have noted that animosities stemming from the absence of effective political structures for conflict resolution manifested themselves in the witchcraft trials. Simply put, the supporters of Reverend Parris and their families and allies tended to be the accusers in 1692, and members of the anti-Parris faction the accused. Once charges of witchcraft were first made in Salem Village, they rapidly became an outlet for years of factional fighting and frustration over Salem Village's political status.[7]

Great Island's efforts to achieve independence parallel Salem Village's in many ways. In fact, Great Island may have used Salem Village as its inspiration when it sought parish status in 1682, for Salem Village's parish standing was rare in early New England. As an island, Great Island was naturally divided from the rest of Portsmouth, just as rural Salem Village differed from distant Salem Town. The petitions submitted by both communities stress their extreme distance to the meetinghouse and their serious need to hire their own minister. At the time of lithobolia, Great Island might even have had a minister lined up, waiting to assume his duties. Salem Village was significantly different from Salem Town. One was a busy port, the other a rural farmland. Likewise, Great Island was the principal port of entry to the Piscataqua, a place frequented by sailors and fishermen. While there certainly were maritime activities elsewhere in the Piscataqua, the mainland was a more rural area dominated by lumbering and farming. On Great Island, as in Salem Village, the fight for independence would result in the fracturing of the community and eventually lead to charges of witchcraft. The assault on George Walton's tavern, which resulted in witchcraft accusations, was triggered by Portsmouth's refusal to approve Great Island's request to form its own town.

In both communities, struggles over hiring a minister were closely related to maintaining Puritan orthodoxy and carrying out a campaign of moral reformation. In 1691 and 1692, Reverend Parris delivered a series of fire-and-brimstone sermons in Salem Village aimed at restoring the moral and religious fiber of the community. In their petition for self-government, Great Islanders, like Salem Villagers, stressed their distance from the meeting-house and the great time it took to travel there. The islanders also emphasized "the great profaning of the Lord's Day by those that stay at home, rather than make the arduous trip to Sabbath services." Furthermore, barely a third of the islanders attended services, and many children were growing up ignorant of religion. Heathenism was threatening to overwhelm the island, and it could only be combated by the erection of a meetinghouse and the hiring of a minister.[8]

The Puritans of Great Island felt themselves threatened by Quakers like the Waltons as well as Anglicans and the godless. Their desire to hire a minister and form a church grew out of this anxiety. When their efforts failed, the Waltons and their allies became scapegoats. In Salem Village, similar concerns among Reverend Parris and the saints of Salem Village about growing commercialism and religious decline would help trigger the witchcraft outbreak. Several scholars have demonstrated that Quakers were at least indirect targets of accusation in 1692, for many people accused of witchcraft in that year had household members, neighbors, or close friends who were Quakers. Several historians have demonstrated that the persecution of these people reflected anxieties felt by Puritans as they saw the Quakers merging into their communities and families. Quaker ties explain some unusual accusations. For example, the conviction of Rebecca Nurse, a member of the Salem Town church and a benevolent and devout woman from a highly respected family, has perplexed many historians. Yet, her household included a ward, Samuel Southwick, who was the orphaned son of a local Quaker family.

This taint on an otherwise devout and worthy home may have led to Nurse's accusation.[9]

In addition to these problems of local control and religious orthodoxy, both Great Islanders and Salem Villagers had to cope with uncertainty about the political status of their respective colonies. In 1682, New Hampshire had been an independent royal colony for only two years, and many important issues remained undecided. The Mason family saw New Hampshire's independence as an opportunity to reassert their proprietary claim. If they succeeded, all land titles in New Hampshire would be invalidated. George Walton's unpopularity stemmed in part from his allegiance to the Mason family and his willingness to go to them to purchase title to his neighbors' lands. A powerful Puritan faction opposed the Masons and their Quaker and Anglican allies and even hoped to reunite New Hampshire with Massachusetts. To add to this uncertainty, when the stones were flying at the Walton tavern in the summer of 1682, the colony was anticipating the arrival of its first royal governor, the Anglican Edward Cranfield.

Likewise, in the spring of 1692, Salem Village and the rest of the Bay Colony were awaiting their first royal governor, Sir William Phips. The New England knight carried with him the new Massachusetts charter, but no one knew precisely what it stipulated, or what to expect from Phips himself. Born in Maine and a resident of Boston, the ship's captain was best known for his successful salvage of a Spanish treasure galleon and his subsequent knighthood. He had virtually no political experience and at best mixed success as a military leader. His Puritan faith was in doubt as well, for he had only recently become a saint in Increase and Cotton Mather's church.

Whatever government Phips brought would be an improvement, for the 1680s were a low point of the Puritan experiment in New England. As the region began to recover from the devastation of King Philip's War, Massachusetts Bay faced a sustained royal effort to bring it under the control of the British crown. In 1684, English courts revoked the 1629 charter, making Massachusetts a royal colony. The charter meant more than just self-government for the colony. It also symbolized their covenant with

God, their bold experiment, the city upon a hill. Two years later, the king combined all of New England into one colony, the Dominion of New England. Governor Edmund Andros ruled the Dominion with an arbitrary power that mirrored the way King James II exercised his authority. Representative government was eclipsed as the elected assembly gave way to a governor and council appointed by the king. Hand-picked juries ruled in favor of the governor, further threatening English liberties. The crown ordered Andros to bring Massachusetts into the imperial system, and his enforcement of the Navigation Acts led to financial hardship and much complaint. Even so basic an issue as land ownership came into question, for the revocation of the charter vacated all property titles in Massachusetts. Andros required all landowners to petition him for a royal patent to their land or risk losing it. Forced to pay a fee for the privilege of re-patenting their land, they would now be directly beholden to the crown, to which they would also have to pay annual rents.[10]

Governor Andros also forced Massachusetts to allow liberty of conscience—the right of all Englishmen to worship in any of the accepted Protestant faiths. Gone was the privileged position of Puritanism. Instead, the Dominion favored the established Church of England. Puritans could practice their faith, but so too could Quakers and Baptists, groups that had existed at the margins of legitimacy under Puritan rule. Upon arrival in Boston, Andros temporarily took over the Old South Church for Anglican services—much to the disgust of its Puritan parishioners. Andros's rule truly seemed to point to the end of the Puritan experiment.[11]

Thus, the arrival of Governor Phips certainly must have been regarded with some optimism, for at the very least it meant an end to the Dominion of New England. However, Massachusetts remained a royal colony with a governor appointed by the king. Residents wondered what rights and liberties would be restored under the new charter. They worried about the position of the Puritan church and the security of their land titles. They were anxious for an end to the devastating three-year-old war with the Wabanaki Indians and their French allies, which now threatened to spread from the frontier to the main settlements of the colony.

Uncertainty ruled the land, creating an atmosphere conducive to witchcraft accusations.

This colony-wide insecurity helps explain one hallmark of Salem witchcraft—the broad geographical spread of accusations. The charges soon radiated out from Salem Village to almost every community in Essex County. People as far south as Boston and as far north as Maine suffered accusation. Events in Salem may have also influenced an outbreak in Connecticut later that same year. This is a remarkable departure from earlier episodes of witchcraft in New England, which appear to have focused mainly on a single individual in a single community. Consider the Hartford outbreak of 1662–63, the largest New England outbreak prior to Salem, with eight people accused and three executed. All but three of the accused witches were from Hartford, and those three came from the neighboring towns of Wethersfield and Farmington.[12]

Lithobolia is noteworthy because it is one of those rare times when the actions of Satan spread from one community to another, traversing considerable distance. The first recorded incident of lithobolia in New England took place in the Morse home in Newbury, Massachusetts, in 1679–1681. Soon after, the stone-throwing devil moved up the coast twenty miles to Great Island, New Hampshire. Later, in the summer of 1682, the panic spread to Berwick, Maine, and all the way to Hartford, Connecticut, using well established lines of communication, including letters between ministers and the word of mouth of sailors and merchants sailing coastal New England.

Word also would have spread through Increase Mather's *Illustrious Providences*, a much read publication. Lithobolia was soon retold in other works, the earliest being Nathaniel Crouch's *Kingdom of Darkness*, published in London in 1688. Crouch began his book with the Morse case and an abbreviation of Mather's account of the lithobolia attacks of 1682. Clearly these cases were popular topics in 1692—the latest news from the kingdom of darkness. Mary Brown may have read or heard of the events while sitting in her Reading home, or perhaps she was just well versed in traditional English stories of witchcraft, which included stone-throwing devils. It does seem more likely that Reverend Emerson would have read *Illustrious Providences* or learned about the Fortados and the Waltons from his nephew.[13]

Participants in the 1692 outbreak might have at least learned about the Fortados' stone-throwing devil from the younger Reverend Emerson, for the former Berwick minister had direct involvement in the proceedings, working to gain confessions of accused witches. After hearing Dorcas Hoar's confession of witchcraft, in September 1692 Emerson and three local ministers petitioned Governor Phips for a delay in her execution so that she might have a month to prepare for her death. Like everyone else who confessed in 1692, Hoar would ultimately avoid the hangman's noose. Emerson also attempted to extract a confession from Martha Tyler, urging her to confess before she lost her soul to the devil. One wonders how much influence the Fortado incident had on John Emerson's determination to root out confessions from witches.[14]

The distinctive nature of lithobolia provides a unique chance to trace the spread of one type of witchcraft and examine the links between a series of cases. The Morse case either directly or indirectly triggered episodes in New Hampshire, Maine, and Connecticut several years after the fact. Lithobolia certainly did not prompt the Salem outbreak, but the signature supernatural stone-throwing was remembered and incorporated into the many other symptoms of witchcraft in 1692.

If lithobolia is any indication, New England witchcraft outbreaks probably had far more connections to each other than the surviving documentary evidence suggests. For example, the cases of the Hartford outbreak (1662–63) are clearly related, as are a second round of accusations made against two of the Hartford witches three years later. Events in Hartford may have influenced the series of accusations that would take place in the ensuing years. Seven different people were accused of witchcraft from 1668 to 1679 in Connecticut River towns ranging from Northampton, Massachusetts, southward to Wethersfield, Connecticut. Though the surviving evidence does not point to any links, one can't help but wonder how the spread of news and gossip up and down the Connecticut River about the Hartford outbreak may have led to these subsequent cases. If the news of a stone-throwing devil in New Hampshire could trigger a similar incident in distant Hartford, it stands to reason that a major outbreak in Hartford may have had repercussions in neighboring valley towns for many years.[15]

In order for any of these witchcraft outbreaks to spread, they needed an initial place to take root. The Walton tavern on Great Island and the Parris home in Salem Village were both likely spots, for both households included outsiders in the form of Native American household servants. Tituba and Indian John were slaves belonging to Reverend Parris. Their precise ethnic identity has been subject to much scholarly debate. Tituba is universally described as an Indian, as opposed to some other slaves in the Salem trials described as "black" or "negro," so it seems most likely that she was an American Indian, rather than an African. Less is known about her husband, Indian John. Possibly he was a New England Indian enslaved at the end of King Philip's War. Tituba was not from New England, for she referred to witchcraft "in her own country." Perhaps she was from the Caribbean, or from coastal Georgia or Florida, where the Spanish enslaved Indians. Some of these captives were sold into New England, where they were sometimes called "Spanish Indians." Regardless of their specific origins, Tituba and Indian John were both outsiders in Salem Village. Suspicions grew against them after they helped to prepare a witches' cake, an effort at countermagic. Tituba would soon be accused of witchcraft, and her confession would implicate a large coven of witches, leading to the growth of the outbreak. In the midst of King William's War, the presence of Native Americans in the Parris household would have been quite notable, and probably disquieting to many villagers.[16]

In the Walton tavern, Mary Agawam and her son William also symbolized the threat of outsiders and the frontier to Puritan New England. A bastard conceived on the Sabbath in the Walton tavern, William Indian would have been a reminder to devout Great Islanders of the need for moral reformation. Neighbors would have also remembered his participation, along with the young men of the Walton clan, in an expedition to loot English homesteads abandoned during King Philip's War. It was rare for Native Americans to be living in English households following the terror and destruction of this war. Although quiet returned to the northern frontier in 1678, it was an uneasy peace, punctuated by recurring fears of renewed warfare. For instance, in March 1681, Samuel Sewall recorded in his diary that there were rumors of Indian attack. So great was the panic that men carried arms to Sunday meeting.[17]

In 1688, the war fears were finally realized as fighting began between the Wabanaki and the English settlers of Maine. The situation was made worse by the outbreak of war between England and France the next year. Soon, minor skirmishing on the frontier gave way to major Native attacks. Between the summer of 1689 and spring of 1690, a series of devastating raids by the Wabanaki and their French allies brought destruction to English settlements from Schenectady, New York, to Pemaquid, Maine. The war would be particularly destructive to communities on the Maine and New Hampshire frontier.

In May 1690 a combined French and Native war party surprised Berwick, burning upwards of twenty homesteads, killing approximately sixty to eighty settlers, and taking at least twenty-two people captive. Antonio and Mary Fortado were among the victims. Their seven-year-old daughter Elizabeth was taken captive and marched north by the raiders to Canada. One of her companions on the trip was her neighbor, Mercy Short. Mercy was the fifteen-year-old daughter of Clement and Faith Short, who lived upriver from the Plaisted's mill at Salmon Falls, not far from the Fortados and their relatives. Clement and Faith and three of their children died during the raid. Mercy was lucky to be taken captive with five or six of her siblings, though she might not have considered herself fortunate at the time.[18]

Mercy and Elizabeth Fortado survived the arduous march to Quebec, where both received baptism into the Catholic faith. Elizabeth's baptism is the last recorded mention of her or any other member of the Fortado family of Berwick. Perhaps she died young, or remained in Canada and married. Mercy was soon redeemed by the Phips Expedition during its unsuccessful siege of Quebec City in November 1690. A teenage orphan, Mercy became a lowly servant in a Boston home. Two years later she would be afflicted by witchcraft, one of the victims of the growing outbreak that started in Salem.[19]

Amid the witch trials, Mercy was sent on an errand to the Boston prison. There, the accused witch Sarah Good saw her and asked her for some tobacco. When Mercy refused, Sarah cursed her. Soon the young girl was afflicted by witchcraft. Cotton Mather was Mercy's minister and he worked closely with her to relieve her suffering, which lasted off and on until the spring of 1693.[20]

Mather recounted in great detail the course of Mercy's afflictions. At times the girl appeared almost to go into a coma. When she came to, she reported that she had been tempted by specters, including those of French Canadians and Indian sagamores that she personally knew. These demons showed her a book of Catholic devotions, tempting her to abandon her faith and become a Catholic. On December 25, she said that the spirits that afflicted her were going to have a dance. To a large degree, Mercy was reliving her captivity and the efforts by the French to convert her and her fellow captives to Catholicism. The very nature of the demon that tormented her was drawn from her experience as a hostage. It was a "Divil having the Figure of A Short Black Man," but "hee was not of a Negro but of a Tawney, or Indian colour; he wore an high-crowned Hat, with straight Hair." Mercy was seeing an Indian—perhaps her master in captivity.[21]

Mather was amazed that a girl who had no book knowledge of witchcraft was able to describe the devil exactly as learned English and European authors described him. Her knowledge is far less remarkable when we realize that Mercy was an impressionable seven-year-old when the lithobolia attack began at the house of her neighbors, the Fortados. She had observed the lithobolia damage or learned of it from family and friends. Surely it and other supernatural events must have been the talk of her household and all of Salmon Falls even long after the year's duration. Although historians have failed to note that Mercy had firsthand experience prior to 1692, they have pointed out that she described Satan completely different from the way someone in Europe would have described him. He was a tawny Native American, with a high-crowned hat and straight hair. Mather may have pictured the pointed hat often attributed to witches or a Catholic bishop's miter, but Mercy Short probably had in mind the high-crowned hat common among the Wabanaki.[22]

Historians have paid much attention to Mercy Short since the early 1980s, when they began to be increasingly interested in the influence of frontier warfare on the witch trials. The timing of the Essex County outbreak, which coincided with the abandonment of frontier townships in King William's War, suggests a general panic among the population. The war threatened to engulf them economically as well as militarily. There were numerous direct ties between Essex County and the frontier. Many families had relatives who had been killed or displaced from frontier homes. Others had to open their Essex County homes to war refugees, while at the same time sending their sons off to fight in the conflict. The war was an expensive undertaking, and the high taxes threatened the economic stability of many families, as well as of the colony itself. The 1680s had been a time of tremendous speculation in frontier lands, as settlers bought and sold properties recently owned by Native Americans. With the outbreak of war, these frontier lands became worthless, and the speculative bubble burst. Many families involved in the Essex County trials owned these lands and suffered financial losses. Indeed, most the witchcraft judges were among the biggest losers, for they held thousands of acres of frontier lands. The judges presided over a court in which thirty-three of the afflicted and accused also had strong connections to the frontier.[23]

By 1692, the link between the frontier and witchcraft would have been firmly in place. One need only look at the then-recent outbreaks of witchcraft to see the connection. With the exception of the 1688 Goodwin case in Boston, the supernatural occurrences of the 1680s had all taken place close to the frontier—Newbury, Hampton, Portsmouth, Berwick, and even Hartford. The link is particularly apparent in the affliction of Mercy Short and in another case, that of Susannah Martin.

Martin lived in Amesbury, one of the northernmost towns of Essex County. She was an elderly widow who had been under suspicion of witchcraft for over thirty years. These fears led to formal charges being filed against her. She was found guilty and executed on July 19, 1692 along with four other convicted witches. Over twenty people signed depositions or testified against Martin, many describing supernatural acts that took place decades before.[24]

Joseph Ring of Salisbury made a vivid deposition against Susannah that even mentioned the former Walton tavern on Great Island. His statement described a chain of events that began in May 1690 when Ring had been a member of militia unit under command of Captain Shadrach Walton, the son of George and Alice Walton. The troops headed north to relieve the beleaguered Fort Loyal in Falmouth (present-day Portland, Maine). On the way, troops spent the night on Captain Walton's home territory of Great Island. From the island they would sail to Fort Loyal. Another solider, Thomas Hardy, entered the room where Ring was billeted and urged him to play shuffleboard, a popular tavern gambling game of the time. Ring declined because he had no money to wager. Presumably, they were staying at the old Walton tavern, The Anchor, for the 1677 inventory of the ordinary included a shuffleboard room—a most unusual feature. Hardy, eager for a game, lent two shillings to Ring so he could play. Hardy then won the game, leaving Ring unable repay the two shillings he had borrowed.[25]

The expedition arrived too late to save Fort Loyal. They sailed into Casco Bay, only to hear the beat of drums and volleys of gunfire. The fifty militia men in the relief party would have been overwhelmed by over 300 French and Wabanaki, so all they could do was watch helplessly as the enemy set fire to Fort Loyal and the surrounding town and killed or captured many settlers. Having no other choice, the relief expedition sailed back to Portsmouth. On the way, they observed that all the settlements between Falmouth and Wells were also on fire. When they arrived in Portsmouth, they found that over 300 refugees from Maine settlements—mostly women and children—crowding the town. Captain Walton, Ring, Hardy, and the rest of the expedition had personally witnessed one of the worst defeats of King William's War and seen the abandonment of most of the English settlements on the Maine frontier.[26]

At the time, though, they had no idea of the true extent of the loss. Only later would they learn the horrible details of the fall of

Fort Loyal. When first attacked, the English settlers fled to Fort Loyal, and together with the garrison, they stubbornly fought for five days, the majority of the defenders being killed or wounded in the process. The survivors watched from inside the fort as the Indians burned down the entire town around them. Finally, Fort Loyal's commander parlayed a truce with the French officers. Under the terms of the agreement, everyone in the fort would be allowed to leave and given safe passage to the nearest English settlement. Unfortunately, when the garrison marched out, the French could not control their Native allies, who set upon the English. Over 200 people were killed or taken captive.[27]

His complete inability to help Falmouth may have haunted Ring—so much so that he soon felt under assault by witches. The month after Fort Loyal fell, Joseph Ring returned home. One day, while walking between Sandy Beach (present-day Rye, New Hampshire) and Hampton, he met Thomas Hardy of Great Island in the company of a fireball and several supernatural beasts. Hardy demanded his two shillings back from Ring. Over the next few months, Ring reported he had a series of supernatural encounters with Hardy. Several times, Hardy and a company of people on horseback—apparently a coven of witches—approached Ring and demanded his two shillings. Once Hardy invited him to have a drink with him. On another occasion, Hardy threatened to gruesomely murder him unless he repaid his debt. Several times Satan himself came to Ring, tempting him to sign his book. Susannah Martin and other unnamed witches were present at some of these meetings where covens gathered. Once, Ring even saw Martin change herself into a black hog. Finally, Ring claimed, he was struck dumb, unable to speak a word from August 1691 to April 1692. After reading Ring's deposition, in which Thomas Hardy is clearly the central figure, it is hard to believe that Susannah Martin was executed for witchcraft, while no formal proceedings appear to have been initiated against her accomplice, Hardy.[28]

There are no known connections between Hardy and Martin, so it is diffcult to explain why Joseph Ring would bring them together in both of his depositions, particularly when his real quarrel was with Hardy. A likely link was Joseph's brother, Jarvis. He also deposed against Susannah, saying that eight years earlier she had repeatedly afflicted him. Martin's Amesbury home was only about twenty miles down the coast from where Hardy resided on Great Island. This proximity probably led Joseph to believe that Martin aided Hardy in his malevolent work.[29]

One possible explanation for Joseph Ring's behavior is that like Mercy Short, he was suffering from what is now known as post-traumatic stress disorder (PTSD). Experts are increasingly diagnosing this affliction among soldiers and civilians who have witnessed the revulsion of war. The vicious fighting on the Maine frontier was just the kind of struggle to bring on PTSD. English towns and Indian villages were put to the torch, and many women and children brutally lost their lives. Ring himself would later suffer a particularly horrible death while fighting in Maine. Taken captive by Native warriors, they tied him to a stake and burned him alive. Other prisoners observed the Natives "barbarously shouting and rejoicing at his cries." In 1692, Ring specifically dated his initial affliction to the month after Fort Loyal fell, so the latter seems to have been an emotional event for him. It is even remotely possible that his stay on Great Island in Captain Walton's company, in a Walton tavern, stirred up memories of lithobolia that fueled his fears of the supernatural.[30]

Ring's anxiety may have been deepened by his wife's experience, for her family suffered horribly at Fort Loyal, as well as in other attacks in King Philip's War and King William's War. Ring's wife was Mary Brackett, a member of a prominent Falmouth family. During King Philip's War, her entire family had been taken captive by the Wabanaki but managed to escape. After the end of the war, the Bracketts returned to Falmouth. Mary's father, Anthony Brackett Jr., was killed by the Wabanaki in the early fighting of King William's War. Her brother was killed at the fall of Fort Loyal. It is unclear if Mary herself was at Fort Loyal, or if at the time she was living with her grandparents at Sandy Beach, or if she had already married Ring. The fact that Ring was accosted by specters while walking toward home from the small settlement at Sandy Beach only a month after Fort Loyal suggests that some bond had already been established with Mary. In September 1691, a Wabanaki raid struck Sandy Beach, killing and taking captive six-teen settlers—mostly members of the Brackett and Rand families. Among the dead were Mary's grandparents. George Walton Jr.'s widow and son Samuel probably also died in the raid, for she had remarried Samuel Rand of Sandy Beach, and she and Samuel disappear from the records after the raid.[31]

Joseph Ring, Mercy Short, and other participants in the Essex County outbreak of 1692 felt the influence of the warfare on the northern frontier with Native Americans and the French. Massachusetts Puritans had long worried about the heathen Native Americans, the Catholic French, and the supposedly godless Englishmen of the region. The fame of the lithobolia outbreak would have only increased these fears, for here was a story of witchcraft set in a disorderly Quaker tavern, and in a household headed by a Portuguese immigrant. By 1692, good Puritans must have been truly convinced that New Hampshire and Maine were the devil's playground.[32]

Frontier warfare was just one of many factors that could lead to witchcraft accusations. The lithobolia outbreak of 1682 and the events in Salem ten years later highlight other causes as well. The presence of an external threat to a community created a climate of fear and uncertainty that could lead to witchcraft accusations. Historians have long recognized that local conflict was usually at the heart of a witchcraft accusation. Neighborly feuds, property disputes, and local political conflict were all too frequent in the early modern world. Those communities that lacked the ability to effectively resolve these disputes ran a heightened risk of witchcraft. The danger level rose even more when external threats such as warfare or regional political or economic crises occurred at the same time. Often these threats came to be represented by outsiders—whether Native Americans, Anglicans, or anyone who deviated from the norms of a society. These outsiders focused and made tangible community fears. They also provided scapegoats.

Finally, witchcraft was, above all else, a religious crime, one that typically occurred in communities suffering from religious conflict or uncertainty. The outsiders, such as the French or Quakers, tended to practice alternative religions perceived as threats to the status quo. On the European continent, witchcraft usually was prosecuted in church courts. Although accusations were made throughout Europe, the charges tended to cluster around those regions that were particularly caught up in the turmoil of the Protestant Reformation and the Catholic Counter-Reformation.

Virginia, an Anglican colony free from the religious tensions of New England, serves as an interesting comparison. The Old Dominion had roughly the same number of residents as Massachusetts, but only a small fraction of the witchcraft accusations. Between 1626 and 1730, only ten Virginians faced formal charges of witchcraft; three are known to have been convicted, and none was executed. The closest Virginia came to slaying a witch was the case of Katherine Sherwood. In 1654, she was executed at sea aboard a ship bound for Virginia, having been found guilty of using witchcraft to cause tempests that threatened to sink the vessel. Two of the convicted Virginia witches were whipped. One of these cases took place in 1730, almost forty years after Salem— quite likely the last conviction for witchcraft in the English colonies. Virginians had local conflicts and colony-wide problems similar to those that afflicted the New Englanders. They suffered Native American uprisings in 1622 and 1644 and Bacon's Rebellion in 1676. As a colony increasingly reliant on tobacco and African slaves, Virginia also had to wrestle with the issue of race and outsiders, as well as a boom-and-bust economy. Characterized by many of the other conditions necessary for major episodes of witchcraft, Virginia lacked the religious turmoil of New England. This helps explain why so few Virginians faced formal charges, or even accusations of witchcraft.[33]

As the 1730 whipping of a convicted Virginia witch indicates, witchcraft accusations did not end at Salem. If anything, the Salem witch trial led to a renewed interest in the supernatural. For the learned members of society, the fascination would prove short lived. For the general population, however, witches and demons would continue to haunt New England for many years. For example, two people were accused of the crime in Kittery in 1725, though neither faced charges and both sued their accusers for slander. One of the alleged witches confided that "she was afraid in the time of the Witchcraft She Should be Taken for a witch" but that she no longer feared such charges.[34]

Richard Chamberlain did not publish his *Lithobolia, or the Stone-Throwing Devil* until 1698, fully sixteen years after the fact, long after he had returned home to England. He must have written a draft of the account or at least made detailed notes during the attack or shortly afterward. Certainly, the signed and dated testimonies of Walter Barefoot and the various Quakers included in the tract were given during the attack, which suggests that Chamberlain was actively recording events as they took place. Furthermore, some of the specific details he notes (such as the day of the week and month on which certain of the events took place) are so precise as to require some contemporary record. Perhaps he was finally urged to publish by Martin Lumley Jr., for Chamberlain begins his account by giving his thanks to this son of former Lord Mayor of London Sir Martin Lumley. In 1695, the junior Lumley married Richard Chamberlain's daughter Elizabeth. Presumably, his new son-in-law had heard the story and convinced Chamberlain to publish it.[35]

Chamberlain was writing in an English tradition of wonder tales that went back over one hundred years. He had little reason to doubt what he believed he saw and he found it hard to accept that anyone could dispute the supernatural nature of lithobolia. The late seventeenth century saw a proliferation of books and pamphlets on providence and the supernatural, even before 1692. Increase Mather's *Illustrious Providences* (1684) was only one of five books published on divine providences at this time. Four English ministers would publish their own books in London between 1672 and 1680. Events in New England helped to re-ignite interest in the 1690s. Cotton Mather's *Memorable Providences Relating to Witchcrafts and Possessions* was first published in Boston 1689, on the heels of the Goodwin case that was the focus of the book. English authors quickly joined in. Two years later, *Memorable Providences* was reprinted in London with a preface from Reverend Richard Baxter, a leading English minister. Later that year, Baxter published his own *Certainty of the World of Sprits*, which featured a rambling account of devils, witches, and hauntings and included references to the books of both Mathers.[36]

Events in Salem soon generated a new series of tracts. Deodat Lawson rushed a brief account to print in 1692, followed the next year by Cotton Mather's *Wonders of the Invisible World*. Mather's detailed work became a bestseller. First published in Boston, it had gone through four London printings by the summer of 1694. In 1693, Increase Mather's observations on Salem, *Cases of Conscience Concerning Evil Spirits*, was published in London. In 1695, Balthazar Bekker's *The World Bewitch'd* was translated from French and published in London. The English audiences hungered for more. John Flavel's *Divine Conduct: or, the Mystery of Providence* was reprinted in 1698, twenty years after its first edition. Deodat Lawson noted the demand for such publications. In 1696 he traveled to England, where friends urged him to reprint a revised edition of his account. He declined at the time, but did publish a new edition in 1704.[37]

England's interest in the supernatural was not rooted solely in Salem. The case of Richard Dugdale, a gardener from Surrey, England, also captured the public's imagination. The nineteen-year-old Dugdale claimed that while drunk he had offered his soul to the devil in return for being made a good dancer. The devil kept his end of the bargain but also subjected Dugdale to fits and other odd symptoms of demonic possession starting in the spring of 1689. Soon dubbed the "Surrey Demoniack," the case gained immediate fame. It also frustrated ministers who tried to help Dugdale and even tested, without success, for witchcraft. Finally Dugdale's symptoms disappeared after almost a year. The much anticipated publication of the account of the Surrey Demoniack did not appear until 1697. It immediately led to a tract war, as some Anglicans declared the case a complete fraud used by the English Puritans (or Dissenters as they were then known in England) behind it to encourage a religious revival. Between the excitement generated by Salem and the Surrey Demoniack, Chamberlain had a ready audience for his old tale in 1698.[38]

As the debate over the Surrey Demoniack demonstrates, learned Englishmen of the 1690s still hotly contested the existence of the supernatural world. A group of Dissenting ministers led the fight against a growing skepticism among learned people who could find no place for witches in the emerging scientific world. A shrinking group of Anglicans also maintained a belief in the supernatural. They were concerned with England's growing atheism and believed that by proving the existence of spirits they also demonstrated the existence and importance of God. Henry More, editor of *Saducismus Triumphatus: Or, Full and Plain Evidence Concerning Witches and Apparitions*, died in 1687, followed four year later by pious scientist Robert Boyle. This left Richard Chamberlain as one of the last Anglicans to state the case for the supernatural. He makes his intent clear at the beginning of *Lithobolia* in a poem dedicated to "RF," which begins:

> To tell strange feats of Daemons, here I am;
> Strange, but most true they are, ev'n to a Dram,
> Tho' Sadduceans cry, 'tis all a Sham.
> Here's Stony Arg'uments of persuasive Dint,
> They'l not believe it, told, nor yet in Print:
> What should the Reason be? The Devil's in't.
> And yet they wish to be convinc'd by Sight,
> Assur'd by Apparition of a Sprite;

The "Sadduceans" or Sadducees were a Jewish sect prominent around the time of Christ whose members did not believe in the existence of angels and spirits or in the resurrection of the dead. Seventeenth-century English religious authorities used the term to describe the atheists and disbelievers of their day. Chamberlain wondered at the extreme skepticism of his age. "SUCH is the Sceptical Humour of this Age for Incredulity, (not to say Infidelity,) That I wonder they do not take up and profess, in terms, the Pyrrhonian Doctrine of disbelieving their very Senses." He hoped the "Stony Arg'uments" of *Lithobolia* would convert the Sadducees and skeptics into believers.[39]

Unlike Richard Chamberlain, Thomas Robie did not believe in witches or the supernatural world. The man one historian has called "the most famous New Englander in science in his day" was born in Boston in 1689 and soon baptized at the Mathers' church. He came from a family of modest means, but that did not prove to be an obstacle to his scholarly potential, for Robie graduated from

Harvard in 1708. At the college Robie developed a keen interest in math and astronomy and after graduation immediately began to publish an almanac, an undertaking he would continue for the next twelve years. He returned to Harvard, where he taught and carried out his astronomical and mathematical research. In a 1719 publication, Robie described the scientific nature of comets, debunking the idea so recently held by all New Englanders that comets were portents of the supernatural world. In 1723, the trustees of Harvard regretfully accepted Robie's resignation upon his marriage to Mehitable, the daughter of Major Stephen Sewall. The couple took up residence in her home town of Salem, where Thomas began a practice as a physician. His career as a doctor was short lived, however, for he died in 1729, four years after his election to the Royal Society of London.[40]

It is a wonderful irony that Robie would help lead New England out of superstition and into the age of science, for his family knew all too well the experience of witchcraft. His father, William Robie, was the nephew of Henry and Samuel Robie. William had been a resident of Great Island in 1679 and probably did not move to Boston until after the lithobolia attack on the Walton tavern. He also would have known of events in nearby Hampton, where in 1680 the witch Goody Cole was alleged to have attacked a man in Uncle Henry Robie's home. Thomas Robie was not yet born when these events took place and only three during the 1692 outbreak. Still, young Thomas and his siblings would have been raised with knowledge of the family's past, including the stories of Goody Cole and the stone-throwing devil. Indeed, the Robie family seems to have been particularly keen on its heritage. In 1726, Thomas's brother traveled to England, where he visited his relations and copied family information out of his great grandmother's Bible.[41]

Thomas Robie's wife, Mehitable Sewall Robie, had her own connections to witchcraft. Not only was she the niece of witchcraft judge Samuel Sewall; her father, Stephen Sewall, was also a Salem Town resident who had served as the clerk of the Court of Oyer and Terminer. Stephen was a friend of Reverend Samuel Parris, and when young Betty Parris's fits worsened in March of 1692, she took up temporary residence in the Sewall homestead, in the hopes that a change of scenery might improve her condition. Unfortunately, the fits continued. In 1710, long after the trials had ended, the General Court appointed Stephen Sewall to a committee to oversee the reimbursement of £578 awarded by Massachusetts as restitution to victims of the trials and their families—the first formal acknowledgement of governmental error during the witchcraft outbreak. Though Mehitable Sewall was born after 1692, given her family history, she must have been well versed in the supernatural events of that year. With such close family ties to witchcraft, eighteenth-century New Englanders like Thomas and Mehitable Robie must have looked to the past as well as to the future, even when it came to observing comets. The Robies and other elites may have embraced the new age of science but belief in the supernatural would only gradually diminish among their less learned neighbors.[42]

Epilogue

In the fall of 1682, the arrival of a new governor, Edward Cranfield, brought an end to the lithobolia attacks on the Walton tavern but ushered in a three-year nightmare for the colony. The governor quickly used the full extent of his office to establish his personal and arbitrary rule, becoming infamous for stripping the colony of its freedoms and liberties. Cranfield established the Anglican Church and jailed Reverend Moody for refusing to perform the Anglican service. He collaborated with Robert Mason to have hand-picked courts and juries enforce Mason's land claims. The governor worked with Edward Randolph to rigorously apply the Navigation Acts. When Cranfield dissolved the legislature, Assemblyman Edward Gove attempted a rebellion that was quickly put down. The governor earned the hatred of most of the colony. Even Edward Randolph, a firm supporter of royal authority, said Cranfield's acts were "of the most arbitrary nature I have heard of."[1]

There were many forms of resistance to Cranfield's rule. The courts, controlled by the governor and his inner circle, continually returned verdicts that supported Cranfield and the Mason faction, but most citizens simply ignored them. When Mason won decisions in land cases, the losers refused to pay the imposed fines or to abandon their properties. When merchants were convicted for violating the Navigation Acts, they too refused to pay their fines. When citizens were dispossessed from their lands, no buyers came forward to bid on the properties at auction.[2]

Cranfield was so unsuccessful and disliked as governor that in the spring of 1685 the king removed him from office. His temporary replacement was Deputy Governor Walter Barefoot, George Walton's friend and neighbor. Unfortunately for Barefoot, his allegiance to Cranfield and the Mason family made him a despised figure and left him vulnerable to attack. On December 30, 1685, Mason was in his lodgings in Barefoot's house when Thomas Wiggin and Anthony Nutter paid a call. An argument quickly ensued between Mason and Wiggin over Mason's land claims. Mason grabbed Wiggin by the arm to throw him out of the house, but Wiggin resisted, seized Mason, dragged him to the hearth, and threw him into the fire. The flames scorched Mason's foot and burned his coat, periwig, and stockings. Wiggin then grabbed Mason by the throat, attempting to strangle him. The elderly Barefoot intervened, and Mason escaped. An enraged Wiggin then threw Barefoot into the fire, breaking two of the doctor's ribs and knocking out a tooth. The astonishing attack on a sitting governor and would-be proprietor indicates just how bitter the Masonian controversy had become. The incident is all the more remarkable considering that Wiggin and Barefoot were brothers-in-law.[3]

Almost all of the colonies subsequently placed within the Dominion of New England saw it as the most repressive era of colonial rule. Only the people of New Hampshire must have viewed it as an improvement, for not even Dominion Governor Edmund Andros ever reached the level of oppression suffered under Cranfield. Furthermore, the majority of New Hampshire's citizens were pleased to be reunited with Massachusetts.[4]

Robert Mason continued to press his land claims under the Dominion, aided by his position as a member of the ruling Council. His ambitions soon ended, however, when he died in 1688 while on a tour of frontier forts in New York with Governor Andros. The Mason title was purchased from his heirs by Samuel Allen, the new governor of New Hampshire. Years of lawsuits followed. After Allen's death in 1707, the cause was taken up by his son and principal heir, Thomas, and his son-in-law, John Usher, the lieutenant governor of New Hampshire. Thomas's death in 1715 brought a hiatus to the conflict. In the late 1730s, John Tufton Mason, the great-great-great grandson of the original proprietor, John Mason, renewed the family's effort one last time. In

1746, he sold the claim for £1,500 to the Masonian Proprietors, a group of twelve wealthy Portsmouth merchants and politicians. The provincial government then authorized the Masonian Proprietors to sell unclaimed lands on the New Hampshire frontier for a modest profit. The cloud that had long hung over the title of New Hampshire lands finally departed, over one hundred years and six generations removed from John Mason's original patents.[5]

The proprietary dispute outlived everyone who had witnessed the odd events at the Walton tavern. George Walton wrote his will on February 14, 1686, and died less than a month later. Still battling to the end, he bequeathed to his grandchildren sixty acres of land granted him by Robert Mason. There is no evidence that Walton's heirs ever tried to pursue these dubious claims. A few months before George's death, midwife Hannah Jones was one of the women granted a warrant to search the Walton home for the bastard child or fetus delivered by Walton's granddaughter. It must have been a satisfying moment for Jones. The deaths of Hannah Jones and Alice Walton are unrecorded, but the elderly women must have soon followed George to the grave. John "the Greek" Amazeen died in 1706. His and wife Mary's descendants still live on Great Island.[6]

George and Alice Walton's son Shadrach would lead a long and storied life. Maintaining his parents' tavern but forsaking their Quaker faith, Shadrach would enjoy a successful military and political career. He served as captain of the militia in King William's War, and was the colonel in charge of the New Hampshire forces that helped capture Port Royal, Nova Scotia, from the French in 1710. He commanded all the New England forces fighting in Maine during Dummer's War, until he resigned in 1723. Shadrach served as a judge of the Supreme Court of New Hampshire and as a counselor to the governor. The wealthy and prominent military leader and politician died in 1741 at the age of eighty-three, survived by his wife Mary Nutter Walton and a large and prosperous family.

Shadrach and Mary's son George would achieve a social standing that his grandfather and namesake could only have dreamed of, for he wed Frances Allen, the daughter of Governor Samuel

Allen—the holder of the Mason claim. George and Frances never inherited a share of the claim, but they were among the heirs granted the township of Allenstown as compensation for Governor Allen's service to the colony. This windfall must have come as a great relief to George, for several years earlier he had declared bankruptcy.[7]

George's sister Abigail also married well and led a successful life. Her husband was Pierse Long, a prosperous and powerful Portsmouth merchant who would become one of the leaders of revolutionary New Hampshire. He participated in the 1774 raid that removed the gunpowder from Fort William and Mary, the British stronghold that stood adjacent to the old Walton tavern, The Anchor. At the outbreak of war, Long became a colonel in the Continental Army and fought at the Battle of Saratoga. After the war, Colonel Long served for two years in the Continental Congress.

In 1790 Pierse and Abigail's daughter Mary Long wed her childhood sweetheart, Tobias Lear, the trusted private secretary to President George Washington. The Lears lived with the Washingtons in the President's House in the temporary capitals of New York and Philadelphia. Mary (better known by the nickname Polly) gave birth to their son, Benjamin Lincoln Lear, in the President's House in Philadelphia, and George Washington served as his godfather. Mary and Martha Washington became close friends. She was a great aid to the First Lady, for she organized the details of all of the president's social gatherings. In 1793, Polly died tragically— possibly one of the first victims of a deadly yellow fever epidemic that would sweep through Philadelphia. The leaders of the new nation came together in their grief for the witty and popular young woman from New Hampshire. Ever concerned about setting presidential precedents, George Washington had pledged not to attend any funerals, for to attend one meant he must attend them all. He broke his rule and attended services for Polly Long. Her pallbearers were three justices of the Supreme Court and three members of the cabinet. Even the bitter enemies Alexander Hamilton and Thomas Jefferson patched up their differences long enough to serve together at the funeral. By all accounts, Polly Long was a remarkable young woman.[8]

In four generations, the Walton family rose from the margins of society to the pinnacle of power. One can only wonder if Polly Long ever entertained George and Martha at the President's House with the remarkable story of the lithobolia attack on her great-grandparents' tavern.

In 1796, three years after Polly Long's death and less than thirty miles from her Portsmouth home, an Arundel, Maine, woman was beaten and almost killed by neighbors who believed she was a witch. When brought before the court the judge tried to reason with the assailants. The newspaper reported he "endeavored to convince them of the gross error into which they had fallen; and the difficulties and dissentions in the neighborhood arose rather from ignorance in themselves than from witchcraft in the poor old woman." The defendants were placed under a bond of good behavior, and the matter quietly disappeared. If the case had been tried before the Court of Oyer and Terminer in 1692, the result might have been quite different.[9]

Traditionally, scholars have associated the decline in witchcraft prosecutions with the advent of the scientific revolution and the age of reason. These advances did bring an end to official prosecutions. Learned judges became unwilling to entertain charges of witchcraft. However, recent scholars have demonstrated that many common folk maintained supernatural beliefs long after the last witch execution. Only gradually, during the eighteenth and nineteenth centuries, did people's fear of the evil power of witches gradually diminish. At the same time society viewed them increasingly as eccentric and pitiable figures. The gradual transformation of the witch from reviled and feared minion of Satan to harmless icon of Halloween trick-or-treat was well underway. Yet, as long as we have prejudice and hatred, we will probably have stone-throwing devils and other demons.[10]

Notes

Introduction

1. The best studies of non-Salem witchcraft are John P. Demos, *Entertaining Satan: Witchcraft and the Culture of Early New England* (New York: Oxford University Press, 1982); Carol Karlsen, *The Devil in the Shape of a Woman: Witchcraft in Colonial New England* (New York: W. W. Norton, 1987); Richard Godbeer, *The Devil's Dominion: Magic and Religion in Early New England* (New York: Cambridge University Press, 1994).

Chapter One: The First Stone Is Cast

1. The account here and in the following paragraphs is from Richard Chamberlain, "Lithobolia: The Stone-Throwing Devil," in George L. Burr, ed., *Narratives of the Witchcraft Cases* (New York: Charles Scribner's Sons, 1914), 62–68, 72–75.
2. Chamberlain, "Lithobolia," 62, 72–73, 75.
3. Chamberlain, "Lithobolia," 60, 74; Ralph Merrifield, *The Archaeology of Ritual and Magic* (New York: New Amsterdam Books, 1987), 159–75; John P. Demos, *Entertaining Satan: Witchcraft and the Culture of Early New England* (New York: Oxford University Press, 1982), 182–84.
4. New Hampshire Historical Society, *Collections* 8 (1866): 100; Chamberlain, "Lithobolia," 76; Carol Karlsen, *The Devil in the Shape of a Woman: Witchcraft in Colonial New England* (New York: W.W. Norton, 1987), 61–63, 262. The property dispute can be traced in *New Hampshire Provincial and State Papers*, 40 vols., (Concord: State of New Hampshire: 1867–1943), 40: 127, 137, 148–149, 413–14, 455–65.
5. Chamberlain, "Lithobolia," 76; Joshua Moody to Increase Mather, in Massachusetts Historical Society, *Collections*, 4th ser., 7:361–62; David Cressy, *Agnes Bowker's Cat: Travesties and Transgressions in Tudor and Stuart England* (New York: Oxford University Press, 2000), 40–45; Karlsen, *The Devil in the Shape of a Woman*, 16–17.
6. Mary Beth Norton, *Founding Mothers and Fathers: Gendered Power and the Forming of American Society* (New York: Alfred A. Knopf, 1996), 245, 250; Demos, *Entertaining Satan*; Robin Briggs, *Witches and Neighbors: The Social and Cultural Context in European Witchcraft* (New York: Viking, 1996).

Chapter Two: Evil Things

1. Pausanias, *Description of Ancient Greece*, trans. W. H. S. Jones (New York: G. P. Putnam's Sons, 1918), 1: 422–23. Gregory Nagy, *Pindar's Homer: The Lyric Possession of an Epic Past* (Baltimore: Johns Hopkins University Press, 1980), 367; B. O. Foster, ed. *Livy, with an English Translation*, 14 vols. (Cambridge: Harvard University Press, 1968), 5: 201–3.

2. Elizabeth Dawes and Norman H. Baynes, *Three Byzantine Saints: Contemporary Biographies Translated from the Greek* (Crestwood, New York: St. Vladimir's Seminary Press, 1977), 14–20. The author is indebted to David Crane for bringing this incident to his attention.

3. Alan Gauld and A. D. Cornell, *Poltergeists* (London: Routledge & Kegan Paul, 1979), 22; Thomas Wright, ed., *The Historical Works of Giraldus Cambrensis* (London: H. G. Bohn, 1863), 408. The quotation is from Thomas Wright and James Halliwell, eds., *Reliquiae Antiquae: Scraps from Manuscripts, Illustrating Chiefly Early English Literature and the English Language*, 2 vols. (New York: AMS Press, 1966), 1: 53.

4. Gauld and Cornell, *Poltergeists*, 27–31; George L. Kittredge, *Witchcraft in Old and New England* (New York: Russell and Russell, 1929), 214–17.

5. Anonymous, *A True Discourse of Such Straunge and Woonderfull Accidents, as hapned in the house of M. George Lee of North-Ashton, in the Countie of Oxford* (London: 1592).

6. David D. Hall, *Worlds of Wonder, Days of Judgment: Popular Religious Belief in Early New England,* (Cambridge: Harvard University Press, 1990), 71–116; Michael P. Winship, *Seers of God: Puritan Providentialism in the Restoration and Early Enlightenment* (Baltimore: Johns Hopkins University Press, 1996).

7. Ronald Hutton, *The Rise and Fall of Merry England: The Ritual Year 1400–1700* (New York: Oxford University Press, 1994), 200–26; Richard P. Gildrie, *The Profane, the Civil and the Godly* (University Park: Pennsylvania State University Press, 1994), 1–15, 133–34; Massachusetts Historical Society, *Winthrop Papers*, 4 vols. (Boston: Massachusetts Historical; Society, 1944), 4: 319–20; Sybil Noyes, Charles T. Libby, and Walter G. Davis, eds., *Genealogical Dictionary of Maine and New Hampshire* (1928–1939; reprint, Baltimore, 1979), 378.

8. Paul J. Lindholt, ed., *John Josselyn, Colonial Traveler: A Critical Edition of Two Voyages to New England* (Hanover: University Press of New England, 1988), 20–21, 196.

9. Lindholt, ed., *John Josselyn*, 21, 188, 192.

10. Robert W. Lovett, ed., "Documents from the Harvard University Archives, 1638–1750," *Publications of the Colonial Society of Massachusetts,* 49 (1975): 150–51; Hall, *Worlds of Wonders, Days of Judgment,* 94; Halsey Thomas ed., *The Diary of Samuel Sewall,* 2 vols. (New York: Farrar, Strauss and Giroux, 1973), 1: 56.

11. Winship, *Seers of God,* 60–63; Increase Mather *An Essay for the Recording of Illustrious Providences* (Boston, 1684), preface.

12. Winship, *Seers of God,* 54–55.

13. The quotation is from Timothy Woodbridge in Cotton Mather, "Notes of Sermons . . . I Mather and Others, 1681–1682," section 25 (n.p. American

Antiquarian Society); Thomas, ed., *Diary of Samuel Sewall*, 1: 49; Winship, *Seers of God*, 54; Chamberlain, *Lithobolia*, 65, 75.

14. Mather, *Illustrious Providences*, 313–19; Stephen Foster, *The Long Argument: English Puritanism and the Shaping of New England Culture, 1570–1700* (Chapel Hill: University of North Carolina Press, 1991), 231–34; Thomas, ed., *Diary of Samuel Sewall*, 1: 52–53.

15. Malcolm Gaskill, *Witchfinders: A Seventeenth-Century English Tragedy* (Cambridge: Harvard University Press, 2005).

16. Keith Thomas, *Religion and the Decline of Magic* (New York: Charles Scribner's Sons, 1971) 577–580; Thomas Birch, *The Works of the Honorable Robert Boyle*, 5 vols. (London, 1744), 5: 244.

17. Joseph Glanvill, *Saducismus Triumphatus: Or, Full and Plain Evidence Concerning Witches and Apparitions* (London, 1688), 313–30; Gauld and Cornell, *Poltergeists*, 43–59.

18. Glanvill, *Saducismus Triumphatus*, 325; Mather, *Illustrious Providences*, 156–58; Gauld and Cornell, *Poltergeists*, 59.

19. Mather, *Illustrious Providences*, 156–67; Alfred O. Aldridge, "Franklin and the Ghostly Drummer of Tedworth," *William and Mary Quarterly*, 7 (1950): 555–67.

20. Mather, *Illustrious Providences*, 142–44. The following account of the Morse case draws heavily upon the excellent work of John P. Demos, *Entertaining Satan: Witchcraft and the Culture of Early New England* (New York: Oxford University Press, 1982), 132–52.

21. The Old Gaol is operated by the Old York Historical Society. The shoes were found during restoration work on it in 1999; Robert St. George, *Conversing By Signs: Poetics of Implication in Colonial New England Culture* (Chapel Hill: University of North Carolina Press, 1998), 184–95.

22. Mather, *Illustrious Providences*, 149–53.

23. David D. Hall, ed., *Witch-Hunting in Seventeenth-Century New England: A Documentary History, 1638–1692* (Boston: Northeastern University Press, 1991), 197–212; Demos, *Entertaining Satan*, 99–131; James Sharpe, *The Bewitching of Anne Gunther: A Horrible and True Story of Deception, Witchcraft, Murder and the King of England* (NY: Routledge, 1999).

24. Charles Bradley, Phil Dunning, and Gerard Gusset, "Material Culture from the *Elizabeth and Mary* (1690): Individuality and Social Status in a Late Seventeenth-Century New England Assemblage," in Christian Roy, Jean Bélisle, Marc-André Bernier, and Brad Loewen, *Mer et Monde: Questions D'Archéologie Maritime* (Québec: Assocation des Archéologues du Québec, 2003), 166–67.

25. This and the following paragraphs are based on Hall, ed., *Witch-Hunting in New England*, 238–39, 249–56; Demos, *Entertaining Satan*, 136–38, 150–52; Christine L. Heyrman, *Commerce and Culture: The Maritime Communities of Colonial Massachusetts, 1690–1750* (New York: W.W. Norton, 1984), 103–5, 107–8.

26. Noyes et al., *Genealogical Dictionary*, 494–95; William Drew, ed., *New Castle Walkabout* (New Castle, NH: Grist Mill Publishing Co., 1993), 25; Rockingham County Registry of Deeds, Kingston, New Hampshire, 3: 151a.

27. New Hampshire Provincial and State Papers, 40 vols., (Concord: State of New Hampshire: 1867–1943), 17: 527; 40: 342; Portsmouth Town Records, typescript at Portsmouth Public Library, 1: 154a–155b.

28. Portsmouth Town Records 1: 209a–211c; Nathaniel B. Shurtleff, ed., *Records of the Governor and Company of Massachusetts Bay in New England*, 5 vols. (Boston: Press of William White, 1853–4), 5: 133, 155.

29. Hall, *Witchcraft in New England*, 242–47, 256–57; Demos, *Entertaining Satan*, 142–43.

30. Stephen Nissenbaum, *The Battle for Christmas* (New York: Knopf, 1996), 16–17.

31. George F. Dow and Mary G. Thresher, eds., *Records and Files of the Quarterly Courts of Essex County, Massachusetts*, 9 vols. (Salem: Essex Institute, 1911–1975), 7: 331–32; Nissenbaum, *The Battle for Christmas*, 17–18.

Chapter Three: The Waltons

1. Walton garners the most attention from Richard Archer, who devotes the first two pages of his book to him. See Archer, *Fissures in the Rock: New England in the Seventeenth Century* (Hanover: University Press of New England), 1–3; Carol Karlsen mentions the case in *The Devil in the Shape of a Woman: Witchcraft in Colonial New England* (New York: W.W. Norton, 1987), 62–63, 262. See also Mary Beth Norton, *Founding Mothers and Fathers: Gendered Power and the Forming of American Society* (New York: Alfred A. Knopf, 1996), 245, 250; Sybil Noyes, Charles T. Libby, and Walter G. Davis, eds., *Genealogical Dictionary of Maine and New Hampshire* (1928–1939; reprint, Baltimore, 1979), 717.

2. In 1685, Walton deposed that he was "seventy years or thereabouts." *New Hampshire Provincial and State Papers*, 40 vols., (Concord: State of New Hampshire: 1867–1943), 1: 47–48; Noyes et al., eds., *Genealogical Dictionary*, 717; Nathaniel B. Shurtleff, ed., *Records of the Governor and Company of Massachusetts Bay in New England*, 5 vols. (Boston: Press of William White, 1853–4), 1: 245.

3. As Michael Winship has demonstrated, the "Antinomian Controversy" is an inaccurate label; however, since it is so widely employed it will be used here. Winship, *Making Heretics: Militant Protestantism and Free Grace in Massachusetts, 1636–1641* (Princeton: Princeton University Press, 2002), 1–27; Archer, *Fissures in the Rock*, 27–52.

4. Louis Breen, *Transgressing the Bounds: Subversive Enterprises among the Puritan Elite in Massachusetts, 1630–1692* (New York: Oxford University Press, 2001), 10, 17–56; Winship, *Making Heretics*, 149–87.

5. Jeremy Belknap, *The History of New Hampshire*, 3 vols. (Boston: 1792), 3: 339.

6. Winship, *Making Heretics*, 45, 209–15; Charles Clark, *The Eastern Frontier: The Settlement of Northern New England, 1610–1763* (Hanover: University Press of New England, 1970), 38–39; *New Hampshire Provincial and State Papers*, 1: 131–33.

7. Wheelwright's home was about forty miles from Threekingham. Noyes et al., *Genealogical Dictionary*, 590–91; "Parish Register Printouts of Threekingham, Lincoln, England; christenings, 1561–1830," accessed through the

International Genealogical Index, The Church of Jesus Christ of Latter-day Saints, Genealogical Department at www.familysearch.org.

8. Winship, *Making Heretics*, 215; Charles H. Bell, *History of the Town of Exeter, New Hampshire*, (Boston: J. E. Farwell, 1888) 15–19; Emery Battis, *Saints and Sectaries* (Chapel Hill: University of North Carolina Press, 1962), 261.

9. Bell, *History of Exeter*, 17–19, 37, 463–67; *New Hampshire Provincial and State Papers*, 40: 27, 41–42; Elmer Page, *Judicial Beginnings in New Hampshire, 1640–1700* (Concord: New Hampshire Historical Society, 1959), 123; John Scales, *Colonial Era History of Dover, New Hampshire* (Manchester: John B. Clark Co., 1923), 233–35.

10. Charles Hayes and John Scales, "Map of Hilton's Point and Dover Neck Village" in Scales, *History of Dover*, front piece.

11. The quotation is from Willem Sewel, *The History of the Rise, Increase, and Progress of the Christian People called Quakers* (Philadelphia: Samuel Keemer, 1728), 330; Noyes et al., *Genealogical Dictionary*, 331–36, 717–18; Scales, *History of Dover*, vii, 310–14; *New Hampshire Provincial and State Papers*, 40: 8.

12. Rockingham County Registry of Deeds, Kingston, New Hampshire, 1: 60, 75, 21: 233; *New Hampshire Provincial and State Papers*, 40: 101, 123, 457; Scales, *History of Dover*, vii.

13. The documents used to provide details on the Walton home are *Inventory of the Estate of Shadrach Walton*, October 26, 1742, New Hampshire State Archives, Concord, New Hampsire; Wolfgang Romer, "Sketch Map of Great Island or New Castle Island, showing plan of Town and Fort, etc. 1699," British Public Record Office, CO 700/North American Colonies, New Hampshire/4; Richard Chamberlain, "Lithobolia: The Stone-Throwing Devil," in George L. Burr, ed., *Narratives of the Witchcraft Cases* (New York: Charles Scribner's Sons, 1914), passim.

14. Portsmouth Town Records, typescript at Portsmouth Public Library 1: 8a, 10, 64a; Kenneth E. Maxam, "The Waltons of Great Island or New Castle, N. H., 1648–1800," typescript on file at the Portsmouth Athenaeum, 1980, 4.

15. *New Hampshire Provincial and State Papers*, 40: 127–28, 218.

16. Richard Archer, "New England Mosaic: A Demographic Analysis for the Seventeenth Century," *William and Mary Quarterly*, 3d Ser., 47 (1990): 488–89.

Chapter Four: The Neighbors from Hell

1. Richard Archer, *Fissures in the Rock: New England in the Seventeenth Century* (Hanover: University Press of New England, 2001), 2.

2. Christopher Hill, *The World Turned Upside Down: Radical Ideas during the English Revolution* (Harmondsworth, Middlesex: Penguin Books, 1972), 231–58; Jonathan Chu, *Neighbors, Friends, or Madmen: The Puritan Adjustment to Quakerism in Seventeenth-Century Massachusetts* (Westport, Conn.: Greenwood Press, 1985), 3–7, 35–51.

3. *New Hampshire Provincial and State Papers*, 40 vols., (Concord: State of New Hampshire: 1867–1943), 40: 130–31, 187–89, 309; Charles T. Libby and

Neal W. Allen eds., *Province and Court Records of Maine*, 6 vols. (Portland: Maine Historical Society, 1931–1975), 2: 18, 91; Charles Banks, *History of York, Maine*, 2 vols. (Boston: The Calkins Press, 1931–1935), 2: 113–19; Archer, *Fissures in the Rock*, 2.

4. Portsmouth Town Records, typescript at Portsmouth Public Library, 1: 85a; Sybil Noyes, Charles T. Libby, and Walter G. Davis, eds., *Genealogical Dictionary of Maine and New Hampshire* (1928–1939; reprint, Baltimore, 1979), 189; Libby and Allen, eds., *Province and Court Records of Maine*, 2: 129.

5. Portsmouth Town Records, 1:, 85a, 87a; *New Hampshire Provincial and State Papers*, 40: 184, 187, 505–6; George F. Dow and Mary G. Thresher, eds., *Records and Files of the Quarterly Courts of Essex County, Massachusetts*, 9 vols. (Salem: Essex Institute, 1911–1975), 2: 180; 3: 3.

6. *New Hampshire Provincial and State Papers*, 40: 228, 236, 241, 266, 269, 272–73, 283, 298, 307, 312, 318, 336, 359, 523, 535–36; Massachusetts Archives, Boston, 60: 263a, 264b, 273

7. Bruce Daniels, *Puritans at Play: Leisure and Recreation in Colonial New England* (New York: St. Martin's Press, 1995) 144–48. The tavern inventory was made after the death of Edward West's son, John. New Hampshire State Archives, Concord, Probate Records, 3: 73–74. *New Hampshire Provincial and State Papers*, 40: 83,

8. Daniels, *Puritans at Play*, 149; Richard Gildrie, *The Profane, the Civil, and the Godly: The Reformation of Manners in Orthodox New England, 1679–1749* (College Station: Pennsylvania State University Press, 1994), 63–83.

9. The best treatment of colonial taverns is Sharon V. Salinger, *Taverns and Drinking in Early America* (Baltimore: Johns Hopkins University Press, 2002).

10. *York Deeds,* 18 vols. (Portland: Maine Historical Society, 1887–1911), 2: 37, 186; 7: 123–24; *New Hampshire Provincial and State Papers*, 40: 193–96.

11. Massachusetts Archives, 38B: 154; *York Deeds*, 1: 13. Bernard Bailyn, *New England Merchants in the Seventeenth Century* (Cambridge: Harvard University Press, 1955).

12. Noyes et al., *Genealogical Dictionary*, 623–24, 691–92.

13. Noyes et al., *Genealogical Dictionary*, 133–34, 263–64, 331–36; Massachusetts Archives, 61: 113.

14. Noyes et al, *Genealogical Dictionary*, 590–91; Mary Walton was born about 1646.

15. *New Hampshire Provincial and State Papers*, 40: 92, 208; Noyes et al, *Genealogical Dictionary*, 590–91. Charles Clark, *The Eastern Frontier: The Settlement of Northern New England, 1610–1763* (Hanover: University Press of New England, 1970), 13, 35; Charles F. Carroll, *The Timber Economy of Puritan New England* (Providence: Brown University Press, 1973); Rockingham County Register of Deeds, Kingston, New Hampshire, 3: 5a.

16. New Hampshire State Archives, Concord, New Hampshire Court Records, 4: 203, 217, 221, 241; Noyes et al., *Genealogical Dictionary*, 672; Dow and Thresher, eds., *Quarterly Courts of Essex County* 1: 202.

17. New Hampshire Court Records, 4: 101; Noyes et al., *Genealogical Dictionary*, Noyes, et al., 672, 717; New Hampshire Archives, Concord, Court file #18231.

18. *New Hampshire Provincial and State Papers*, 40: 353, 357; Noyes et al. eds., *Genealogical Dictionary*, 574, 717; New Hampshire Archives, Concord, Court file #18231.

19. *New Hampshire Provincial and State Papers*, 31: 198–99, 233, 533; Noyes et al., *Genealogical Dictionary*, 182, 533, 740, 672. At least two of the maids were Walton's granddaughters; Richard Chamberlain, "Lithobolia: The Stone-Throwing Devil," in George L. Burr, ed., *Narratives of the Witchcraft Cases* (New York: Charles Scribner's Sons, 1914), 66–67; New Hampshire State Archives, Concord, New Hampshire Court Papers, 8: 419; Elwin Page, *Judicial Beginnings in New Hampshire, 1640–1700* (Concord: New Hampshire Historical Society, 1959), 105, following 128.

20. *New Hampshire Provincial and State Papers*, 40: 245.

21. *New Hampshire Provincial and State Papers*, 40: 107, 249, 283–84, 490, 523–24. Specifically, the inquest was concerning the death of "George Barton Mr. Job Waltons man brought into Court and is on file." The court recorder almost certainly made a transcription error, meaning to say "Job Barton, Mr. George Waltons man," for there are no other references in any surviving records for a George Barton or Job Walton.

22. *New Hampshire Provincial and State Papers*, 40: 263, 523; Noyes et al., *Genealogical Dictionary*, 189; Rockingham Deeds, 3: 51a. New Hampshire State Archives, Concord, Court file #26335.

23. *New Hampshire Provincial and State Papers*, 40: 129, 131. The quotation is from M. Halsey Thomas, ed., *The Diary of Samuel Sewall, 1674–1729*, 2 vols. (New York: Farrar, Straus and Giroux, 1973), 1: 10; Supreme Judicial Court of Massachusetts, dockets 1339, 1363, Massachusetts Archives; Noyes et al., *Genealogical Dictionary*, 208.

24. *New Hampshire Provincial and State Papers*, 31: 477–78, 514–19; Noyes et al., *Genealogical Dictionary*, 626; New Hampshire Archives, Concord, Court file #18231; Emerson W. Baker, "Trouble to the Eastward: The Failure of Anglo-Indian Relations in Early Maine," Ph.D. diss., College of William and Mary, 1985, 221–27; Colin Calloway, ed., *Dawnland Encounters: Indians and Europeans in Northern New England* (Hanover: University Press of New England, 1991), 96–100.

25. James D. Drake, *King Philip's War: Civil War in New England* (Amherst, University of Massachusetts Press, 1999), 168–196; Jill Lepore, *The Name of War: King Philip's War and the Origins of American Identity* (New York, Alfred A. Knopf, 1998). Drake, Lepore and others end the war in August 1676, with the death of King Phillip. However, hostilities continued in Maine and New Hampshire until 1678. See Emerson Baker and John Reid, *The New England Knight: Enrichment, Advancement, and the Life of Sir William Phips, 1651–1695* (Toronto: University of Toronto Press, 1998), 135–37.

26. Most of the fishing crews appear to have been from Essex County, though there could have been some from the Piscataqua region as well. Baker and Reid, *New England Knight*, 135–36.

27. New Hampshire Court File #18231.

28. New Hampshire Court File #18231; Noyes et al., *Genealogical Dictionary*, 355, 526–27.

29. Chamberlain, "Lithobolia," 72. Clark, *The Eastern Frontier*, 105; York Deeds, 4: 15.

Chapter Five: Fences and Neighbors

1. Portsmouth Town Records, typescript at Portsmouth Public Library, 1: 47b, 67b.

2. Gary T. Lord, "The Politics and Social Structure of Seventeenth-Century Portsmouth, New Hampshire," Ph.D. diss., University of Virginia, 74–77.

3. Portsmouth Town Records, 1: 9a, 45a, 187a; Lord, "Seventeenth-Century Portsmouth," 74–81.

4. David G. Allen, *In English Ways: The Movement of Societies and the Transferal of English Local Law and Custom to Massachusetts Bay in the Seventeenth Century* (Chapel Hill: University of North Carolina Press, 1981).

5. "List of Estates taken by Robert Elliott and Captain Stileman made townsmen for the year 1680," North Parish Records, Portsmouth Athenaeum.

6. Richard Chamberlain, "Lithobolia: The Stone-Throwing Devil," in George L. Burr, ed., *Narratives of the Witchcraft Cases* (New York: Charles Scribner's Sons, 1914), 60–61.

7. Chamberlain, "Lithobolia," 72, 75.

8. Charles F. Adams, *Three Episodes of Massachusetts History* (Boston: Houghton Mifflin, 1892) 135–55, 161, 321, 336–37.

9. Robert C. Anderson, *The Great Migration Begins: Immigrants to New England, 1620–1633*, 3 vols. (Boston: New England Historic Genealogical Society, 1995), 3: 1904–905; Sybil Noyes, Charles T. Libby, and Walter G. Davis, eds., *Genealogical Dictionary of Maine and New Hampshire* (1928–1939; reprint, Baltimore, 1979), 275, 712–13.

10. Noyes et al., *Genealogical Dictionary*, 712–13; Anderson, *The Great Migration Begins*, 3: 1902–903; Kenneth Maxam, "New Castle, New Hampshire Circa 1630–1700," manuscript on file at the Portsmouth Athenaeum, 3–5; Portsmouth Town Records, 1: 25a.

11. Portsmouth Town Records, 1: 14a, 20a, 118a.

12. New Hampshire Provincial Deeds, New Hampshire State Archives, Concord, 3: 54a.

13. Noyes et al., eds., *Genealogical Dictionary*, 384–85; Charles T. Libby and Neal W. Allen, eds., *Province and Court Records of Maine*, 6 vols. (Portland: Maine Historical Society, 1928–1931), 1: 118, 162, 168; 2: 433, 450; "List of Estates taken by Robert Elliott and Captain Stileman, 1680."

14. Portsmouth Town Records, 1: 11a.

15. *New Hampshire Provincial and State Papers*, 40 vols., (Concord: State of New Hampshire: 1867–1943), 40: 127, 137, 413–14.

16. *New Hampshire Provincial and State Papers*, 40: 148–49.

17. Noyes et al., *Genealogical Dictionary*, 712; *New Hampshire Provincial and State Papers*, 31: 43–44

18. The wedding date is based on the birth of their son. See Noyes et al., *Genealogical Dictionary*, 64; Portsmouth Town Records 1: 122a, 125b, 254a, 272b; Index, 8; New Hampshire State Archives, Concord, New Hampshire

Court Records, 7: 246, 275, 296, 313. The author is indebted to Alexandros Kyrou for ideas on the origins on John Amazeen.

19. *New Hampshire Provincial and State Papers*, 40: 2, 244; Portsmouth Town Records, 1: 122a, 125b, 219b.

20. *New Hampshire Provincial and State Papers*, 40: 264; "List of Estates taken by Robert Elliott and Captain Stileman, 1680."

21. *New Hampshire Provincial and State Papers*, 40: 2, 215.

22. *New Hampshire Provincial and State Papers*, 31: 87, 90; Walford signed his will on November 15, 1666; Noyes et al., *Genealogical Dictionary*, 698. The boy's sister, Martha Walford only received one sow as well.

23. *New Hampshire Provincial and State Papers*, 31: 91–92, 223.

24. *New Hampshire Provincial and State Papers*, 31: 92; Noyes et al., eds., *Genealogical Dictionary*, 112, 276–77, 609;

25. *New Hampshire Provincial and State Papers*, 31: 224; 40: 397.

26. Portsmouth Town Records, 1: 8–12; George F. Dow and Mary G. Thresher, eds., *Records and Files of the Quarterly Courts of Essex County, Massachusetts*, 9 vols. (Salem: Essex Institute, 1911–1975), 1: 202.

27. *New Hampshire Provincial and State Papers*, 40: 252–53. Portsmouth Town Records, 1: 83a, 85a.

28. *New Hampshire Provincial and State Papers*, 31: 299–300, 40: 246, 252; Noyes et al., *Genealogical Dictionary*, 249, 537;

29. Portsmouth Town Records, 1: 49a–b, 89a, 90b; *New Hampshire Provincial and State Papers*, 40: 203.

30. Increase Mather, *An Essay for the Recording of Illustrious Providences* (Boston, 1684), 208; New Hampshire Historical Society, *Collections* 8: (1866), 99–100.

Chapter Six: Neighbors and Witches

1. New Hampshire Historical Society, *Collections* 8: (1866), 100; Richard Chamberlain, "Lithobolia: The Stone-Throwing Devil," in George L. Burr, ed., *Narratives of the Witchcraft Cases* (New York: Charles Scribner's Sons, 1914), 76.

2. Carol Karlsen, *The Devil in the Shape of a Woman: Witchcraft in Colonial New England* (New York: W.W. Norton, 1987), 62–63, 262. *New Hampshire Provincial and State Papers*, 40 vols., (Concord: State of New Hampshire: 1867–1943), 40: 38.

3. David D. Hall, ed., *Witch-Hunting in Seventeenth-Century New England: A Documentary History, 1638–1692* (Boston: Northeastern University Press, 1991), 95–96; *New Hampshire Provincial and State Papers*, 1: 217–19.

4. Hall, *Witch-Hunting in New England*, 96.

5. Hall, *Witch-Hunting in New England*, 97; John Demos includes Mrs. Evans in his list of witchcraft accusations. John P. Demos, *Entertaining Satan: Witchcraft and the Culture of Early New England* (New York: Oxford University Press, 1982), 403.

6. Hall, *Witch-Hunting in New England*, 97. Trimmings referred to "Old Ham" a clear reference to William Ham senior. Ham was a West Country fisherman who had arrived in the region in the 1630s. Sybil Noyes, Charles T.

Libby, and Walter G. Davis, eds., *Genealogical Dictionary of Maine and New Hampshire* (1928–1939; reprint, Baltimore, 1979), 303.

7. Keith Thomas, *Religion and the Decline of Magic* (New York: Charles Scribner's Sons, 1971), 177–252.

8. *New Hampshire Provincial and State Papers,* 1: 219; Hall, *Witch-Hunting in New England,* 97.

9. Demos, *Entertaining Satan,* 292–300; Thomas, *Religion and the Decline of Magic,* 535–69; Alan Macfarlane, *Witchcraft in Tudor and Stuart England: A Regional and Comparative Study* (London: Routledge and Kegan Paul, 1970), 147–85.

10. *New Hampshire Provincial and State Papers,* 1: 87–88; Demos, *Entertaining Satan,* 275–312.

11. Noyes et al., *Genealogical Dictionary,* 79, 598; *New Hampshire Provincial and State Papers,* 40: 36–39, 46; Portsmouth Town Records, typescript at Portsmouth Public Library, 1: 33a.

12. Malcolm Gaskill, *Hellish Nell: Last of Britain's Witches* (New York: Harper Collins, 2002); Brian Levack, *The Witch-Hunt in Early Modern Europe* (New York: Longman, 1987), 21–26; Macfarlane, *Witchcraft in Tudor and Stuart England,* 186–89.

13. Karlsen, *Devil in the Shape of a Woman,* 47, 280–81; P. G. Maxwell-Stuart, *Witchcraft in Europe and the New World* (New York: Palgrave, 2001), 96–99; Carson O. Hudson Jr., *These Detestable Slaves of the Devill: A Concise Guide to Witchcraft in Colonial Virginia* (Haverford, PA.: Infinity Publishing, 2001), 35.

14. Levack, *The Witch-Hunt in Early Modern Europe,* 133–56; Robin Briggs, *Witches and Neighbors: The Social and Cultural Context of European Witchcraft* (New York: Viking, 1996), 17–59; *New Hampshire Provincial and State Papers,* 40: 129.

15. Gary T. Lord, "The Politics and Social Structure of Seventeenth-Century Portsmouth, New Hampshire," Ph.D. diss., University of Virginia, 120–28.

16. Hall, *Witch-Hunting in New England,* 97; Portsmouth Town Records, 14a, 15a, 18a, 33a.

17. Richard Archer, *Fissures in the Rock: New England in the Seventeenth Century* (Hanover: University Press of New England), 59–66, 180.

18. Lord, "Seventeenth-Century Portsmouth,"121–22; *New Hampshire Provincial and State Papers,* 40: 142–43; Portsmouth Town Records, 1: 52.

19. The following discussion of Eunice Cole and witchcraft in Hampton relies heavily on Demos, *Entertaining Satan,* 315–39. Many of the documents in the Cole case are reprinted in Hall, *Witch-Hunting in New England,* 213–29.

20. Demos, *Entertaining Satan,* 315–22; George F. Dow and Mary G. Thresher, eds., *Records and Files of the Quarterly Courts of Essex County, Massachusetts,* 9 vols. (Salem: Essex Institute, 1911–1975), 1: 88.

21. Demos, *Entertaining Satan,* 322–26.

22. Nathaniel B. Shurtleff, ed., *Records of the Governor and Company of Massachusetts Bay in New England,* 5 vols. (Boston: Press of William White, 1853–4), 4: pt. 2, 554, 572–73. The quotation is on 554.

23. Noyes et al., *Genealogical Dictionary*, 41, 184–85; *New Hampshire Court Records*, 3: 375–86. The quotation is from page 377.
24. *New Hampshire Court Records*, 3: 375–86; James P. Baxter, ed., *Documentary History of the State of Maine*, 24 vols. (Portland: Maine Historical Society, 1889–1916), 6: 45–88.
25. Demos, *Entertaining Satan*, 326–31.
26. Increase Mather, *An Essay for the Recording of Illustrious Providences* (Boston, 1684), 85–86; Hall, *Witch-Hunting in New-England*, 192.
27. Hall, *Witch-Hunting in New-England*, 192–94; Demos, *Entertaining Satan*, 330–31.
28. Demos, *Entertaining Satan*, 330–31.
29. Paul Boyer and Stephen Nissenbaum, *Salem Possessed: The Social Origins of Witchcraft* (Cambridge: Harvard University Press, 1974), 133–51.
30. Karlsen, *Devil in the Shape of a Woman*, 101–15; L. S. Davidson and John O. Ward, ed. and trans., *The Sorcery Trial of Alice Kyteler* (Binghamton, NY: Medieval and Renaissance Texts and Studies, 1993), 8–11.
31. Mary Beth Norton, *Founding Mothers and Fathers: Gendered Power and the Forming of American Society* (New York: Alfred A. Knopf, 1996), 250.
32. James Sharp, *The Bewitchment of Anne Gunter: A Horrible and True Story of Deception, Witchcraft, Murder, and the King of England* (New York: Routledge, 1999).

Chapter Seven: Great Island's Great Matter

1. *New Hampshire Provincial and State Papers*, 40 vols., (Concord: State of New Hampshire: 1867–1943), 40: 188, 506, 514; Gary T. Lord, "The Politics and Social Structure of Seventeenth-Century Portsmouth, New Hampshire," Ph.D. diss., University of Virginia, 123.
2. Roger Thompson, *Divided We Stand: Watertown, Massachusetts, 1630–1680* (Amherst: University of Massachusetts Press, 2001).
3. Philip Greven, *Four Generations: Population, Land, and Family in Colonial Andover, Massachusetts* (Ithaca: Cornell University Press, 1970), 40–62.
4. Greven, *Four Generations*, 53–65, 72–124.
5. Kenneth Lockridge, *A New England Town: The First Hundred Years* (New York: W.W. Norton and Co., 1970).
6. Lord, "Seventeenth-Century Portsmouth," 85.
7. Lord, "Seventeenth-Century Portsmouth," 248.
8. Nathaniel B. Shurtleff, ed., *Records of the Governor and Company of Massachusetts Bay in New England*, 5 vols. (Boston: Press of William White, 1853–54) 5: 231; Portsmouth Town Records, typescript at Portsmouth Public Library 1: 219; Lord, "Seventeenth-Century Portsmouth," 248–50.
9. Lord, "Seventeenth-Century Portsmouth," 250–51; Massachusetts Archives 10: 155; Portsmouth Town Records 1: 148.
10. Lord, "Seventeenth-Century Portsmouth," 252; Portsmouth Town Records 1: 206, 219; Shurtleff, *Massachusetts Bay Records*, 5: 76.
11. Lord, "Seventeenth-Century Portsmouth," 251–52; Portsmouth Town Records 206–7, 219; Shurtleff, *Massachusetts Bay Records*, 5: 249; Massachusetts Archives 10: 154.

12. Lord, "Seventeenth-Century Portsmouth," 247–58; *New Hampshire Provincial and State Papers*, 19: 685.

13. Richard Chamberlain, "Lithobolia: The Stone-Throwing Devil," in George L. Burr, ed., *Narratives of the Witchcraft Cases* (New York: Charles Scribner's Sons, 1914), 65, 75; Sybil Noyes, Charles T. Libby, and Walter G. Davis, eds., *Genealogical Dictionary of Maine and New Hampshire* (1928–1939; reprint, Baltimore, 1979), 768–69; John L. Sibley et al., *Biographical Sketches of Graduates of Harvard University, in Cambridge, Massachusetts*, 17 vols. (Cambridge: Harvard University Press, 1933), 1: 20–27; 2: 155–59, 464–70, 536.

14. Noyes et al, *Genealogical Dictionary*, 769; Henry Burrage, *History of the Baptists in Maine* (Portland: Marks House Printing, 1904), 16–17; Sibley, *Graduates of Harvard University*, 2: 464–70, 536. Reverend Moody counted on Woodbridge to provide him with details of lithobolia.

15. Lord, "Seventeenth-Century Portsmouth," 250; *New Hampshire Provincial and State Papers*, 19:672; Massachusetts Archives, 10: 155.

16. "List of Estates taken by Robert Elliott and Captain Stileman made townsmen for the year 1680," North Parish Records, Portsmouth Athenaeum.

17. The quotation is from *New Hampshire Provincial and State Papers*, 12: 672. Italics have been added for emphasis; Noyes et al., eds., *Genealogical Dictionary*, 219, 249, 337–38, 375–76; Chamberlain, "Lithobolia," 75.

18. William Edmundson, *A Journal of the Life, Travels, Sufferings, and Labour of Love in the Work of the Ministry, of that Worthy Elder and Faithful Servant of Jesus Christ, William Edmundson* (Dublin: 1820), 105–6; Charles Pettingell, "Quakerism in the Piscataqua: A Historical Address Delivered Before the Piscataqua Pioneers at Exeter, New Hampshire August 7, 1945," (n.d.: n.p.), 11–13.

19. *New Hampshire Provincial and State Papers*, 12: 672.

20. Christopher Hill, *The World Turned Upside Down: Radical Ideas During the English Revolution* (Harmondsworth, UK: Penguin Books, 1975), 231–41; Philip Gura, *A Glimpse of Sion's Glory: Puritan Radicalism in New England, 1620–1660* (Middletown: Wesleyan University Press), 144–45; Jonathan Chu, *Neighbors, Friends, or Madmen: The Puritan Adjustment to Quakerism in Seventeenth-Century Massachusetts* (Westport, Conn.: Greenwood Press, 1985), 106–9;

21. Hill, *The World Turned Upside Down*, 241.

22. Chu, *Neighbors, Friends, or Madmen*, 35–48; Gura, *A Glimpse of Sion's Glory*, 144–52; Carla Gardina Pestana, *Quakers and Baptists in Colonial Massachusetts* (New York: Cambridge University Press, 1991), 25–38.

23. Pestana, *Quakers and Baptists*, 36–40.

24. George Bishop, *New England Judged by the Spirit of the Lord* (London: T. Sowle, 1703), 227–29.

25. Bishop, *New England Judged*, 229–30.

26. Chu, *Neighbors, Friends, or Madmen*, 105–10; William Sewel, *History of the Rise, Increase and Progress of the Christian People called Quakers* (Philadelphia, 1728), 330.

27. Sewel, *History of the Rise of Quakers*, 330.

28. James P. Baxter, ed., *Documentary History of the State of Maine*, 24 vols. (Portland: Maine Historical Society, 1889–1916), 4: 113; 6: 46–47; Noyes et al., *Genealogical Dictionary*, 331–32, 624, 691–92.

29. Pettingell, "Quakerism in the Piscataqua;" Noyes et al., *Genealogical Dictionary*, 251.

30. Peter Elmer, "'Saints or Sorcerers: Quakerism, Demonology and the Decline of Witchcraft in Seventeenth-Century England," in Jonathan Barry, Marianne Hester, and Gareth Roberts, eds., *Witchcraft in Early Modern Europe* (Cambridge: Cambridge University Press, 1996), 145–49; Richard Godbeer, *The Devil's Dominion: Magic and Religion in Early New England* (New York: Cambridge University Press, 1994), 193–96. The quotation is from Richard Baxter, *The Certainty of the World of Spirits* (London: 1691), 175.

31. Godbeer, *The Devil's Dominion*, 194–95; Christine L. Heyrman, *Commerce and Culture: The Maritime Communities of Colonial Massachusetts, 1690–1750* (New York: W.W. Norton, 1984), 96–142. The quotation is from James Allen, Joshua Moodey, and Samuel Willard, *The Principles of Protestant Religion Maintained* (Boston, 1690), preface.

32. David Underdown, *Revel, Riot and Rebellion: Popular Politics and Culture in England 1603–1660* (New York: Oxford University Press, 1985), 252–55.

33. George F. Dow and Mary G. Thresher, eds., *Records and Files of the Quarterly Courts of Essex County, Massachusetts*, 9 vols. (Salem: Essex Institute, 1911–1975), 8: 222–26, 340–43.

34. Bishop, *New England Judged*, 267; Chamberlain, "Lithobolia," 69.

35. Burrage, *Baptists in Maine*, 13–17; Noyes et al., eds., *Genealogical Dictionary*, 177–79, 421, 615; T. L. Underwood, ed., *The Acts of the Witnesses: The Autobiography of Lodowick Muggleton and Other Early Muggletonian Writings* (New York: Oxford University Press, 1999), 27, 63–65, 212.

36. Burrage, *Baptists in Maine*, 13–17; Noyes et al., *Genealogical Dictionary*, 135–37, 177–78.

37. Gura, *A Glimpse of Sion's Glory*, 93–125; Pestana, *Quakers and Baptists*, 45–65, 85.

38. Shurtleff, *Massachusetts Bay Records*, 5: 347; Burrage, *Baptists in Maine*, 16–17; Charles T. Libby and Neal W. Allen eds., *Province and Court Records of Maine*, 6 vols. (Portland: Maine Historical Society, 1931–1975), 3: xxxiv–xxxviii.

Chapter Eight: The Mason Family Stakes Its Claim

1. W. Noel Sainsbury et al, eds., *Calendar of State Papers, Colonial Series, American and the West Indies*, 42 vols. (London: Her Majesty's Stationary Office, 1860–1953), 11: 27.

2. David Van Deventer, *The Emergence of Provincial New Hampshire, 1623–1741* (Baltimore: Johns Hopkins University Press, 1976), 40–51; Elwin Page, *Judicial Beginnings in New Hampshire, 1640–1700* (Concord: New Hampshire Historical Society, 1959), 183–234; Theodore Lewis, "Royal Government in New Hampshire and the Revocation of the Charter

of the Massachusetts Bay Colony, 1679–1683," *Historical New Hampshire* 25 (1970), 3–45.

3. Charles Clark, *The Eastern Frontier: The Settlement of Northern New England, 1610–1763* (Hanover: University Press of New England, 1970), 16–17. Charles W. Tuttle, *Captain John Mason, the Founder of New Hampshire* (Boston: The Prince Society, 1887), 9–17; James P. Baxter, ed., *Documentary History of the State of Maine*, 24 vols. (Portland: Maine Historical Society, 1889–1916), 7: 27. Van Deventer, *Province of New Hampshire*, 40–61; Page, *Judicial Beginnings in New Hampshire, 1640–1700*, 183–234.

4. Baxter, ed. *Documentary History of Maine*, 7: 64–65; Tuttle, *Captain John Mason*, 44–48.

5. Jere Daniell, *Colonial New Hampshire: A History* (Millwood, NY.: KTO Press, 1981), 21; Tuttle, *Captain John Mason*, 17–18; Faith Harrington, "'Wee Tooke Great Store of Cod-Fish,': Fishing Ships and First Settlements on the Coast of New England, 1600–1630," in Emerson Baker et al., eds., *American Beginnings: Exploration, Culture and Cartography in the Land of Norumbega* (Lincoln: University of Nebraska Press, 1994), 214–15.

6. Tuttle, *Captain John Mason*, 20–21; 255–56; Robert C. Anderson, *The Great Migration Begins: Immigrants to New England, 1620–1633*, 3 vols. (Boston: New England Historic Genealogical Society, 1995), 2: 794–95.

7. Clark, *Eastern Frontier*, 16–17; John Reid, *Acadia, Maine, and New Scotland: Marginal Colonies in the Seventeenth Century* (Toronto: University of Toronto Press, 1981), 90.

8. Jeremy Belknap, *The History of New Hampshire*, 3 vols. (Dover: S.C. Stevens & Wadleigh, 1831), 1: 9–12.

9. Francis Bremer, *John Winthrop: America's Forgotten Founding Father* (New York: Oxford University Press, 2003), 230–36.

10. This and the following paragraphs are drawn from Tuttle, *Captain John Mason*, 28–30; Belknap, *History of New Hampshire*, 1: 14–15; Van Deventer, *Provincial New Hampshire*, 40–44; Clark, *Eastern Frontier*, 42–46, 53–54; John Scales, *Colonial Era History of Dover, New Hampshire* (Manchester: John B. Clark Co., 1923), 105–6, 145–50.

11. Reid, *Acadia, Maine, and New Scotland*, 90; Clark, *The Eastern Frontier*, 44–51. John Reid, *Maine, Charles II, and Massachusetts : Governmental Relationships in Early Northern New England* (Portland: Maine Historical Society, 1977), 11–14.

12. Massachusetts Archives, 3: 289–93; Sybil Noyes, Charles T. Libby, and Walter G. Davis, eds., *Genealogical Dictionary of Maine and New Hampshire* (1928–1939; reprint, Baltimore, 1979), 436–37, 464–65; Baxter, *Documentary History*, 4: 312, 318–19, 323; *New Hampshire Provincial and State Papers*, 40 vols., (Concord: State of New Hampshire: 1867–1943), 17: 517–19; Page, *Judicial Beginnings of New Hampshire*, 190–92; Reid, *Maine, Charles II and Massachusetts*, 118.

13. Noyes et al., eds., *Genealogical Dictionary*, 468, 772; *New Hampshire Provincial and State Papers*, 40: 79.

14. *New Hampshire Provincial and State Papers*, 40: 110–11, 118–19, 123. Noyes et al., *Genealogical Dictionary*, 698, 772.

15. Van Deventer, *Provincial New Hampshire*, 43. Reid, *Maine, Charles II and Massachusetts*, 60–77.

16. Sainsbury et al., eds., *Calendar of State Papers*, 5: 307–8, 314; *New Hampshire Provincial and State Papers*, 17: 537; Reid, *Maine, Charles II, and Massachusetts*, 86–88.

17. Sainsbury et al., eds., *Calendar of State Papers*, 5: 307–8; *New Hampshire Provincial and State Papers*, 17: 510–12.

18. Massachusetts Archives, 3: 291; Baxter, ed., *Documentary History*, 4: 318–19; Noyes, et al., *Genealogical Dictionary*, 436–37, 465; Van Deventer, *Provincial New Hampshire*, 46.

19. This and the following paragraphs are based on Michael Hall, *Edward Randolph and the American Colonies, 1676–1703* (New York, W.W. Norton, 1960), 4, 19–20, 36–52; Van Deventer, *Provincial New Hampshire*, 44–46; Lewis, "Royal Government in New Hampshire," 21–22.

20. *New Hampshire Provincial and State Papers*, 17: 526–27; John P. Demos, *Entertaining Satan: Witchcraft and the Culture of Early New England* (New York: Oxford University Press, 1982), 332–33.

21. Sainsbury et al., eds., *Calendar of State Papers*, 11: 43–44; *New Hampshire Provincial and State Papers*, 40: 371, 373; Daniell, *Colonial New Hampshire*, 83–84.

22. Sainsbury et al., eds., *Calendar of State Papers*, 11: 43–34, 111; Clark, *Eastern Frontier*, 59.

23. Richard Chamberlain, "Lithobolia: The Stone-Throwing Devil," in George L. Burr, ed., *Narratives of the Witchcraft Cases* (New York: Charles Scribner's Sons, 1914), 55–57.

24. Daniell, *Colonial New Hampshire*, 82; Belknap, *History of New Hampshire*, 1: 90–94.

25. Sainsbury et al., eds., *Calendar of State Papers*, 11: 48.

26. Page, *Judicial Beginnings in New Hampshire*, 33–34; Daniell, *Colonial New Hampshire*, 83.

27. Sainsbury et al., eds., *Calendar of State Papers*, 11: 41–46, 138–39; Page, *Judicial Beginnings in New Hampshire*, 196–200; Daniell, *Colonial New Hampshire*, 84–85.

28. Sainsbury et al., eds., *Calendar of State Papers*, 11: 47, 62–64; Page, *Judicial Beginnings in New Hampshire*, 200–1; Clark, *Eastern Frontier*, 60.

29. Sainsbury et al., eds., *Calendar of State Papers*, 11: 11, 174.

30. Sainsbury et al., eds., *Calendar of State Papers*, 11: 186, 199, 201, 213; Daniell, *Colonial New Hampshire*, 86.

31. Robert Toppan and Alfred Goodrick, eds., *Edward Randolph*, 7 vols. (Boston: Prince Society, 1898–1909), 3: 154–55.

32. Sainsbury et al., eds., *Calendar of State Papers*, 11: 213. The quitrent rate was 6 pence per pound of value.

33. The author thanks Nancy Schultz for suggesting the Mason-Pyncheon link. Sir William Phips may have also served as the inspiration for the Pyncheons; Emerson Baker and James Kences, "Maine, Indian Land Speculation, and the Essex County Witchcraft Outbreak of 1692," *Maine History*, 40, no. 3 (2001), 182.

34. Chamberlain, "Lithobolia," 72.
35. Chamberlain, "Lithobolia," 68, 70, 71, 72.
36. Rockingham County Register of Deeds, Kensington, New Hampshire, 3: 181b.
37. *New Hampshire Provincial and State Papers*, 31: 224; 40: 397. The fate of Walford's appeal is unknown.
38. New Hampshire Historical Society, *Collections* 8 (1866): 118.
39. Sainsbury et al., eds., *Calendar of State Papers*, 11: 409, 526, 542, 574, 580; *New Hampshire Provincial and State Papers*, 392.
40. Page, *Judicial Beginnings in New Hampshire*, 204–10.

Chapter Nine: The Spread of Lithobolia

1. Increase Mather, *An Essay for the Recording of Illustrious Providences* (Boston, 1684), 167.
2. Mather, *Illustrious Providences*, 164–65.
3. Mather, *Illustrious Providences*, 165–66.
4. Mather, *Illustrious Providences*, 166–67.
5. Charles T. Libby and Neal W. Allen, eds., *Province and Court Records of Maine*, 6 vols. (Portland: Maine Historical Society, 1928–1931), 2: xvii–xviii, 237; Massachusetts Archives, Boston, Suffolk County Court File, 1126.
6. David Cressy, *Bonfires and Bells: National Memory and the Protestant Calendar in Elizabethan and Stuart England* (Berkley: University of California Press, 1989), particularly 141–155.
7. Stephen Innes, *Creating Commonwealth: The Economic Culture of Puritan New England* (New York: W.W. Norton, 1995), 295–96; Bernard Bailyn, *New England Merchants in the Seventeenth Century* (Cambridge: Harvard University Press, 1955), 83–84; Libby and Allen, eds., *Province and Court Records of Maine*, 2: 271.
8. Sybil Noyes, Charles T. Libby, and Walter G. Davis, eds., *Genealogical Dictionary of Maine and New Hampshire* (1928–1939; reprint, Baltimore, 1979), 657.
9. The quotation is from Richard Dunn, James Savage and Laetitia Yeandle, eds., The *Journal of John Winthrop*, 1630–1649 (Cambridge: Harvard University Press), 432; Charles Banks, *History of York, Maine*, 2 vols. (Boston: The Calkins Press, 1931–1935), 120–30, 2: 110–25.
10. Noyes, et al., *Genealogical Dictionary*, 705; Charles Banks, *History of York, Maine*, 2 vols. (Boston: The Calkins Press, 1931–1935), 1: 217–18; Libby and Allen, eds., *Province and Court Records of Maine*, 2: 214, 228, 483.
11. Libby and Allen, eds., *Province and Court Records of Maine*, 2: 483–84.
12. *York Deeds*, 18 vols. (Portland: Maine Historical Society, 1887–1911), 2: 188; 8: 204; Noyes, et al., eds., *Genealogical Dictionary*, 762–63, 771–72; Everett Stackpole, *Old Kittery and Her Families* (Lewiston, ME: Press of the Lewiston Journal, 1903), 132–35; Libby and Allen, eds., *Province and Court Records of Maine*, 2: 271, 480–84.
13. Noyes, et al., *Genealogical Dictionary*, 762, 560; *York Deeds*, 3: 1, 125–26; 4: 8, 50; 6: 21–22, 112–13; Halsey Thomas ed., *The Diary of Samuel Sewall*, 2 vols. (New York: Farrar, Strauss, and Giroux, 1973), 1: 149.

14. Jonathan Chu, *Neighbors, Friends, or Madmen: The Puritan Adjustment to Quakerism in Seventeenth-Century Massachusetts* (Westport, Conn.: Greenwood Press, 1985), 105–17.

15. Banks, *History of York*, 1: 206–8. Charles E. Banks, "Scotch Prisoners Deported to New England by Cromwell 1651–52," Massachusetts Historical Society *Proceedings*, 61 (1927), 4–29; Malcolm Atkin, *Cromwell's Crowning Mercy: The Battle of Worcester, 1651* (Thrupp, Gloucestershire: Sutton Publishing, 1998), 123–133.

16. Banks, "Scotch Prisoners Deported to New England," 4–29. Another community established itself a few miles away at "Scotland" on the upper reaches of the York River.

17. Chu, *Neighbors, Friends or Madmen*, 105–17; Libby and Allen, eds., *Province and Court Records of Maine*, 2: 184, 226, 306; 3: 54, 117, 284; Noyes, et al., eds., *Genealogical Dictionary*, 721; *Collections of the Massachusetts Historical Society* 4th Ser., 8: (1868), 359–61; Emerson is first noted as preaching in Berwick in 1680, but may not have taken residence there until 1681 or 1682. John L. Sibley, et al., *Biographical Sketches of Graduates of Harvard University, in Cambridge, Massachusetts*, 17 vols. (Cambridge: Charles William Sever, 1881), 2: 472–74.

18. Mather, *Illustrious Providences*, 165. Chamberlain does not mention the Fortado case.

19. Mary Beth Norton, *Founding Mothers and Fathers: Gendered Power and the Forming of American Society* (New York: Alfred A. Knopf, 1996), 77–80; Noyes, et al., eds., *Genealogical Dictionary*, 771; Libby and Allen, eds., *Province and Court Records of Maine*, 4: 88, 91.

20. Mather, *Illustrious Providences*, 167.

21. Alan C. Dessen and Leslie Thomson, *A Dictionary of Stage Directions in English Drama 1580–1642* (Cambridge: Cambridge University Press 1999), 187.

22. Mather, *Illustrious Providences*, 167; *Collections of the Massachusetts Historical Society* 4th Ser., 8: (1868), 361–62.

23. David Cressy, *Agnes Bowker's Cat: Travesties and Transgressions in Tudor and Stuart England* (New York: Oxford University Press, 2001), 29–50; For details on the Antinomian monstrous births see Carol Karlsen, *The Devil in the Shape of a Woman: Witchcraft in Colonial New England* (New York: W.W. Norton, 1987), 16–17; Dunn et al., eds., *Journal of John Winthrop*, 253–35.

24. Dunn et al., eds., *Journal of John Winthrop*, 255, 330; Karlsen, *Devil in the Shape of a Woman*, 16–18, 123–24.

25. Henry Waters, *Genealogical Gleanings in England*, 2 vols. (Baltimore: Genealogical Publishing Company, 1969), 1: 251–52; Robert St. George, *Conversing By Signs: Poetics of Implication in Colonial New England Culture* (Chapel Hill: University of North Carolina Press, 1998), 22–26; Michael S. Disbrow, comp., "Descendants of Thomas and Mercy (Holbridge) Disbrow, Part I: The First Six Generations," Manuscript on file at the Connecticut State Library, Hartford, 1992. There is no evidence of a family tie to Mercy Holbridge Desborough, who was accused of witchcraft in Fairfield, Connecticut in 1692. John Desborough's brother Samuel lived close to Hartford, in Guilford, Connecticut, from 1639 until he returned to England in 1651.

26. Laurence Hauptman, "The Pequot War and its Legacies," in Laurence Hauptman and James Wherry, eds., *The Pequots in Southern New England: The Rise and Fall of an American Indian Nation* (Norman: University of Oklahoma Press, 1990), 71–77.

27. *Collections of the Connecticut Historical Society* 6: (1897), 130; William D. Love, *The Colonial History of Hartford* (Hartford: The Plimpton Press, 1914), 146–47. Technically, Desborough was a joiner, a man who attached pieces of wood with mortise and tenon joints.

28. The quote is from "Records of the Particular Court of Connecticut, 1639–1663," *Collections of the Connecticut Historical Society*, 22: (1928), 10, 12; "Hartford Town Votes," *Collections of the Connecticut Historical Society* 6: (1897), 83, 103, 137, 148 and 158. The population estimate is derived from the 1669 listed of freemen, which numbered 120 men. See J. Hammond Trumbull, *The Public Records of the Colony of Connecticut, from 1665 to 1678* (Hartford: F.A. Brown, 1852), 2: 518–19.

29. Hartford Probate Records, Connecticut State Archives, 1: 155. Helen S. Ullmann, ed., *Hartford County Court Minutes, Volumes 3 and 4, 1663–1687, 1697* (Boston: New England Historical Genealogical Society, 2005), 127.

30. *Collections of the Massachusetts Historical Society* 4th Ser., 8: (1868), 86–88; Ullmann, ed., *Hartford County Court Minutes*, 323.

31. *Collections of the Massachusetts Historical Society* 4th Ser., 8: (1868), 86–87.

32. *Collections of the Massachusetts Historical Society* 4th Ser., 8: (1868), 87; Mather, *Illustrious Providences*, 159–60.

33. *Collections of the Massachusetts Historical Society* 4th Ser., 8: (1868), 87.

34. *Collections of the Connecticut Historical Society*, 22: 77.

35. Richard Chamberlain, "Lithobolia: The Stone-Throwing Devil," in George L. Burr, ed., *Narratives of the Witchcraft Cases* (New York: Charles Scribner's Sons, 1914), 69; For early communication networks, see Richard D. Brown, *Knowledge is Power: The Diffusion of Information in Early America, 1700–1865* (New York: Oxford University Press, 1989), 16–41; *New Hampshire Provincial and State Papers*, 40 vols., (Concord: State of New Hampshire: 1867–1943), 18: 922–23. The shipping figures are for 1681.

36. Ullmann, ed., *Hartford County Court Minutes*, 175, 196, 297, 320, 372; Noyes, et al., *Genealogical Dictionary*, 768–69.

37. Noyes, et al., *Genealogical Dictionary*, 444; The Wyllys Papers, *Collections of the Connecticut Historical Society* 21: (1924), xxxv–xxxvii, 307–9, 484; Wyllys was a leading Connecticut magistrate. His papers are an invaluable source for the Connecticut witchcraft outbreak of 1692.

Chapter Ten: To Salem

1. Paul Boyer and Stephen Nissenbaum, eds., *The Salem Witchcraft Papers: Verbatim Transcripts of the Legal Documents of the Salem Witchcraft Outbreak of 1692* (New York: Da Capo Press, 1977), 1: 225–26.

2. Boyer and Nissenbaum, eds., *Salem Witchcraft Papers*, 1: 233.

3. "A Faithful and Wonderful Account of the Surprising Things which happened in the Town of Glocester, in the Year, 1692" by JE (John Emerson), May 19, 1693, in Cotton Mather, *Decennium Luctuosum* (Boston, 1699),

104–112; the quote is from page 105. Christine L. Heyrman, *Commerce and Culture: The Maritime Communities of Colonial Massachusetts, 1690–1750* (New York: W.W. Norton, 1984), 105–6.

4. Paul Boyer and Stephen Nissenbaum, *Salem Possessed: The Social Origins of Witchcraft* (Cambridge: Harvard University Press, 1974), 37–59. In their brilliant study, *Salem Possessed*, Paul Boyer and Stephen Nissenbaum have explored the religious and political limbo and local conflict that Salem endured. They stress that the village's unusual status seriously disrupted the community. The following paragraphs are basedly largely on this work.

5. Boyer and Nissenbaum, *Salem Possessed*, 40–43.

6. Boyer and Nissenbaum, *Salem Possessed*, 43; Kenneth Lockridge, *A New England Town: The First Hundred Years* (New York: W.W. Norton and Co., 1970), 93–118; Sumner Powell, *Puritan Village: The Formation of a New England Town* (Middletown: Wesleyan University Press, 1963), 116–46.

7. Boyer and Nissenbaum, *Salem Possessed*, 43–59.

8. *New Hampshire Provincial and State Papers*, 40 vols., (Concord: State of New Hampshire: 1867–1943), 12: 672; Richard Latner, "'Here Are No Newters': Witchcraft and Religious Discord in Salem Village and Andover," *New England Quarterly* 79: (2006), 92–122.

9. Heyrman, *Commerce and Culture*, 108–17; Richard Godbeer, *The Devil's Dominion: Magic and Religion in Early New England* (New York: Cambridge University Press, 1994), 193–99.

10. David Lovejoy, *The Glorious Revolution in America* (New York: Harper and Rowe, 1972), 150–59, 175–95. New York and New Jersey were added to the Dominion in 1688.

11. Lovejoy, *The Glorious Revolution*, 191–95.

12. Mary Beth Norton, *In the Devil's Snare: The Salem Witchcraft Crisis of 1692* (New York: Alfred A. Knopf, 2002) 77–78; Richard Godbeer, *Escaping Salem: The Other Witch Hunt of 1692* (New York: Oxford University Press, 2004), 8–9; John P. Demos, *Entertaining Satan: Witchcraft and the Culture of Early New England* (New York: Oxford University Press, 1982), 405; David D. Hall, ed., *Witch-Hunting in Seventeenth-Century New England: A Documentary History, 1638–1692* (Boston: Northeastern University Press, 1991), 147–63.

13. Nicholas Crouch, *The Kingdom of Darkness* (London: 1688), 15–42.

14. Boyer and Nissenbaum, eds., *Salem Witchcraft Papers*, 2: 404, 3: 778.

15. The list of cases from 1662 to 1679 is drawn from Demos, *Entertaining Satan*, 405–6.

16. Norton argues convincingly that Tituba was a Native American. See *In the Devil's Snare*, 20–21, 334–35; John McWilliam, "Indian John and the Northern Tawnies," *New England Quarterly* 69: (1996), 580–604; Elaine Breslaw, *Tituba, Reluctant Witch of Salem: Devilish Indians and Puritan Fantasies* (New York: New York University, 1997).

17. M. Halsey Thomas, ed., *The Diary of Samuel Sewall, 1674–1729*, 2 vols. (New York: Farrar, Straus and Giroux, 1973), 1: 49.

18. Sybil Noyes, Charles T. Libby, and Walter G. Davis, eds., *Genealogical Dictionary of Maine and New Hampshire* (1928–1939; reprint, Baltimore, 1979), 631, 762–63; Emma Coleman, *New England Captives Carried to Canada Be-*

tween 1677 and 1760 During the French and Indian War, 2 vols. (Portland: The Southworth Press, 1925), 1: 182–95; James P. Baxter, ed., *Documentary History of the State of Maine,* 24 vols. (Portland: Maine Historical Society, 1889–1916), 5: 57.

19. Coleman, *New England Captives Carried to Canada,* 1: 188–89, 192–93; Noyes et al., eds., *Genealogical Dictionary,* 631.

20. Cotton Mather, "A Brand Pluck'd out of the Burning," in George L. Burr, ed., *Narratives of the Witchcraft Cases* (New York: Charles Scribner's Sons, 1914), 253–87. Chadwick Hansen, *Witchcraft at Salem* (New York: George Braziller, 1969), 172–78; Norton, *In the Devil's Snare,* 176–81.

21. Mather, "A Brand Pluck'd out of the Burning," 261, 274, 282; Norton, *In the Devil's Snare,* 180.

22. Mather, "A Brand Pluck'd out of the Burning," 261; Ruth Holmes Whitehead, *Elitekey: Micmac Material Culture from 1600 to Present* (Halifax: The Nova Scotia Museum, 1980), 19–22; Emerson Baker and John Reid, *The New England Knight: Sir William Phips, 1651–1695* (Toronto: University of Toronto Press, 1998), following 104; Norton, *In the Devil's Snare,* 179–81.

23. For an overview of the extensive literature on witchcraft and the frontier see Emerson Baker and James Kences, "Maine, Indian Land Speculation, and the Essex County Witchcraft Outbreak of 1692," *Maine History* 31: (2001), 160–61, 183; Norton, *In the Devil's Snare,* 319–20.

24. Marilynne Roach, *The Salem Witch Trials: A Day-by-Day Chronicle of a Community Under Siege* (New York: Cooper Square Press, 2002), 101–2, 106–8; Boyer and Nissenbaum, eds., *Salem Witchcraft Papers* 2: 550–81

25. Boyer and Nissenbaum, eds., *Salem Witchcraft Papers,* 2: 564–67; New Hampshire State Archives, Probate Records, 3: 73–74. Norton, *In the Devil's Snare,* 222.

26. Baxter, ed., *Documentary History of Maine,* 5: 104–5.

27. William Willis, *The History of Portland* (1831–2; reprint, Portland: Maine Historical Society, 1972), 282–87; Norton, *In the Devil's Snare,* 105–6.

28. Boyer and Nissenbaum, eds., *Salem Witchcraft Papers,* 2: 564–67.

29. Boyer and Nissenbaum, eds., *Salem Witchcraft Papers,* 2: 564.

30. The quote is from Samuel Penhallow, *The History of the Wars of New-England, with the Eastern Indians* (Boston: 1726), 10; Boyer and Nissenbaum, eds., *Salem Witchcraft Papers,* 2: 564–67.

31. Noyes et al., eds., *Genealogical Dictionary,* 102–3; 573–74, 717. Herbert Brackett, *Genealogy: Descendants of Anthony Brackett of Portsmouth and Captain Richard Brackett of Braintree* (Washington, D.C.: Herbert Brackett, 1907), 57.

32. Christopher Hill, "Puritans and the Dark Corners of the Land," in Hill, *Change and Continuity in Seventeenth-Century England* (Cambridge, Massachusetts: Harvard University Press, 1975), 3–47; Richard P. Gildrie, *The Profane, the Civil and the Godly* (University Park: Pennsylvania State University Press, 1994), 133–56; Baker and Reid, The *New England Knight,* 134–55.

33. Carson O. Hudson Jr., *These Detestable Slaves of the Devill: A Concise Guide to Witchcraft in Colonial Virginia* (Haverford, PA.: Infinity Publishing, 2001).

34. Charles T. Libby and Neal W. Allen eds., *Province and Court Records of Maine*, 6 vols. (Portland: Maine Historical Society, 1931–1975), 6: 192, 208–9, 213.

35. Richard Chamberlain, "Lithobolia: The Stone-Throwing Devil," in George L. Burr, ed., *Narratives of the Witchcraft Cases* (New York: Charles Scribner's Sons, 1914), 58–59.

36. Michael P. Winship, *Seers of God: Puritan Providentialism in the Restoration and Early Enlightenment* (Baltimore: Johns Hopkins University Press, 1996), 54–56; David D. Hall, *Worlds of Wonder, Days of Judgment: Popular Religious Belief in Early New England*, (Cambridge: Harvard University Press, 1990), 71–80.

37. Balthazar Bekker *The world bewitch'd, or, An examination of the Common Opinions Concerning Spirits* (London, 1695); John Flavel *Divine Conduct: or, the Mystery of Providence* (London, 1678; reprint 1698); Deodat Lawson, *Christ's Fidelity the Only Shield Against Satan's Malignity* (London, 1704); Winship, *Seers of God*, 119–21.

38. Winship, *Seers of God*, 117–18, 126–28.

39. Chamberlain, "Lithobolia," 59.

40. John L. Sibley et al., *Biographical Sketches of Graduates of Harvard University, in Cambridge, Massachusetts*, 17 vols. (Cambridge: Harvard University Press, 1933), 5: 450–455. Thomas Robie, *A Letter to a Certain Gentleman, &c.* (Boston, 1719), 8; David Hall, Worlds *of Wonder, Days of Judgment*, 108.

41. Sibley et al., *Graduates of Harvard*, 5: 450–53; Noyes et al., eds., *Genealogical Dictionary*, 590–591.

42. Norton, *In the Devil's Snare*, 65, 169; Roach, *The Salem Witch Trials*, 569–71.

Epilogue

1. Robert Toppan and Alfred Goodrick, eds., *Edward Randolph*, 7 vols. (Boston: Prince Society, 1898–1909), 4: 4; Elwin Page, *Judicial Beginnings in New Hampshire, 1640–1700* (Concord: New Hampshire Historical Society, 1959), 206–27.

2. Jere Daniell, *Colonial New Hampshire: A History* (Millwood, NY.: KTO Press, 1981), 91.

3. Page, *Judicial Beginnings in New Hampshire*, 225; Daniell, *Colonial New Hampshire*, 92–93; "Deposition of Robert Mason," March 8, 1686, New Hampshire Historical Society Papers.

4. David Lovejoy, *The Glorious Revolution in America* (New York: Harper and Rowe, 1972), 197.

5. David Van Deventer, *The Emergence of Provincial New Hampshire, 1623–1741* (Baltimore: Johns Hopkins University Press, 1976), 59–61.

6. Sybil Noyes, Charles T. Libby, and Walter G. Davis, eds., *Genealogical Dictionary of Maine and New Hampshire* (1928–1939; reprint, Baltimore, 1979), 385, 717; New Hampshire State Archives, Court Papers, 8: 419; *New Hampshire Provincial and State Papers*, 40 vols., (Concord: State of New Hampshire: 1867–1943), 31: 299–300.

7. Noyes et al., *Genealogical Dictionary*, 63, 717; *New Hampshire Provincial and State Papers*, 17: 755.

8. Ray Brighton, *The Checkered Career of Tobias Lear* (Portsmouth: Portsmouth Marine Society, 1985), 91–99, 114–15.

9. *The Eastern Herald and Gazette of Maine*, November 17, 1796, 2; Dane Yorke, *A History and Stories of Biddeford* (Biddeford, ME: McArthur Library, 1994), 144–46.

10. John P. Demos, *Entertaining Satan: Witchcraft and the Culture of Early New England* (New York: Oxford University Press, 1982), 389–92; Owen Davies, *Witchcraft, Magic and Culture, 1736–1951* (Manchester: Manchester University Press, 1999); Owen Davies and Willem de Blecourt eds., *Witchcraft Continued: Popular Magic in Modern Europe* (Manchester: Manchester University Press, 2004).

Index

Acknowledgements

While one person gets the credit for writing a book, such a task is impossible without the help and support of many people. I should start my thanks with the History Department at Salem State College, what I call my "academic family." The faculty members and staff provide a friendly, stimulating, and supportive atmosphere that helps nourish the historian's soul. Dane Morrison and Donna Vinson read early sections of the book, and helped steer me in the right direction. David Crane and Alexandros Kyrou gave me several valuable references. Everyone has been patient and understanding when their department chair took an occasional day off to research and write. My good colleague in the English Department Nancy Schultz read the entire manuscript and provided me with many good ideas. Several of my classes have served as sounding boards for the book, and I thank my students for at least never appearing to grow tired of hearing about stone-throwing devils. The students in my graduate seminar on witchcraft and magic read a draft of the entire manuscript. Special thanks to Maria Pride, Karen Goodno, Michael Powers, and Wendy West for their detailed comments.

Many other friends and scholars have aided me. Mary Beth Norton has encouraged and advised me from the beginning. Benjamin Ray made useful comments on the original book proposal. My neighbor Richard Candee provided insights into the architecture of the Walton tavern. A number of friends have read the entire manuscript: Dennis Robinson, Wilson Ring, Virginia Spiller, James Kences and Christine Cataldo all helped with their suggestions.

Several people were instrumental in bringing this manuscript to press. Special thanks to my agent Matthew Carnicelli whose enthusiasm for *The Devil of Great Island* has never dimmed. My editor at Palgrave Macmillan, Airié Stuart, was of invaluable assistance, particularly in helping this academic produce a book for a wider audience. My old friend Mark Mastromarino used his editing talents to craft the index.

Every summer I run an archaeology dig for the Old Berwick Historical Society in South Berwick, Maine, at the Chadbourne site. This homestead was destroyed in the Salmon Falls raid of 1690, and is a couple miles away from the location of the Fortado and Short homesteads that were lost at the same time. The project staff and volunteers are always keen to hear about the stone-throwing devil, and other pieces of history that relate to the site, and they have been a great source of friendship and support, as well as intellectual exchange. For anyone who is not an archaeologist, it may be hard to believe that some of the best ideas are discovered when you are exhausted, covered in sweat and dirt, and sitting in a hole three feet underground. So, thanks to Brad Fletcher, Gordon Russell, Dick Lunt, Rich Fernald, George Langlais, Wendy Pirsig, Peter Sablock, Bruce Tucker, Tom Osborne, Norm Buttrick, and the many others who have participated in this project.

I have drawn upon the resources of many libraries and archives in the course of my research. Thanks to the Salem State College Library, Massachusetts Archives, Essex County Registry of Deeds, Rockingham County Registry of Deeds, Maine State Archives, Maine Historical Society, Maine State Library, Old York Historical Society, Kittery Town Clerk's Office, New Hampshire Division of Archives and Records Management, New Hampshire Historical Society, New Castle Public Library, Portsmouth Public Library, Connecticut State Archives, John Carter Brown Library at Brown University, and the National Archives of the United Kingdom. Barbara Austen, Manuscript Archivist for the Connecticut Historical Society, gladly examined a manuscript for me, saving a trip to Hartford. The staff of the Portsmouth Athenaeum, particularly Keeper Thomas Hardiman, deserves special thanks for fielding my many questions and requests.

I have been blessed to have fine teachers help guide my historical career. James Leamon introduced me to the history of northern New England in the first history class I took as an undergraduate at Bates College, and he has remained a mentor and friend ever since. James Axtell, James Whittenburg, Alaric Faulkner, Anne Yentsch, and the late Robert Bradley all helped me hone my skills as an historian and an archaeologist.

As a public historian, I believe we must make the past accessible to the general audience, so the *The Devil of Great Island* has been written with this readership in mind. To achieve this goal, I have streamlined the endnotes, and also minimized the often complex historiography behind the book. I would prefer to acknowledge historians by name in the text but most have been relegated to the notes. This has been a painful process, for I draw upon numerous scholars, and want to give full credit to them for their ideas and hard work. It would have been impossible to write this book without the work of John Demos, Carol Karlsen, Keith Thomas, Paul Boyer, Stephen Nissenbaum, David Hall, Richard Godbeer, and other witchcraft historians. The influence of Robin Brigg's *Neighbors and Witches* can even be seen in the title of chapter six. The modern study of colonial northern New England began with Charles Clark's *The Eastern Frontier.* I lean heavily on Gary Lord's excellent dissertation for my interpretation of early Portsmouth's history. The work of other New Hampshire historians, including Elwin Page, David Van Deventer, and Jere Daniel also provided valuable background information. Other authors, too numerous to name here, have provided important insights along the way. I can only hope that no one feels slighted by the abbreviated citations and if they do, they will realize it was done with a worthy goal in mind.

Finally, I owe an incalculable debt to my family. Anyone who knows my wife, Peggy, realizes that she is a candidate for sainthood. She has welcomed our messy house guest, the stone-throwing devil, into our home. She had done this without complaint, even as chores are forgotten and stacks of books and papers pile up in our family room. Despite a hectic life, a busy career, and just a passing interest in the subject, she has sacrificed much time to read drafts of chapters, and to listen to endless discussions about lithobolia. Our daughters Megan and Sarah and our basset hound Snowshoe have also shared their lives with the stone-throwing devil, even though it meant I was not always available to do all the fun things they might like.

Snowshoe Rock, York, Maine
February 2, 2007.